THE BIG LIE

THE BIG LIE

ELECTION CHAOS, POLITICAL OPPORTUNISM,
AND THE STATE OF AMERICAN POLITICS
AFTER 2020

JONATHAN LEMIRE

FLATIRON
BOOKS
NEW YORK

www.flatironbooks.com

Designed by Steven Seighman

Library of Congress Cataloging-in-Publication Data

Names: Lemire, Jonathan, 1979– author.
Title: The big lie : election chaos, political opportunism, and the state of American politics after 2020 / Jonathan Lemire.
Description: First edition. | New York : Flatiron Books, 2022. | Includes bibliographical references.
Identifiers: LCCN 2022016642 | ISBN 9781250819628 (hardcover) | ISBN 9781250819635 (ebook)
Subjects: LCSH: Presidents—United States—Election—2020. | United States—Politics and government—2017–2021.
Classification: LCC E912 .L45 2022 | DDC 324.973/0905—dc23/eng/20220506
LC record available at https://lccn.loc.gov/2022016642

Our books may be purchased in bulk for promotional, educational, or business use. Please contact your local bookseller or the Macmillan Corporate and Premium Sales Department at 1-800-221-7945, extension 5442, or by email at MacmillanSpecialMarkets@macmillan.com.

First Edition: 2022

10 9 8 7 6 5 4 3 2 1

For Carrie, Beckett, and Flynn

CONTENTS

Prologue: "Rigged"   1

1. The Beginning   7

2. 2016   21

3. The Trump Presidency   39

4. The Democrats   59

5. Conservative Reinforcements   77

6. 2020   97

7. The Election   119

8. January 6   148

9. The Grip Tightens   174

10. The States   201

11. Challenges   225

12. The Campaigns to Come   253

Acknowledgments   281

Sources   287

THE BIG LIE

PROLOGUE: "RIGGED"

In retrospect, it was an unlikely place to begin history's greatest assault on American democracy.

The Greater Columbus Convention Center sits where Interstate 670 and Route 23 intersect, just north of the Ohio capital city's downtown. There are acres of parking, the usual nondescript convention center–style hotels, and outposts of the standard chain restaurants. Famously, Ohio State's football stadium sits three miles to the north; less famously, the home of the National Hockey League's Blue Jackets is just a few blocks to the south.

Though not nearly as well known as Ohio's other big cities that all happen to start with the same letter—Cleveland to the north, Cincinnati to the south—Columbus is actually by far the largest, home to over nine hundred thousand people, a top-twenty city in the nation. And any metropolis, particularly one home to a massive university, state government offices, and a burgeoning e-commerce industry, needs a big convention center.

This one fits the bill, clocking in at 1.8 million square feet. Each year it hosts a pleasant slate of wildly diverse events, with highlights including what is dubbed the largest annual horticulture trade show in America; a three-day anime convention dubbed Ohayocon, whose name is a mix of the words "Ohio" and "*ohayou*" (Japanese for "good morning"); and, of course, the Arnold Sports Festival, which was founded by bodybuilder/actor/governor Arnold Schwarzenegger and draws more than two hundred thousand attendees every March.

But on August 1, 2016, the Greater Columbus Convention Center served as the birthplace of the Big Lie.

Little about the setting or the timing suggested that history was about to forever tilt off its axis.

A few thousand people, a decent crowd but not one that packed the space, had filed into one of the convention center wings, which had been partitioned to create a modest-sized room amid a cavernous hall. It was early in the day and the energy was very much on—and not off—the charts. Those in attendance fit the profile of a typical midwestern crowd, many middle-aged or older, perhaps whiter than most gatherings. Many wore red hats.

It was a run-of-the-mill campaign rally, sure to be just like the ones in Colorado a few nights before and those scheduled for Pennsylvania later that day and in Virginia the next.

Instead, with one seemingly off-the-cuff remark uttered within the walls of the convention center that day, Donald Trump threatened the tradition of peacefully contested American elections and challenged the very essence of a fair democratic process.

"I'm afraid the election is going to be rigged, I have to be honest," Trump said.

It had begun. The seeds of the Big Lie had been planted. A celebrity candidate with little regard for the truth had publicly doubted the intrinsic fairness of America's most sacred democratic institution, taking the first step on a journey that would undermine the integrity of the presidency, fuel a violent insurrection at the US Capitol, imperil voting rights ahead of the 2022 and 2024 elections, and forever change both political parties.

For the first time, Trump cast doubt on the results of the 2016 general election and, weeks later, he would become the first major presidential candidate to not promise to abide by those results. In times of war, in times of peace, in times of deep civil unrest, one of the few American constants was the firm conviction that an election would be held on its appointed date and that its results would be honored by the winners and losers alike, with a smooth and amicable transfer of power.

Not by Trump. He had never been one to go quietly, to accept defeat, to cede the stage. He had whined months earlier that the Iowa caucuses, which he lost narrowly, had been conducted unfairly. Hell, he once thought that the Emmys—for which his reality TV show *The Apprentice* and its spin-off, *Celebrity Apprentice*, were nominated a total of nine times but never won—were fixed.

But this was different. In the months and years that followed, it was clear that the ripples in the water from the rock Trump had thrown that day in Ohio would turn into tidal waves, swamping political discourse and nearly drowning a democracy.

Everything had irrevocably changed, but no one knew how just yet. Reporters in the convention center quickly pinged their editors, realizing that what they had thought might be the day's lead story—Trump's ongoing war of words with the family of a Muslim serviceman killed in Iraq—would no longer be what drove the headlines. But there was no way to immediately grasp the magnitude of what had just happened.

I was there that day. My lede for the Associated Press, which was on the wire and online within minutes and then printed the next day in newspapers throughout the country and mirrored on websites around the world, was simple and stark:

"COLUMBUS, Ohio (AP)—Republican presidential nominee Donald Trump suggested Monday that he fears the general election 'is going to be rigged'—an unprecedented assertion by a modern presidential candidate."

We had never been here before. And what would come over the next four and a half years would test every institution in American democracy, from the government to the courts to the free press. Trump had already been an unconventional candidate: vulgarly casting aside political norms; feuding with Republicans and Democrats alike; hugging flags and tweeting with abandon. He would generate headlines, stir controversy, and dominate the political and media landscape like no one before him. He was, and is, a singular figure.

His eventual presidency would strain alliances, upend traditions, and plunge Washington into chaos—before, in a remarkable third act, being overwhelmed by a global pandemic. I covered all of it. And yet his mismanagement of the nation's response to COVID-19, which saw more than four hundred thousand deaths under his watch, would somehow not be his defining moment.

Instead, what will be forever linked to Donald Trump is the mob that committed violence in his name on January 6, 2021. They were convinced by his Big Lie that the election had been stolen, that there had been widespread voter fraud, that their president was being unfairly deposed. None of that had happened. But Trump told them it had. And they believed him.

And they chose violence.

Holding Trump signs and using American flags as weapons, the rioters stormed the US Capitol, a building symbolic as a citadel of democracy, and in doing so stirred echoes of the angst and blood of the Civil War era. Only this time the violence was instigated by a duly elected president unwilling to honor the foundational principle of a peaceful transfer of power.

The scene that unfolded—the mob pushing through police barricades, breaking windows, occupying seats of power—was one that Americans are accustomed to watching from afar, unfolding in distant lands with authoritarian regimes. But this violence, which included gunshots fired in the Capitol, five deaths, and an armed occupation of the Senate floor, was born of the man who had sworn an oath to protect the very democratic traditions that rioters tried to undo in his name.

The moment led to swift bipartisan rebukes and another impeachment—and acquittal—for Trump, who slunk out of office two weeks later. It could have been a moment of true repudiation, of Trump being forced from the political stage, of a nation rattled by the violence and the pandemic recommitting itself to the democratic values on which it was founded.

It was not.

Instead, Republicans seized upon Trump's lies and used them as justification to undermine voting rights and election security across the nation. Nearly twenty GOP-controlled state legislatures used the aftermath of the 2020 election, preying upon the distrust fomented in voters by Trump's falsehoods, to push forward long-desired efforts to tighten access to voting, installing roadblocks to the ballot that disproportionately impacted voters—minorities, the young, recent immigrants—who tend to vote Democratic.

One crisis of democracy had birthed another.

This would shape the years to come, as Democrats deemed the election efforts not just an existential threat to democracy, one that continued to roll back the 1965 Voting Rights Act that protected Black citizens' ability to vote, but an assault squarely aimed at keeping them out of power in the 2022 midterms and the 2024 presidential election.

President Joe Biden, who fairly vanquished Trump's reelection bid, was confronted with the task of leading a sizable portion of the electorate who did not believe he was their legitimate commander in chief. He was faced with making the defense of voting rights a central piece of his presidency, deeming it "the most significant test of our democracy since the Civil War," a charge that would require a balancing act: pursuing his agenda to bring the nation out of the pandemic while protecting the franchise for the very voters that put him in office.

Few Republicans broke with their party's ranks to reject the Big Lie, and those who did suffered political ostracization as Trump's hold on the GOP only tightened from his exile at his gilded golf courses in

Florida and New Jersey. It was there, stripped of his powerful Twitter account but still wildly popular with rank-and-file Republicans, where Trump mulled his own political future while stoking the conspiracies and fueling the Big Lie that rapidly redefined politics for both major political parties.

American democracy was brought to the brink. And the journey to that edge truly began that sleepy Monday in Ohio.

I

THE BEGINNING

The crowd wasn't quite sure what to think.

Donald Trump, the unlikeliest major party presidential nominee in more than a century, had drawn several thousand people to the Greater Columbus Convention Center. They laughed at his jokes, they chanted "Lock Her Up!" about Hillary Clinton, they seemed to think Mexico might pay for a border wall. They did not expect to hear that the most basic and vital element of American democracy was a sham.

After suggesting that the process might be rigged, Trump declared that he had been hearing "more and more" that the election might not be contested fairly, though before elaborating further, he changed the subject to a tangent about one of his first real estate deals, in (somewhat) nearby Cincinnati.

He made his incendiary accusation after suggesting that the Democrats had fixed their primary system so Clinton could defeat Bernie Sanders, making some wild link to a batch of hacked emails from the national party that appeared to indicate a preference for the former secretary of state. But emails aside, Clinton had received 3.7 million more votes than Sanders nationwide and had established a clear lead in delegates months before her party's convention, which had concluded just days earlier in Philadelphia.

This followed Trump's own evidence-less claim that the Republican nomination would have been stolen from him had he not won by significant margins. Part of his pitch was that he was an outsider, someone who was not from Washington and not beholden to its traditions and informal and formal rules. He wielded that status as a weapon, and at times made it appear that he was running in opposition to the Republican Party as much as representing it.

He accused the GOP of plotting against him, with claims that the system was fixed against him becoming frequent catchphrases during low-water marks of his primary campaign, months earlier, first when he lost Iowa and then when forces allied with Republican rival Ted Cruz managed to pack state delegations with supporters of the Texas senator. He claimed that the whole thing was "rigged" and also asserted that the Republican Party had changed the delegate allocation in the Florida primary to favor a native candidate, like Jeb Bush or Marco Rubio, at Trump's expense.

The celebrity businessman had long been known to dabble in conspiracy theories, including jump-starting his political career by falsely claiming that President Barack Obama was not born in the United States and then, incredibly, that Cruz's father was hanging out with President John F. Kennedy's assassin (he was not). But this was the first time Trump had asserted that November's general election might not be on the up-and-up.

And it wasn't just a slip of the tongue, a stray thought that crossed his lips, never to be uttered again. Those happened plenty. But veteran Trump watchers knew from hundreds of campaign rallies that if one of his sentiments played well with the crowd—the candidate, truly skilled in reading a room, liked to test material on the audience, like a comic workshopping a joke—it could then become part of his nightly routine.

And truly, his campaign was, at its heart, just one rally to the next: outside of a few core tenets (the nation's trade deals were bad, its immigration system worse), there was very little in the way of political philosophy to Trump. The core goal was simply to seize attention, to get the crowd to cheer, to spawn a cable news chyron, to dominate Twitter, to own the libs.

And Trump stuck to this idea, repeating the charge that night on Fox News channel's *Hannity*: "I'm telling you, November eighth, we'd better be careful, because that election is going to be rigged. And I hope the Republicans are watching closely or it's going to be taken away from us.

"I've been hearing about it for a long time," Trump continued. "And I just hope that there's really—I hope the Republicans get out there and watch very closely because I think we are going to win this election."

The host did not push back. They rarely did.

Trump's lies did not remain confined to the rally stage. They needed life; they needed amplification. He did some of that himself, via his Twitter account, which was in the early stages of a five-year reign as the most potent political weapon on the planet, one that would rattle global capitals, leave political foes cowering in fear, and, at times, weigh in on pressing matters like the quality of Diet Coke. But he needed accomplices, he needed coconspirators, he needed a way to reach those who did not live their lives 140 characters at a time.

He needed cable news.

Every network was guilty of giving Trump too much time, including those without conservative leanings. He was a welcome guest on panel shows, even if conversations got contentious, and his rallies received wall-to-wall coverage, far more than any other Republican candidate. His rivals cried out that it was unfair, but the networks didn't care. Trump was compelling TV; people couldn't look away. Trump was ratings gold.

But it was conservative media, and Fox News in particular, with which Trump eventually formed a symbiotic relationship. It's true that Rupert Murdoch, the head of News Corporation, which ran Fox News, was at first deeply skeptical of Trump. But the programming didn't reflect that. In Fox, Trump had a huge platform: the number one cable channel in the country, and one on which he was never challenged. One that gave him free media and, often enough, regurgitated his lies.

Fox News became a wing of the Trump campaign. The celebrity maybe-billionaire called in at will to its morning show *Fox & Friends* and then later did the same with his prime-time pal Sean Hannity. As Trump took power, stations launched and rebranded themselves, catering to those for whom Fox News just wasn't conservative enough. Newsmax and One America News Network (OAN) each grabbed a foothold with those on the Right and showed a willingness to parrot Trump's lies.

And he lied a lot. He lied about his wealth. He lied about his sex life. He lied about how many times he was on the cover of *Time* magazine, hanging a fake on the walls of his New Jersey and Florida golf courses. He repeatedly claimed things that did not happen. He said Obama was born in Kenya, then falsely claimed that Hillary Clinton's campaign team had started the "birther" movement that questioned Obama's origins. He said he saw thousands of Muslims in New Jersey celebrate the collapse of the World Trade Center after the attacks on September 11, 2001. He said Russian president Vladimir Putin called him a "genius" when in fact Putin called him something like "colorful" or "bright."

He lived in his own world and created his own reality. He refused to accept hard truths. He appeared to think that if he just said things over and over, he could will them into reality—and persuade his followers to believe them. At times, it was hard to know whether he knew he was lying or if he had somehow convinced himself of the alternate, and incorrect, reality.

Steve Bannon, the conservative provocateur who ran Breitbart News, took over the Trump campaign for its 2016 stretch run and then spent a tumultuous seven months inside the White House as the president's chief strategist. A firebrand whose website would run sensational and at times offensive headlines, who derided the media as the "opposition party" but happily spoke off the record to reporters to help shape their stories, Bannon was not shy about coloring or shading the truth.

But even for Bannon, Trump was something new. The chief strategist told me that Trump "was not looking to win a news cycle, he was looking to win a news moment, a news second." An at-times shell-shocked Bannon would relay to aides that "Trump would say anything, he would lie about anything to win that moment, to win whatever exchange he was having at that moment." Entire campaign proposals had to be written on the fly, policy plans reverse engineered, teams of aides immediately mobilized to meet whatever floated through Trump's head in that moment to defend his record, put down a reporter, or change a chyron on CNN.

A hurricane map had to be redrawn after the president made a mistake. A task force was created to fight an imaginary caravan of immigrants that was getting big play on Fox News. A commission was formed to look into whether illegal votes had cost him the popular vote.

And so much of it—so, so, so much of it—was to avoid the impression that Trump was wrong. Or, more dangerously, that he was a loser.

* * *

Donald John Trump hates losing. He hates the idea of appearing weak, hates that anyone might think he was not as rich/handsome/skinny/smart/successful/well-endowed as would be required to perpetuate the gold-plated Trump brand. He hated being laughed at.

His campaign was based on a central idea that the world was laughing at the United States, that the once-mighty and respected nation had fallen so steeply that it had become nothing but a global joke. "The world is laughing at us," he said in May 2016. "They're laughing at us, at our stupidity."

Who was doing the laughing? It varied by the day, but it could be China or Mexico or the Arab League or OPEC or Vladimir Putin. His great fear was to be the subject of ridicule, which is why, aides would later say, one of his angriest moments in office was at the United Nations in September 2018 when, with typical hyperbole, he declared, "In less than two years, my administration has accomplished more than almost any administration in the history of our country."

He drew audible laughter from the heads of state from around the world. Trump, taken aback, paused, and said, "Didn't expect that reaction, but that's okay," and went ahead with his speech. He later screamed at his aides.

He couldn't stand being bested; he always had to have an excuse at the ready. When Trump Tower was eclipsed as the tallest building in its section of Midtown Manhattan, he simply renumbered the floors in the elevator. The fifty-seventh floor became the sixty-seventh, the fifty-eighth-floor penthouse became the sixty-eighth, and so on. Voilà! The building had not grown an inch, but in the Trump Organization's promotional materials, it suddenly was sixty-eight floors. Still the tallest.

When pundits roundly declared him the loser, to Hillary Clinton, of the first general election debate in September 2016, Trump was ready with an excuse: his microphone was not working properly. When he didn't want his tax returns released for fear they would reveal that he was worth a lot less than he claimed—and potentially showcase the true sources of his wealth—he said the IRS had been auditing him for years (it wasn't) and that he couldn't release them (he could). He simply couldn't publicly face the possibility of being defeated or shamed.

And maybe that's all that day in Columbus was, some thought.

Maybe Trump had glanced at the polls that morning, which showed him down an average of four and a half points to Clinton with just over three months until Election Day. Maybe he saw a defeat coming, the same expectation that would lead aides to hurriedly scramble to write an acceptance speech on Election Night because no one had thought he could win. Maybe the statement was simply Trump's effort to lay the groundwork of an excuse if he went on to lose the general election.

But if it was a deception, he didn't immediately let aides into his thinking. Later that day, as his private jet made the short flight to Harrisburg, Pennsylvania, for his next rally, a few of his senior aides, including press secretary Hope Hicks and head of security Keith Schiller, raised the question of fears of a rigged election.

Trump snapped that it was a threat, that "Many people have told me that it's happening, that they are going to steal it from us."

Schiller, a grizzled former New York cop who was rarely not by his boss's side, nodded agreement. Hicks was in some ways an unusual part of Trump's core group, a twenty-seven-year-old former model from Connecticut who had first worked for the candidate's daughter Ivanka. She wondered if the idea came from a conservative news host, maybe other Republicans on the ground in battleground states? Mr. Trump didn't elaborate. But Mr. Trump was usually right, she thought.

If Trump were to be defeated in November and then to publicly declare that the election results were bogus, his claim could yield unpredictable reactions from his supporters and fellow Republicans. His musings in Ohio and on *Hannity* would soon become a rally routine, one that would be repeated night after night in front of thousands.

He did not yet have the Republican Party fully in his grasp. There were some, as the campaign entered its stretch run, who hoped Trump would be an aberration, that his populism and obscenity would fade away. But Trump saw the moment differently. It was a prod, a test. How far would the party go with him? The GOP leadership was uncertain.

Its voters were not.

* * *

The line outside Trump's second stop that August day—Cumberland Valley High School in Mechanicsburg, Pennsylvania—stretched for blocks beyond the school's parking lot.

Trump often boasted to the crowds inside his rallies that far more people were waiting outside, unable to get in. Often, that wasn't true. But it was accurate that day, as reporters in the motorcade nudged each other and took note of the size of the crowd in a state that had become Republicans' white whale, one in which they spent an extraordinary amount of time and money but hadn't won since 1988.

Trump's crowds, he always bragged, were far bigger than those Clinton drew. How much they mattered was the subject of fierce debate; political reporters and operatives alike could remember four years before, when Mitt Romney had drawn megacrowds in his campaign's final days, including more than thirty thousand near Pittsburgh, and how his aides had told everyone that he'd won. He lost the popular vote by nearly four points to Obama.

But surely the crowds meant something. It must have meant something in October when Trump drew twenty thousand to a rally in Tampa and, just a few days and 280 miles away across the state, Clinton attracted only a few hundred people in Miami. It must have meant something—what seemed to be the sheer size of the energy gap—that Trump was drawing bigger and louder audiences.

Born into wealth and living in a penthouse atop a Manhattan skyscraper emblazoned with his name in gold, Trump was the least likely representative of deep-red America. But he struck a chord and spoke to people's anger about immigration and political correctness. To some, it was undeniable: he gave voice to their darkest, sometimes racist thoughts, their fear and hatred of the Other. For other white voters, he seemed to bring to light the frustration of being forgotten, of living at a time in America when it was no longer sure that your children would have a better life than your own. When you hadn't had a raise in ten years or when the factory that employed seemingly half the town shut down. When opioids were everywhere, even in the hands of your own teenager. When suicides and overdoses were up. When the post–Great Recession recovery worked out fine for others but passed you by. When the elites got richer and smarter and more arrogant. And when the government moved to help *them*, the immigrants, the people of color, and gave them an unfair advantage over you, the hardworking American who got left behind and didn't get a fair share.

Clinton was in a race for history, aiming to become the first woman president, and the power of that barrier potentially breaking could not be overstated. But Clinton also had been in Americans' lives for decades; there was little new to learn, as voters' opinions about her had hardened long before. She had been vilified by the Right for years, by Republicans and in the conservative media. Among conservatives, a whole cottage industry was born that seemed intent on floating the wildest possible conspiracy theory about her and her husband. She was a victim of extraordinary sexism. Even some who voted for her did so unenthusiastically.

For decades, she had loomed on the Right as a bogey(wo)man. Far more than her husband, she was the target of the conservatives' venom. She was seen as the puppet master, pulling the strings behind the scenes. The deep national political polarization that Trump accelerated had its origins decades earlier and really exploded in the late 1990s, when the Right—with the aid of the new cable network Fox News—seized upon the Clintons as an existential threat to their values. No conspiracy was too far-fetched: murder, rape, pedophilia. Hillary Clinton, a brilliant, successful, accomplished woman, was triggering, and that only grew after her husband left office and her own presidency appeared a possibility. She was blamed for a terror attack in Benghazi; she was accused of being in league with socialists.

Lots of people hated Trump too, in what became a race of two candidates with the highest unfavorability ratings in modern times. But polls after the election showed that, among voters who disliked both candidates, far more broke for Trump. They had their doubts, but they wanted to try something new, someone brash who seemed to understand and vocalize their frustrations.

And in many ways, Clinton was the perfect foil for Trump. Trump played into voters' worst instincts when it came to racism and sexism. He could be elected only as a reaction to the nation's first Black president and its first potentially winning female candidate. And some of the tactics being considered to stop her set a template for what would happen five years later.

* * *

Roger Stone was, by reputation and his own admission, a dirty trickster. His résumé is almost too audacious to examine: He worked for Richard Nixon and later tattooed a giant image of the disgraced thirty-seventh president on his back. He later, along with his partner Paul Manafort, founded a Washington lobbyist firm that specialized in representing clients no one else would touch. He helped bring down Eliot Spitzer, associated with the Proud Boys, and found himself the subject of a 2019 FBI raid based on charges of witness tampering and lying to investigators.

He also was Donald Trump's first political adviser.

He tried unsuccessfully to get Trump to run several times before 2016 and was one of the first staffers aboard the celebrity developer's eventual campaign. He didn't stay in the official role long—Stone says he quit, Trump says he fired him—but the political provocateur didn't go far, always remaining in Trump's orbit and on the other end of the phone. Eventually, he—and Manafort, who went on to run Trump's campaign for a while in 2016—was pardoned by Trump in the waning days of his term.

And it was Stone who, the week of Trump's Ohio rally, amplified the message; Stone who would make the direct link between the seemingly harmless words uttered from a convention center stage to the insurrection at the United States Capitol.

"I think we have widespread voter fraud, but the first thing that Trump needs to do is begin talking about it constantly," said Stone in an interview with a Breitbart producer that was largely ignored by the mainstream media but picked up significant traction on the Right.

"He needs to say for example, today would be a perfect example: 'I am leading in Florida. The polls all show it. If I lose Florida, we will know that there's voter fraud. If there's voter fraud, this election will be illegitimate, the election of the winner will be illegitimate, we will have a constitutional crisis, widespread civil disobedience, and the government will no longer be the government.'"

As if gazing into a warped crystal ball, Stone got the candidate wrong but offered a foreboding preview of one of the darkest days in America's history, predicting what would happen if Trump's supporters believed his victory had been stolen.

"The government will be shut down if they attempt to steal this and swear Hillary in. No, we will not stand for it. We will not stand for it."

* * *

The crowd in Mechanicsburg, wearing their red "Make America Great Again" hats, was fired up, nearly drowning out Trump as he spoke.

They were the voters—mostly white and working class—whom Trump had drawn into the system. A number of them told reporters that day that they had not voted in decades or had never voted before. But they were going to this year; they were going to vote for *him*, they'd say, as they pointed to the stage. Trump had struck a chord with them.

And they were willing to follow Trump, to believe him when he said that the system was biased against them. Others got the handouts, got the leg up. The establishment—from government to media to Wall Street to Hollywood to Silicon Valley—was designed to keep the rich and well-connected in power and regular folks out. And maybe, just maybe, the elites would rig an election to do so.

The rest of that rally in Pennsylvania passed uneventfully. But the threat of a rigged election became a theme of Trump's closing argument, as the campaign moved into its stretch run. The fear that the race could be stolen manifested itself in a new and dangerous way, and Trump would soon do the unthinkable for an American presidential candidate: he would not commit to honoring the results of the election. He refused to promise that he would concede if he lost.

He hammered home the theme night after night, even after his candidacy was nearly derailed by the release of the *Access Hollywood* tape in which he was heard boasting about sexually assaulting women. That moment was the closest that the Republican Party ever came to severing itself from Trump. But while some in the GOP abandoned him, his followers did not, and he soon recovered in the polls to again draw close to Clinton heading into their third and final debate, on a sweltering late October night in Las Vegas.

About two-thirds of the way through the debate, the moderator, Fox News' Chris Wallace, turned to Trump.

"Your running mate, Governor Pence, pledged on Sunday that he and you, his words, will absolutely accept the result of this election," Wallace said. "Today your daughter Ivanka said the same thing. I want to ask you here on the stage tonight: Do you make the same commitment that you'll absolutely accept the result of this election?"

Trump glared at him. His answer drew gasps from the audience.

"I will look at it at the time. I'm not looking at anything now, I'll look at it at the time," he said. "What I've seen, what I've seen, is so bad."

Wallace tried to interrupt twice, but Trump kept going, reciting unproven allegations about voter rolls and media bias. When the anchor finally jumped in, his voice was a mix of frustration, incredulity, and concern.

"But, sir, there is a tradition in this country, in fact, one of the prides of this country is the peaceful transition of power and no matter how hard fought a campaign is that at the end of the campaign, that the loser concedes to the winner," Wallace said. "Not saying you're necessarily going to be the loser or the winner, but that the loser concedes to the winner and the country comes together in part for the good of the country. Are you saying you're not prepared now to commit to that principle?"

Trump almost seemed to sneer in response.

"What I'm saying is that I will tell you at the time. I'll keep you in suspense, okay?"

As the audience murmured, Clinton jumped in.

"Chris, let me respond to that because that's horrifying. You know, every time Donald thinks things aren't going in his direction, he claims whatever it is, is rigged against him," she said. She then ticked off some of Trump's claims about his Iowa caucus defeat, his Wisconsin primary loss, a legal defeat for Trump University, all setbacks Trump deemed unfair.

"There was even a time when he didn't get an Emmy for his TV program three years in a row and he started tweeting that the Emmys were rigged against him," she said.

"Should have gotten it," Trump said to laughter. Clinton was not amused.

"This is a mindset. This is how Donald thinks, and it's funny, but it's also really troubling. That is not the way our democracy works," she said. "We've been around for 240 years. We've had free and fair elections. We've accepted the outcomes when we may not have liked them, and that is what must be expected of anyone standing on a debate stage during a general election."

When the night ended, the talk was of Trump's refusal to promise to honor the results of the election. Two of the cable channels (MSNBC and CNN) treated it as an existential threat to democracy, the third (Fox News) decidedly less so. Headlines screamed, ledes blared, all about Trump threatening to violate one of the sacred tenets of the nation's democracy.

It still seemed unreal. Would Trump really refuse to concede?

Would some of his followers actually not accept Clinton's election? Surely, pundits thought, Trump would walk away if he lost.

Trump, of course, didn't lose. But a step had been taken, a journey toward Republicans seizing upon false claims of voter fraud to restrict ballot access, forcing Democrats to make voting rights the defining political issue of the decade.

But a step was also taken toward violence, a step toward the events of January 6, 2021.

2

2016

All politicians lie in one way or another. Some shade the truth, some exaggerate, some practice the sin of omission. And without question, some dwell in outright falsehoods.

Among the most famous:

> George H. W. Bush: "Read my lips: no new taxes."
> Bill Clinton: "I did not have sexual relations with that woman."
> Richard Nixon: "I'm not a crook."

Sometimes these were misstatements, sometimes complete fabrications. George W. Bush cited faulty intelligence in the run-up to the Iraq War. Ronald Reagan swore that arms would not be traded to Iran for hostages until, well, they were. But there had never been a politician like Donald Trump, whose relationship with the truth was so casual. It didn't begin when he threw his hat in the ring for president: his entire public platform and persona were built on mistruth.

Even as a young developer, Trump understood the power of a lie or an exaggeration, especially when it was put to use to make him—or his buildings—seem bigger, better, bolder. It was all about promotion.

Because promotion, and the resulting publicity, equaled prestige and power and, of course, money. At first he lied about his buildings, not just saying that they were taller than they were, but that they were home to the most famous and sensational people. Several different times in the 1980s and 1990s, he planted stories that the British royal family was interested— for whatever reason—in buying property in one of his Manhattan buildings. He capped that off by telling Howard Stern in 1993 that Princess Diana was interested in becoming his neighbor in Trump Tower.

"I hope she's looking at—she is really hot. She has gained twenty to twenty-five pounds, she looks great," Trump told the shock jock. "There could be a love interest. I'd become King of England. King of England. I'd have to leave, I'd have to lose the New York accent quickly."

Sure. A good old-fashioned lie to promote himself is one thing. But how to get that lie out there? How to get people to see that lie, consume that lie, believe that lie? That's where the media came in.

Donald Trump had some undeniable skills. He was adept at reading a room, telling people what they wanted to hear, and ingratiating himself to others, particularly the rich and powerful who could give him what he wanted (read: money, fame, and power). He was shameless, seemingly free of the intrinsically human ability to be embarrassed, a neat trick when occasionally the lies backfired. And he was very good at knowing what the media wanted.

Trump became a public figure in the 1980s and 1990s, at a time when the New York media world was booming and insatiable and rife with competition. The city was home to multiple national and local television stations, much of the nation's magazine industry, and a number of daily newspapers. There were the *New York Times*, the paper of record, and the *Wall Street Journal*, the paper of business. Trump certainly cared about those, but his appearances in their pages were vastly outnumbered by the times he showed up as a boldface name in the city's two tabloids, the *New York Daily News* and the *New York Post*.

The *News* was the paper of the city's working-class residents of the boroughs outside Manhattan, the read for city workers as they commuted on the subway. The *Post* was more of a scandal sheet, the second read for the city's elite in their homes on the Upper East Side or the Hamptons. Both papers had good sports sections; both covered cops and crimes and murder and mayhem in a city that at the time averaged around two thousand homicides a year; both had screaming headlines on the front page—known as "the wood," a term dating back to typesetting days—meant to capture a reader's eye on the newsstand and become watercooler talk later in the day; and both had rather extensive gossip sections to cover the ups and downs of the city's famous and infamous.

Trump liked being in the news pages. He loved being in the gossip pages.

It was there he built his reputation as a young real estate mogul on the make, a rising force on Manhattan's real estate scene, a budding celebrity who dated only the most beautiful women. He was obsessed with appearing in the papers, believing that all publicity is good publicity, certain that New Yorkers would want to buy one of his apartments in an effort to steal a piece of the life Trump was leading, one of glamour and gold, for themselves.

"The final key to the way I promote is bravado: I play to people's fantasies. People may not always think big themselves, but they can still get very excited by those who do," Trump wrote in his 1987 best-selling book *The Art of the Deal*. "That's why a little hyperbole never hurts. People want to believe that something is the biggest and the greatest and the most spectacular. I call it truthful hyperbole. It's an innocent form of exaggeration—and a very effective form of promotion."

And to shape the impression created in the tabloids, Trump needed a reliable spokesperson, an advocate well acquainted with the developer's innermost thoughts and secrets and wishes and desires. A publicist with a very familiar voice.

The tone and cadence were just so distinct, so unique, so Trumpian. A man would call the newsroom of the *News* or the *Post* or *People* magazine and declare that he was a spokesman named John Miller—or sometimes John Barron—and would then vigorously defend or promote his client, one Donald J. Trump. They were public relations men who sounded just like Trump and, well, they *were* Trump, masquerading as an unusually insightful advocate for the man himself.

New York newsrooms of the 1980s and 1990s got used to these calls from Trump posing as someone else. Linda Stasi, then a *New York Daily News* gossip columnist, said Trump once left her a voice mail from an "anonymous tipster" who wanted it known that Trump had been spotted going out with models. Another time, John Miller (or was it Barron?) claimed that the actress Kim Basinger had been trying to date Trump. Starlets wanted to live in Trump Tower. And, yes, Madonna had tried to put the moves on Trump during an event at the Plaza Hotel.

But the PR man assured the reporter that, despite Madonna's intentions, nothing untoward occurred between the developer and the biggest pop star on the planet: "He's got zero interest that night."

Other times, all Trump wanted to sell was his sex life. Even if little of it was true.

Few pre-politics stories better displayed Trump's ability to control a news cycle with his sensationalism, shamelessness, and lies than the drama over his divorce from his first wife, Ivana. Trump had been having an affair with Marla Maples when his mistress brazenly confronted his wife in Aspen in 1989. In Ivana's book, she recalled, "This young blond woman came up to me out of the blue and said, 'I'm Marla and I love your husband. Do you?'"

The subsequent divorce was tabloid gold.

The front page of the *Daily News* on February 13, 1990, was "'Ivana Better Deal': Mrs. T Brands Donald's $25M Pre-Nuptial Pact a Fraud."

The same day's *Post*: "Ivana to Donald at Secret Sitdown: Gimme the Plaza! . . . the Jet and $150 Million, Too."

People magazine got in on the act, with the cover tagline reading: "Billion Dollar Blowup: She wants the Plaza, he'll take Manhattan. America's gaudiest couple square off in an old-fashioned battle over babes and bucks. Direct from Aspen, Palm Beach and New York City, here's the latest dish."

And then the coup de grâce, the most famous Trump-related headline of the period, one simply invented by Trump or Miller or Barron—all the same man—to push his narrative, to make him seem more successful and famous than possible: "Marla Boasts to Her Pals About Donald: 'Best Sex I've Ever Had,'" screamed the headline in the *Post*.

The subhead, though not as infamous, was just as braggadocious or hilarious or nauseating, suggesting that the city "always knew that Trump was a tiger in the corporate boardroom" but now it had learned that "he was wildcat in the bedroom too."

Trump lost $14 million in the divorce. He only grew more famous.

But trouble was on the horizon and bankruptcies followed. Trump's Taj Mahal casino opened with great fanfare in April 1990 in Atlantic City, but six months later defaulted on interest payments to bondholders as his finances went into a tailspin. It filed for bankruptcy in 1991, while two other Atlantic City hotels and the Plaza Hotel in Manhattan—the Central Park South jewel Ivana so desperately wanted—filed for bankruptcy the following year. Eventually, only one bank, Deutsche Bank, continued to lend Trump money, and his real estate empire began to cool.

Still, Trump had made it; he was a celebrity, his standing bolstered by lies as much as truth.

But was it enough?

* * *

Trump was the second son of Fred Trump, a Queens-based real estate developer who had never made it across the East River to become a player amid the gleaming skyscrapers of Manhattan. Donald Trump could not handle that, driven by an insecurity to move beyond the forgotten, middle-class neighborhoods where his father built.

He pushed the company into Manhattan and, like in the outer boroughs before, immediately ran into accusations that it discriminated against minority renters. Despite his holdings on the nation's most famous island, the true New York elite never admitted Trump into their circle, looking down upon his Queens roots and shameless self-promotion. He continued, as best he could, to be a man about town, to seek out the limelight and attention. He'd hold random stunt press events, cold call journalists, happily talk to reporters at any time on any topic. He'd slip into the movies after the lights went down—during a late 2001 screening of *Vanilla Sky*, he was spotted sneaking in his own snacks—but yet would be sure to linger after the film was over so he'd get noticed.

Once, in the summer of 2001, he stayed behind a rote news conference to give a few unrelated quotes to a *New York Daily News* intern, only to grow distracted when he noticed that the intern had the same color of red hair as a young television producer nearby.

"Are you guys together?" Trump asked.

"Uh, no," I answered, somewhat baffled, since I had never seen the young woman before in my life.

"Are you sure?" Trump asked. "But you have the same hair."

Apparently, couples came color-coded in the celebrity developer's mind. And then Trump went one step further, offering to play matchmaker.

"I mean, would you like to be together?" he asked, as he stepped into his waiting limo. "Because I can make that happen."

But what made Trump *Trump*—the gauche need for publicity; the boasting, the need to emblazon his name in giant gold-plated letters on the side of every building he owned; the constant Page Six presence; even his odd hair—made him toxic for Manhattan's blue bloods. They mocked him and excluded him if they thought about him at all. The insecurity drove Trump. How to fit in, to finally be accepted and envied? There were two main possibilities.

First: television.

* * *

Everyone watched television. Trump was initially skeptical when approached by producer Mark Burnett about hosting a reality show, but he warmed to the pitch that he would appear as a glamorized version of himself, a successful mogul with a luxurious lifestyle.

What *The Apprentice* did for Trump cannot be overstated. It ran for fifteen seasons, showcased his properties and his adult children, gave him an iconic catchphrase—"You're fired!"—and made him tens of millions of dollars. But more than that, it changed how he was perceived.

In Manhattan, he was still an afterthought, even a joke. But for much of America, this was their introduction to Trump, and, like so much else about his life, it wasn't a truthful one.

In reality, Trump did live large in his gilded penthouse and had a fleet of helicopters and planes. But the version of Trump depicted in the show was supersized: it exaggerated his wealth and business prowess; even his signature line was bogus, since Trump himself hated firing people and usually delegated that unpleasant task to others. The show portrayed him at the pinnacle of his powers, a Master of the Universe in Manhattan, as opposed to a celebrity sideshow who at that point had largely stopped developing projects in favor of licensing deals, having his name attached to buildings at home and, at times, with dubious business partners abroad.

It was that glossy depiction of Trump that was beamed weekly into the living rooms of six or seven million homes across America, many of whom were getting their first dedicated look at someone they knew, at best, in passing as a vaguely famous person. Though later lost in the chaos of his presidency, much of Trump's 2016 campaign—especially the early stages—was built on the idea that he was a successful businessman who was the perfect CEO to hire in order to turn around the nation's economy.

Voters at rallies across the country thought they knew "Mr. Trump"—as he was inevitably called on the show—as a corporate tycoon perfectly suited to strike a favorable international trade deal and start bringing American jobs home.

And maybe they knew one other thing about him: that he was the leading proponent of the idea that President Barack Obama was not born in the United States. And that, too, was not the truth.

* * *

Trump had once been a Democrat. He flirted with a presidential campaign as far back as 1999, even briefly attaching himself to the fledgling Reform Party in 2000, putting forth some vague economic proposals before dropping out. There was far more serious talk in 2010 and 2011, as he became a darling of the fringe GOP because of his obsession with Obama's birthplace, a fixture on the conservative media circuit, a favorite at right-wing events.

He opted against running that year but he had laid the foundation. His political career was born, the seeds of his 2016 campaign planted. And it was all based on a lie. A racist lie.

It wasn't his first: in 1989, he took out a full-page ad to call for the death penalty for the "Central Park Five," a group of Black teenagers arrested for an assault of a female jogger. Their convictions were later overturned. But birtherism was, in many ways, Trump's first Big Lie. It was an idea plucked from the fever swamps of the Right when confronted with an out-of-nowhere presidential candidate from Illinois with an unusual name that, to some in the years after September 11, evoked a deposed Iraqi dictator and a vague sense of Muslim menace.

Barack. Hussein. Obama. When Trump really wanted to lean in on the racism, he'd add and accentuate the middle name, one that didn't sound like it would belong to a man whose mother was from Kansas. Now, Trump wasn't the first to question the heritage of Obama, who was born in Hawaii. When Obama burst onto the national scene ahead of the 2008 election, he had to fend off all sorts of accusations that he wasn't American—Kenyan was the most popular guess—and therefore not eligible to be president.

Memorably, his GOP opponent that year, Senator John McCain, corrected a woman who, at a town hall, declared that Obama was an Arab. McCain said that, no, his opponent was "a decent family man." Though hailed as a unifying moment—the transformative election of the nation's first nonwhite president, the ascension to power of a Black man a century and a half after the end of slavery—Obama's victory did little to quell the conspiracies. Entire cottage industries were set up on the fringes of the right-wing media—all too often seeping onto the airwaves on Fox News—that suggested that Obama was Other, that he was not qualified or eligible to be president.

No one stoked those hateful flames more than Trump. In 2010, as he eyed a possible challenge to Obama's reelection bid, he had his then-fixer Michael Cohen plant stories with the Trump-friendly editors at the *National Enquirer* that questioned the president's birthplace. Trump himself upped the ante the following year, doing a series of interviews that spring in which he declared himself "skeptical" of Obama's heritage.

With no evidence, Trump theorized on *The View* that "there [was] something on that birth certificate that Obama doesn't like," which prompted this understated response from host Whoopi Goldberg: "That's the biggest pile of dog mess I've heard in ages." On a near-daily basis, Trump questioned Obama's citizenship and demanded to see his long-form birth certificate, even suggesting he would send private investigators to Hawaii to prove that the president was not born there.

Well, Obama released the long-form birth certificate. Trump, always trying to claim a victory and twist a moment to boost his own stature, shamelessly took credit, somehow trying to spin a humbling defeat into a personal triumph, saying, "I am really honored and I am really proud, that I was able to do something that nobody else could do." Obama, though, didn't let him off the hook, turning that spring's White House Correspondents' Association Dinner into a roast of Trump, who was in attendance.

Obama unloaded one cutting joke after another while Trump sat there, trapped, his smile frozen in place. He managed a few waves.

"No one is happier, no one is prouder to put this birth certificate matter to rest than the Donald," Obama said. "And that's because he can finally get back to focusing on the issues that matter—like, did we fake the moon landing? What really happened in Roswell? And where are Biggie and Tupac?"

Obama didn't let up: "All kidding aside, obviously, we all know about your credentials and breadth of experience. For example—no, seriously, just recently, in an episode of *The Celebrity Apprentice* at the steak house, the men's team cooking did not impress the judges from Omaha Steaks. And there was a lot of blame to go around. But you, Mr. Trump, recognized that the real problem was a lack of leadership. And so ultimately, you didn't blame Lil Jon or Meat Loaf. You fired Gary Busey. And these are the kind of decisions that would keep me up at night. Well handled, sir."

The president's victory only became more astounding the next day, when it was revealed that he was humiliating Trump just hours after he had authorized the raid that killed Osama bin Laden in Pakistan. It was, in many respects, Obama's highest moment and Trump's lowest.

But Trump did not fade away. The birtherism lie had found traction on the Right and it allowed Trump to grab a foothold within the

Republican Party. His spots on Fox News only increased, and his was a coveted endorsement among Republicans in 2012 after he passed on his own candidacy that year. The unease that more establishment Republicans felt about Trump was obvious when the party's nominee that year, Mitt Romney, accepted the developer's backing. The event wasn't at Romney's campaign headquarters in Boston, a short distance from Fenway Park, but rather at an awkward, halting news conference in the lobby of the provocateur's Las Vegas hotel.

"There are some things that you just can't imagine happening in your life," an uncomfortable-looking Romney told the crowd. "This is one of them."

And when Romney lost to Obama, Trump was quick to blame the former Massachusetts governor for ignoring his advice, for not fighting dirty; privately, he even suggested the defeat was because birtherism voters were ignored. Lies should be embraced, he reasoned, if they helped a candidate win.

He would not make the same mistake.

* * *

On June 16, 2015, a small crowd of onlookers—some of whom, it was later discovered, were paid to be there—and a crush of reporters crowded into the gilded basement lobby of Trump Tower. Trump had teased running so many times before, and he was perceived by official Washington as such a sideshow, that many news outlets didn't send their top political reporters. The campaign editor at the Associated Press, for instance, didn't bother sending up a reporter from Washington and just had its New York–based political reporter cover the event. Expectations were low: the editor had booked a story for just three hundred words.

Then Trump descended the golden escalator. A lot more words were needed.

What followed was the beginning of the most tumultuous and likely most vicious presidential campaign in modern history. In the Tower that day, I watched Trump spew a hard-line anti-immigration policy, declaring that many Mexicans were rapists. He became the day's top political story. And he held that title just about every day for the next year and a half.

Trump was vulgar, outrageous, shameless, thrilling. His campaign was a mix of celebrity, wealth, racism, and political incorrectness, and he became a phenomenon, drawing both outsize media attention and massive crowds to swamp his far more established Republican rivals. As his signature 757 airplane crisscrossed the nation, he'd insult Republican and Democrat alike, no cow too sacred to attack. He turned politics on its head and did so in front of the unblinking eyes of TV cameras that allowed him to dominate cable in a way that left his rivals hopelessly jealous and helplessly outgunned.

The campaign was built on one after another seemingly indestructible lie. By noon nearly every day, Trump would have already committed three political gaffes so severe that any one of them would have ended Mitt Romney's career. Yet he moved on without seemingly suffering a scratch.

And his Biggest Lie, the one that would redefine politics for the upcoming decade, also first took root during what ended up being that victorious campaign.

Trump faced voters for the first time that February in Iowa, a state where he failed to dominate the GOP polls like he did so many of those that followed. Anxious about the race, his behavior turned (more) erratic: he tossed off allegations that the Republican Party had fixed the election, and he pulled out of the final debate to instead hold a fundraiser for veterans that didn't pay out what it raised until it came under media scrutiny many months later.

He lost Iowa narrowly. And it was in Iowa where he first floated the idea that an election, the most sacred element of American democracy, was "rigged." It wasn't the claim of full-fledged voter fraud that would define his bid four years later, but he still assailed the integrity of the process. His target wasn't some vast federal conspiracy, but rather the man who captured the caucus, Texas senator Ted Cruz.

"Based on the fraud committed by Senator Ted Cruz during the Iowa Caucus, either a new election should take place or Cruz results nullified," Trump tweeted. And another one: "Ted Cruz didn't win Iowa, he stole it. That is why all of the polls were so wrong and why he got far more votes than anticipated. Bad!"

The celebrity businessman made some half-baked assertion that Cruz—perhaps with help from the Republican Party—had made some efforts to improperly woo backers of another candidate, Ben Carson, but Trump never followed up with any support for his claims. And his supporters in the media were also not willing to back him up, as they would in the future, when he wielded presidential power. He looked like a whiner, they said, a sore loser. One cable television personality even visited Trump in his New Hampshire hotel days later and screamed at him to knock it off.

Trump's allegation didn't last: he rolled on to massive victories in New Hampshire and South Carolina, and the nomination was quickly in his grasp. But a marker had been placed.

Politics had never seen anything like Trump's shamelessness. He compared hand size with Marco Rubio. He called a former *Apprentice* contestant overweight. He feuded with a Gold Star family. He praised authoritarians. And he tried to ban an entire religion.

After a terror attack by Islamic State terrorists in Paris in November 2015, Trump proposed tracking Muslims in the United States, putting surveillance teams on mosques and creating a database for all members of the religion in the United States. It was met with sharp bipartisan rebukes but, a few weeks later, after an attack by a married couple of ISIS sympathizers in San Bernardino, California, the candidate went even further, calling for "a total and complete shutdown of Muslims entering the United States until our country's representatives can figure out what is going on."

It was his most outrageous statement of the campaign to that point, one that was immediately denounced by the Pentagon—which feared it could inspire more terror—as well as by leaders in the United Kingdom and France. But Trump for days repeated the call at his rallies, drawing cheers from the crowds.

Republican leaders wondered what was going on. Would Trump's supporters follow him anywhere, even when he proposed stifling the nation's defining creed to protect freedom of religion?

Would they follow him after he made a racist attack on a federal judge?

Trump University, the candidate's real estate development course, turned out to offer no college credit and very little value. It became the subject of a series of lawsuits that charged that it was nothing more than a scam to line Trump's pockets. In one case, after Trump was dealt a setback, he unleashed an attack on Gonzalo Curiel, the presiding judge in two of the cases, stating that Curiel's Mexican heritage served as a conflict of interest.

"Now, this judge is of Mexican heritage. I'm building a wall, okay? I'm building a wall."

Curiel was from Indiana. Trump was denounced by Republican leaders, including House Speaker Paul Ryan. His crowds continued to cheer.

Trump's campaign was dealt its lowest blow in October, just before the second presidential debate, when a 2005 recording emerged of Trump on *Access Hollywood* bragging about sexually assaulting women. For forty-eight hours, his campaign seemed on the verge of collapse; Trump, appearing in what looked like a hostage video, even offered a pseudo-apology for the "locker-room talk" heard on the clip. Republican leaders called for him to drop out. He holed up in his penthouse. His campaign seemed finished. But the day after the tape was released, he went downstairs and ventured into a crowd of supporters who had gathered outside Trump Tower. They mobbed him. He felt energized, he felt loved again, and he vowed to keep fighting. The next day, just before the debate with Hillary Clinton began in St. Louis, the campaign press pool was told to gather for a last-minute event. We reacted with surprise. Who holds an event within an hour of a debate? We were then told we'd simply be getting a quick glimpse of Trump rehearsing. But that's not at all what we saw.

Instead, Trump was sitting with four women, three of whom—Paula Jones, Kathleen Willey, and Juanita Broaddrick—had accused Clinton's husband, the former president, of sexual misconduct. The fourth, Kathy Shelton, was there because when she was raped as a twelve-year-old, Hillary Clinton, then a lawyer, defended her assailant in court. The Trump campaign was answering the *Access Hollywood* tape with its own allegations of women being mistreated.

Reporters who had covered Trump for more than a year—who felt they were beyond being shocked—were left with their mouths hanging open, as Steve Bannon smiled wide with glee behind them. I was slack-jawed. A news photographer hardened by a brutal time in Iraq who was too tough to be stunned—well, he audibly gasped. The secret was so closely held that Stephanie Grisham, the campaign staffer whose job it was to wrangle the press pool, keeping them in line and on time, wasn't told in advance about it, instead thinking, like the reporters, that she was simply giving them a chance to observe debate prep.

Grisham later broke down and wept, telling confidants that she was horrified by the stunt and just as upset to be kept out of that loop. She would later become White House press secretary and First Lady Melania Trump's closest aide.

It was a reckless gambit, but it steadied the campaign. But even that wasn't enough. Months later, when he took office, Trump revised his story, walking back his public acknowledgment of the recording's authenticity. To the amazement of staffers and a handful of Republican senators with whom he addressed the matter, Trump began raising questions as to whether it was his voice on the tape at all.

"We don't think that was my voice," Trump privately told a senator, according to an aide who overheard the conversation. He suggested that he might order an investigation into the matter. The probe never materialized.

* * *

The St. Louis stunt worked. Trump had changed the conversation; the race stabilized. And, soon after, the Republican moved back into striking distance when FBI director James Comey ordered the investigation into Clinton's private email server reopened. Trump forged ahead with the campaign, moving into darker rhetoric, avoiding interviews, dodging events where reporters might ask him about further accusations of sexual harassment.

When he did hold a small business roundtable in West Palm Beach, Florida, on October 13, just a few weeks before the election, I tried to ask him if he had ever touched or kissed a woman without her consent. As the crowd of business leaders booed me and staffers pushed the press pool out the door, Trump could be heard speaking as he gestured toward me: "What a sleazebag."

That night, at a packed downtown arena in Cincinnati, the audience was so vitriolic toward the press that the Secret Service moved the press pool out of its normal position on the floor near the rally goers, away from the ugly crowd and back toward an exit bay behind the parked motorcade and the SWAT team. The agents told us it was the only way that they could guarantee our safety.

The final few weeks of the campaign were relentless: Comey had given Trump an opening, raising those (often sexist) questions about Clinton's trustworthiness. The new emails had been found on the computer of Anthony Weiner, the former congressman who had resigned after a sexting scandal. Weiner, who suffered a relapse that cost him a chance at the 2013 New York City mayoral election, was married to Huma Abedin, Clinton's most trusted aide. Trump hammered it home night after night, his campaign also happily embracing the help offered by WikiLeaks, which took a batch of hacked Clinton campaign emails—stolen by Russian operatives—and slowly doled them out over months. Later, the media would have a collective soul-searching over the appropriateness of reporting on the stolen materials; but in 2016, it for the most part eagerly reported on the materials, and the drip, drip, drip wounded Clinton.

The race tightened dramatically in the final week. Trump relentlessly pushed across the map, holding five or six rallies a day. His finale was supposed to be on Election Day eve in New Hampshire, the site of his first primary victory, but some late data prompted Bannon to schedule another one, post-midnight, in Grand Rapids, Michigan.

Democrats in that state—as well as the others in the blue firewall, Wisconsin and Pennsylvania—saw the same things. They frantically signaled to the Clinton campaign that they could glimpse troubling omens: Trump signs and hats were everywhere, and new voters—the most difficult thing to find in politics—were emerging for the Republican. Independents broke his way too at the end. Bill Clinton also sensed trouble, but his wife's campaign was focused on expanding the map, rather than simply getting the needed 270 Electoral College votes. Still, a final rally in Philadelphia, featuring the Obamas and Bruce Springsteen, felt like a coronation.

Clinton's choice of setting for her expected Election Night victory was full of symbolism. She would stand under the glass ceiling of the Jacob K. Javits Convention Center in Manhattan as she shattered the last one remaining in American politics. The night started well: the exit polling and some early states looked strong. But within a few hours, in newsrooms across America, journalists looking at the data could all see the same thing: Florida was going hard for Trump, fueled by an overwhelming turnout in Republican counties. A few hours later, it was clear that the rural areas in Michigan, Pennsylvania, and Wisconsin were coming out in record numbers for Trump and, combined with softer Democratic turnout in the cities, would give him those states too.

Clinton conceded the next morning. The glass ceiling remained intact. It was instantly one of the unlikeliest electoral triumphs in the nation's history. The political world had been upended.

Trump won.

3

THE TRUMP PRESIDENCY

The presidency began with a lie.

President Donald J. Trump, the forty-fifth president of the United States, a man who had transformed from laughingstock to the most powerful man on the planet in five short years, woke up on January 21, 2017, in the White House. Here was a man who cared about status and power above all else, and on a blustery Saturday morning in Washington, Trump stirred early at the world's most famous address, a place he now called home. He had done it.

He woke up angry.

Trump had long been an obsessive cable TV watcher, a habit that only accelerated once he became president, despite the demands of the office. And it was fitting, in a way, that his TV fixation played a role in his very first full day in office. It would be far from the last.

The news on January 21 was, of course, wall-to-wall coverage of the new commander in chief. Trump had, again, achieved his ultimate goal of being the center of conversation, the name on everyone's lips. But what the anchors were saying—and displaying—infuriated him.

The hosts that day were showing photos of the National Mall and the crowd that fanned out from the Capitol's west steps, where Trump had delivered his sixteen-minute inaugural address: dark, almost dystopic remarks, quickly dubbed the "American carnage" speech after a stunningly bleak line that prompted former president George W. Bush to deem the whole thing some "weird shit."

The crowd was sizable. But it was not nearly as large as the one that had welcomed President Barack Obama's 2009 inauguration. Obama's crowd was packed shoulder to shoulder and stretched all the way to the Washington Monument. Trump's was nowhere near that.

And that was unacceptable to the new president, as was the footage that dominated the TVs that day of the Women's March, as women—and some men—thronged cities across the globe, many wearing pink hats, as a protest against one common cause: Trump. These crowds, too, dwarfed what Trump's inauguration had drawn. Crowd size was a particular obsession with Trump, who night after night during the campaign would brag that his crowds were bigger than those drawn by his competitors (that was almost always true) and that thousands more people were lined up outside unable to get into the sold-out venue (that was almost always not true).

He was furious. He felt he was the target of mockery. What came next was the birth of the first lie of Trump's presidency.

* * *

The day after Trump's inauguration was Sean Spicer's first full day as White House press secretary.

It was a career pinnacle for a good GOP soldier, one who had climbed the ranks in the Republican National Committee and earned a reputation among political journalists as a solid guy, one who could be slippery but, in the right moment, could give you a more unvarnished take on his party's power brokers. Spicer was closely linked to Reince Priebus, Trump's first White House chief of staff, both party loyalists who fit uneasily in Trump's orbit. It was Priebus, in fact, who told Trump he should bow out after the release of the *Access Hollywood* tape. And it was

Spicer who had offered an off-the-record briefing to reporters just before the election, mapping out how Trump would likely lose.

But, short of better options and at the time (nominally) still trying to remain in the party's good graces, Trump put them both in key posts. Spicer was nervous but also proud and excited. He had grown up in New England; he would defend Tom Brady to the death; and while he had mixed feelings about the man for whom he now worked, he also believed that Trump could change, could moderate some of his positions once he got to office.

"Reince," Spicer would tell his longtime colleague, "the president has the right people around him and we can keep him in check." Priebus was less sure.

Spicer's first press briefing was slated for Monday. That Saturday, the first full day in the West Wing, was meant for staffers to move in and figure out how to work the light switches and overhead intercom (it took a while on both). Spicer, wearing a suit that didn't fit quite as well as it should have, was unpacking his office when he was summoned.

Trump wanted him out there. He wanted a briefing. And he wanted Spicer to say that Trump's crowd was bigger than Obama's. It was a lie, by any measure. But it was the first full day, and Spicer's job and proximity to power were already on the line. So he did it. He lied.

In the grand scheme of things, an exaggeration about crowd size seems quaint, trivial. And indeed, most Republicans on Capitol Hill laughed it off. But it set a template, and not just because Spicer's credibility was thrown away in his first moments on the job. This was a lie that had come from the White House podium. The levers and power and symbols of government were behind the lie, even if it was a fairly inconsequential one. White House staffers could have snuffed out the lie but they didn't, for fear of losing power and access. A year later, a National Park Service employee admitted he edited photos to cut out empty spaces to make the crowd look bigger, an early example of a government employee misusing power to make the president look good.

Trump got ridiculed, to be sure, but no one told him no. There were no real consequences. He could lie and put the power of the government behind it.

And soon, he turned his attention to the vote.

* * *

Fueled by a refusal to admit any sort of defeat, even though he now called the White House home, Trump went on a crusade and, for the first time at the executive mansion, made repeated and unsubstantiated claims of voter fraud. How many votes, in Trump's estimation, were cast illegally? Well, just about exactly the number by which he lost the popular vote to Hillary Clinton.

Clinton won the popular vote by nearly 2.9 million ballots, handing Trump the largest popular vote defeat of any president who won the Electoral College. That didn't sit well with the president-elect, who sought ways to explain why such a humbling defeat couldn't possibly be legitimate.

The answer included a golfer.

Trump began privately telling confidants—and then a group of Republican lawmakers soon after taking the oath of office—that his friend professional golfer Bernhard Langer had tried to vote near his Florida home on Election Day only to be turned away. Worse yet, people who didn't "look like they should be allowed to vote" were permitted to stay in line, the president claimed, citing potential Latin American countries of origin for the would-be voters. He told the story to Senate and House Republicans, who were noshing on pigs in a blanket as they gathered in the White House's State Dining Room for a get-to-know-you just a few days after Inauguration Day.

Langer later denied that the story had happened that way, and his daughter noted that he, as a German citizen, was not permitted to vote in the United States anyway. But it took hold in Trump's mind, as did the apocryphal tale that Democrats were loading up buses to drive voters from deep-blue Massachusetts across the border into swing state New Hampshire, causing the president's narrow defeat in a state that, since his primary win there in February, he deeply prized. And all those votes in California must be from illegal immigrants, Trump thought.

A framework was established: the Republicans eating hors d'oeuvres at the White House said nothing to dispute Trump's claims of voter fraud. White House chief of staff Priebus prodded Trump to change the subject, according to those in attendance, but none of the lawmakers pushed back, even slightly, to the president's wildly erroneous claims. Nor did they object when he took to Twitter to announce a major federal investigation into his evidence-free claims.

"The president does believe that there was election fraud," said Spicer. "It's a belief that he's maintained for a while, a concern that he has about voter fraud. And that's based on information that's provided."

Republicans had advanced claims of voter fraud, large and small, for years, though virtually no evidence of such improprieties has been discovered—and none had neared the magnitude of the claims put forth by Trump. He wrote on Twitter, "In addition to winning the Electoral College in a landslide, I won the popular vote if you deduct the millions of people who voted illegally."

Then that May, Trump announced a new commission to chase down the allegations of voter fraud—ones thoroughly debunked since Election Day—and while it would be nominally led by Vice President Mike Pence, symbolizing its importance, it would be run by Kris Kobach, the Kansas secretary of state known for sharing the president's hard-line immigration views. The idea of the commission had been percolating behind the scenes for a while, but the formal announcement of its creation—done in typical slapdash Trump fashion—was rushed, hurriedly sent out to distract from the constitutional crisis the president had sparked that week by firing FBI director James Comey, which led to the appointment of special counsel Robert Mueller, whose Russia investigation would shadow the White House for two years.

The commission went nowhere fast. With no credible evidence of fraud in hand to validate the conclusion that both Trump and Kobach had clearly already reached, it had to turn up something quickly before the famously impatient president lost his temper. In June, Kobach sent a letter to states asking for all publicly available voter data, including names, addresses, voting history, party affiliation, felony convictions, and the last four digits of Social Security numbers.

That was a bridge too far for some state Republicans who, while long advocates of more restrictive voting laws, also bristled at the idea that they had overseen a fraudulent election. Foreshadowing the stands taken by GOP secretaries of state in places like Georgia and Arizona years later, some officials balked, with Bill Gardner, New Hampshire's secretary of state and a commission member, rejecting the group's efforts to probe fraud in his home state. And even a few Republicans from Trump strongholds said no, including Mississippi secretary of state Delbert Hosemann, who addressed the commission's request by memorably saying, "My reply would be: they can go jump in the Gulf of Mexico and Mississippi is a great state to launch from."

The commission was put out of its misery in January 2018, having found no evidence of voter fraud and disbanding without even disclosing its findings. After a lawsuit filed by Maine's secretary of state forced the release, the final report was put out there for the nation to see: there was unequivocally no widespread voter fraud in the 2016 election. It was over. Trump had lied. The tangible impact was minimal: some taxpayer money was spent and plenty of ink spilled, but for the most part the nation shrugged and moved on, the nonsensical probe overshadowed by the daily dramas consuming the West Wing.

But there were ripple effects. According to polls, the number of Republicans who believed there was the potential for voter fraud increased. The conservative media more freely tossed around accusations without penalty. And the national Republicans had largely stayed silent, allowing Trump to make the false claims with impunity. He paid no price for his lies. The message from the GOP seemed to be: Yes, Trump's election fraud claims were unseemly, inaccurate, and embarrassing, but what harm did they do?

What harm could they possibly do?

* * *

The election fraud claims became the Big Lie, but there were many (many, many, many) other falsehoods. While it's tempting to say that Trump told too many lies to count, that's not accurate since the fact-checkers at the *Washington Post* did, in fact, tally them. During the president's four years in office, he uttered 30,573 false and misleading claims, according to the newspaper. That's 7,643 a year, nearly 21 a day. And those are only the ones he told in public.

There was the time he told reporters on Air Force One that he knew nothing about the payments made to purchase the silence of Stormy Daniels, the porn star with whom Trump had sex. He claimed to have ended Obama's family separation program when in fact he dramatically grew it and enforced it to draconian levels. He lied repeatedly that Joe Biden's health care plan eliminated coverage for those with preexisting conditions.

Some lies were pointless, like when he claimed that the head of the Boy Scouts told him that his address to their national jamboree was the best speech ever given to the organization—when in actuality it was an inappropriate ramble and the group's leader never said such a thing. Some lies were silly, like when he'd make up tales of burly men crying and addressing him as "sir" to thank him for, well, whatever it is Trump felt like talking about that day.

Some lies were dangerous, like when he claimed that Representative Ilhan Omar supported Al Qaeda, leading to death threats to the

Somali-born congresswoman from Minnesota. Some lies showcased his willingness to take advantage of dirty politics, like when he was able to name Neil Gorsuch to the Supreme Court in 2017 on the back of the lie told by Senate Majority Leader Mitch McConnell that Obama was not eligible to fill a vacant Supreme Court seat the year before because there was an election upcoming.

And some lies were just plain hard to categorize, like Trump's insistence that windmills cause cancer.

But a deeper dive into a pair of his falsehoods reveals how, over his four years in office, Trump was willing to repeatedly tell shameless lies, overrun any allies' objections to them, and abuse the power of his office to insist they were true.

One way Trump pushed his lies was simply by repetition, by sheer force of will and personality, fueled by the belief that if he just said something over and over again he could will it to be true or at least confuse or convince others to go along with it.

The Veterans' Access to Care through Choice, Accountability, and Transparency Act—shorthanded as the Veterans Choice Program—was signed into law by President Obama in 2014. That is true. On June 6, 2018, President Donald Trump signed the John S. McCain III, Daniel K. Akaka, and Samuel R. Johnson VA Maintaining Internal Systems and Strengthening Integrated Outside Networks Act—the MISSION Act—which was a modest and good update to the law. That is also true.

Very little of what happened next was.

White House aides and allies of the president were not quite sure how it started, or if Trump made a conscious choice to erase Obama's contribution. But in the coming weeks, Trump began systematically rewriting history, eliminating not just Obama's role but also that of Senator John McCain of Arizona, a Republican rival who was a fierce critic of Trump and who cast the deciding vote to scuttle his health care legislation. McCain was one of the three senator sponsors for whom the

MISSION Act was named, and yet Trump would go on to say that McCain—a veteran himself who had spent years as a prisoner of war in Vietnam—had nothing to do with the bill.

"McCain didn't get the job done for our great vets and the VA, and they knew it," Trump said during a 2019 campaign stop in Ohio. Over the next two years, Trump told more than 150 false and misleading statements about the bill, according to terrific reporting in the *Washington Post*, his story changing until, in his version, he was the sole force behind it.

The president's handling of the Veterans Choice legislation offers a sharp look into the evolution of a Trump lie: the initial false claim, the subsequent embellishment, the incessant repetition, and clear signs that he knows the truth but chooses to keep telling the lie—all enabled by aides either unwilling or unable to stop him.

Stakeholders acknowledge that Obama's 2014 legislation was well intentioned but flawed, and Trump could have just touted his own measure as an improvement. But that wasn't good enough, especially for a president looking to burnish his ties to the military ahead of a reelection effort.

The Veterans Choice Program sprang up in the aftermath of a massive Veterans Affairs scandal in 2014, in which scheduling staff at VA hospitals across the country had been instructed to falsify their waiting lists to cover up the long waits for even basic care. The woes at one VA medical center in Phoenix made national headlines, with an inspector general's report finding that officials there falsified records to cover up the fact that veterans on average waited 115 days for an appointment—and some died while waiting. The legislation Trump signed made it easier for veterans to seek private care and offered improvements such as allowing veterans to see non-VA doctors for primary care if the VA faced delays.

There were some West Wing aides who, behind the scenes, tried to get Trump to change his language, suggesting that it unnecessarily left them open to fact-checking and diluted the impact of what was, by any measure, a successful piece of legislation. But the president refused.

"No one loves veterans like me. Obama and McCain didn't do anything, they didn't do what I did," Trump would say, according to multiple aides. He'd sometimes toss in an expletive and just steamroll over the aides' concerns. But the president and his speechwriters were wedded to the language of "Veterans Choice," the language of the Obama bill, because they wanted to take full credit and because they believed "choice" was an appealing word, and no one knew, they believed, what the "MISSION Act" was.

So Trump continued to just use "Choice," erasing Obama's role and taking full credit. It was not a dangerous lie, but a blatant one, and one on which he did not like to be challenged. He finally was pushed in August 2020, during a coronavirus news conference at his tony Bedminster, New Jersey, golf club, when CBS News White House correspondent Paula Reid asked him, "Why do you keep saying that you passed Veterans Choice?"

As Trump tried to call on another reporter instead, Reid continued, "You said that you passed Veterans Choice. It was passed in 2014 . . . it was a false statement, sir."

Trump paused and looked around the room. He then abruptly ended the news conference and walked out. Later, when an aide pointed out that the offending question was built on a correct premise, Trump ignored him. And, in the weeks ahead, he continued telling the same lie.

Another—and more ominous—way Trump pushed a lie was to use his presidential power to make it appear true.

Hurricane Dorian was massive and deadly. With winds reaching more than 220 miles per hour, it grew to be a Category 5 storm, one that could wipe a community off the map, as it gained power in the Atlantic Ocean. Before it was done, it would tear through the Bahamas, becoming the most destructive storm to ever smash through the islands.

As it moved menacingly toward the United States, the National

Weather Service and local and government officials who, due to climate change, had become depressingly practiced at warning the populace about extreme weather, began to send out the usual alerts. It certainly was not uncommon for a president of the United States to use his platform and visibility to do the same. It was just everything that followed that was unusual.

Trump tweeted on September 1, 2019, that "In addition to Florida—South Carolina, North Carolina, Georgia, and Alabama, will most likely be hit (much) harder than anticipated."

Most of that was true, to be sure. But Trump's claim that Alabama was in harm's way was not. A National Oceanic and Atmospheric Administration forecast from two days earlier found that a tiny portion of southeastern Alabama might be affected by Dorian because the "cone of uncertainty" extended a few miles into the state. But NOAA forecasts current at the time of Trump's tweet showed the storm not impacting the state at all, since it was moving north instead of west.

Within a half hour, due to fears that the president's erroneous statement could lead to panic in the state ahead of the storm, the Birmingham, Alabama, Twitter account for NOAA's National Weather Service tweeted that the state would not be affected by the hurricane: "Alabama will NOT see any impacts from #Dorian. We repeat, no impacts from Hurricane #Dorian will be felt across Alabama. The system will remain too far east."

This was what government agencies typically do: they deal in facts and try to provide the most current information possible for the citizens who rely on them, particularly ahead of a looming crisis. But an hour later, during a briefing at the Federal Emergency Management Agency's headquarters, Trump again referred to supposed new information that "just came up, unfortunately."

"And, I will say, the states—and it may get a little piece of a great place: It's called Alabama. And Alabama could even be in for at least some very strong winds and something more than that, it could be.

This just came up, unfortunately. It's the size of—the storm that we're talking about. So, for Alabama, just please be careful also."

But, again, that was not true. And by the night, the contradiction began to get traction in the media, as the Birmingham NOAA tweet went viral. Trump only dug in. He went on to argue that "certain original scenarios" had suggested Alabama could be affected. But that claim was plainly contradicted by all three of his Sunday comments, in which he had suggested he was referring to new information.

A few days later, the saga took a turn for the absurd. On September 4, after the worst of the storm had cascaded across the United States, Trump called reporters into the Oval Office. Though some Americans had died in the storm, that was not what was on the president's mind: instead he held up a NOAA forecast from the morning of August 29—altered with a crudely drawn black line that took the hurricane forecast into Alabama.

Reporters in the room looked at one another. One pulled up an image of the original version of the map on his phone—the image did not display a black line extending into Alabama. No, it was only this map, being held by this president, that featured a black line, obviously drawn by a black Sharpie of the type that Trump favored.

"What the fuck?" one reporter whispered to himself. Trump pushed forward, declaring again that "Alabama was in the original forecast." He insisted: "They actually gave that a 95 percent chance—probability." But again, that never happened. Advisers later admitted that Trump had demanded a map to justify his original claim and, outraged that it did not show Alabama impacted, grabbed a marker to alter it.

The story could have ended there, as the latest example of Trump's ego running out of control and his refusal to admit a mistake leading to an embarrassing display. Twitter had a field day, as did the late-night talk shows, and Trump, again, looked petty and unserious, unable to admit a mistake. But the story took a more serious turn. And once more, it showed that Trump was not above using the levers of power, the tools of the federal government, to back up a lie.

As the focus shifted to rebuilding in the wake of Dorian, the NOAA on September 6 suddenly published an unsigned statement in support of Trump's initial claim. Its key line: that National Hurricane Center models "demonstrated that tropical-storm-force winds from Hurricane Dorian could impact Alabama." Trump crowed that he was right. Democrats and good government watchdogs fretted that the White House had exerted undue influence to push a nonpartisan government agency—a team of scientists! meteorologists!—to do the president's bidding. Was there nothing, Democrats feared, that Trump would not corrupt?

Investigations were launched and the results were not surprising. By the following summer, a pair of probes—one internal, one launched by the inspector general of the Commerce Department—found that the acting NOAA administrator, Neil Jacobs, a Trump appointee, and other officials inappropriately used their positions during the flap. Jacobs, the probes found, had ordered the drafting of the September 6 statement and criticized the employees in Birmingham for contradicting Trump. He had "engaged in the misconduct intentionally, knowingly, or in reckless disregard" for the agency's scientific integrity policy, according to a panel commissioned by the agency to investigate complaints against him. And the Commerce Department inspector general concluded that some department employees—NOAA falls within the Commerce Department—had received instructions from the White House itself to support Trump's claims.

This was no longer a sideshow about a bad tweet or even a Sharpie drawing on a map. This was no longer a moment meant for Stephen Colbert. This was something far more serious: Trump knew no bounds, and there were few checks on his power. The guardrails were gone.

And as Trump so casually pulled the levers of power in support of his lies, he changed the very nature of the nation's politics and deliberately exacerbated the mistrust many Americans already had in their government. Faith in the nation's institutions first began to waver after the Kennedy assassination and then fell dramatically after Vietnam and Watergate. The government, which after the New Deal and World War II was largely seen as a force for good, suddenly couldn't be trusted to do the right thing or do anything well.

That erosion in confidence only accelerated after the September 11, 2001, terror attacks; the faulty justification for the Iraq War; the federal government's mishandling of the response to Hurricane Katrina that left a proud American city to nearly drown; and the government's response to the financial crisis of 2008–9, with bank bailouts, home foreclosures, and the sense that the rich were getting richer at the expense of everyone else.

Similarly, the partisan warfare had intensified in the decades before 2016. The 1990s, which featured an explosion in conservative media, saw the fault lines grow, with fury over culture wars and the impeachment of President Bill Clinton. That fight—Team Red versus Team Blue—grew far more vicious during the contested election of 2000, which was captured by George W. Bush with the support of fewer voters than Al Gore but more Supreme Court justices.

There were accusations of dirty tricks, claims that the Republicans had stolen the election, and, for the first time in a century, questions about a president's legitimacy. The bitter partisan anger grew after the misguided invasion of Iraq and the near collapse of the financial market, with many placing the blame for both catastrophes squarely at Bush's feet. Obama's election provided a brief, fleeting moment of national exultation, but it too was soon lost to pure Republican obstructionism—with a meeting of powerful Republicans declaring on the very night of Obama's inauguration that they would kill his legislative agenda, and then–Senate minority leader Mitch McConnell soon declaring, "The single most important thing we want to achieve is for President

Obama to be a one-term president"—and the rise of the Tea Party, as well as a surge in racist rhetoric and violence. The Republican Party was already becoming more anti-science and antiestablishment, a party that jettisoned a lot of policy in favor of fighting along cultural lines.

Trump threw gasoline on those smoldering flames. Coherent party ideology? Gone. Long-held policy beliefs? Gone. Respect for the sanctity of the judiciary and military? Gone. Being tough on Russia? Gone. Leaning on international alliances? Gone.

Upholding the dignity of the office? Gone. As was rarely made clearer than on Saturday, March 4, 2017.

Washington woke up that morning to be greeted by a series of incendiary tweets from the commander in chief. They were jaw-dropping, with one Democratic congressional staffer awakening his wife with a shouted "Oh shit!" when he first glanced at his phone. They came in quick succession:

"Terrible! Just found out that Obama had my 'wires tapped' in Trump Tower just before the victory. Nothing found. This is McCarthyism!"

"Is it legal for a sitting President to be 'wire tapping' a race for president prior to an election? Turned down by court earlier. A NEW LOW!"

"I'd bet a good lawyer could make a great case out of the fact that President Obama was tapping my phones in October, just prior to Election!"

"How low has President Obama gone to tapp [*sic*] my phones during the very sacred election process. This is Nixon/Watergate. Bad (or sick) guy!"

The president of the United States, without any evidence, had claimed that his predecessor had wiretapped him, which would have been one of the gravest misuses of power in the history of the office. The ramifications would be massive. Had a sitting president used the powers of the office to try to put his thumb on the scale to rig the results of an election?

Trump himself, of course, would try to do just that four years later. But Obama had not. And Trump's claim came not from the US intelligence agencies or federal law enforcement, but from an influential conservative radio host who would occasionally wade into the right-wing fever swamps.

Mark Levin wasn't a boldface name, like Rush Limbaugh or Glenn Beck, but he had amassed a devoted following on the Right, aiming to add intellectual heft to some of the arguments espoused by conservative figures who, to put it charitably, were not intellectuals. Levin was antagonistic and combative, known for calling out media figures by name on his radio show and, at times, penning critical open letters (and posting them on Facebook) when he disagreed with a reporter's coverage of his show. Brian Stelter, CNN's media reporter, got one. So did yours truly.

Levin had stitched together material—including from such "liberal" media outlets as the *New York Times* and *Washington Post*—on Foreign Intelligence Surveillance Act (FISA) court warrants sought during the election. He went on to claim that the Obama administration had used unspecified "police state" surveillance tactics against the Trump campaign throughout the stretch run of 2016.

That claim was then amplified in a Breitbart piece that ran on Friday, the day before Trump's tweets, and it was passed along by Priebus in a phone call with the president. There was no hard evidence. But for Trump, there was enough to spew the falsehood.

"This is bigger than Watergate," Trump immediately told Priebus in that call, engaging in his favorite game—whataboutism—as he was eager for anything to deflect from the growing questions about his ties to Russia.

The institutional guardrails, this time, held against the lie. But there were consequences. Over the next forty-eight hours, the director of National Intelligence, James Clapper, and the FBI director, James Comey, both put out public statements refuting the accusation and making it clear that the Obama administration had not done any spying. Trump leaned on Spicer, once again, to back up the lie, and the embattled press secretary pushed Congress to investigate.

One GOP congressman happily led the charge.

Devin Nunes was the chair of the House Intelligence Committee and, therefore, tasked with running the investigation into Trump's claims. Nunes, whose family ran a dairy farm and who now represented inland California, was very much in Trump's thrall and would spend the remainder of his time in Congress bowing before the forty-fifth president. About two weeks into the wiretap matter, Nunes raced to the White House to meet with a source at a secure location to discuss possible evidence of surveillance.

Within a day, Nunes had largely backed off his claim, but the howls of protest about his behavior were deafening. Nunes was accused of collaborating with the White House, compromising the independence and integrity of his investigation.

"[Nunes] will need to decide whether he is the chairman of an independent investigation into conduct which includes allegations of potential coordination between the Trump campaign and the Russians, or he is going to act as a surrogate of the White House, because he cannot do both," said Representative Adam Schiff, the ranking Democrat on the committee.

Citing ethical complaints lodged against him, Nunes would eventually step down from his post, though he deemed the claims scurrilous and denied any wrongdoing. Four years later, after Trump had departed office, Nunes would actually announce his resignation from Congress as a whole, turning down a possible spot helming the powerful Ways and Means Committee in favor of taking a leadership post in Trump's fledgling social media start-up. Nunes, once more, tied himself to Trump.

But more significantly, Nunes was an early example of a Republican congressman defying tradition and breaking congressional norms in order to help Trump. He, like so many Republicans who would follow him, seemed to toss aside his integrity and loyalty to the job in order to back his party's president.

The Russia probe would come to define Trump's first two years in office. Democrats and certain cable news hosts deified the man put in charge of it, former FBI director Robert Mueller, as a man above the political fray, above Washington, a man with impeccable integrity and a crackerjack team who would surely—surely!—prove that Trump had conspired with Russia to get him elected in 2016. Russia had meddled in the election—that much was known—but the role that Trump and his campaign may have played was the source of 24/7 speculation.

It drove Trump crazy. He demanded loyalty from others on the payroll, acting more like a mob boss than commander in chief. He demanded subservience from officials, whom he treated as if they had sworn allegiance to him and not to the Constitution. Soon after Comey refused to publicly clear his name in the Russia probe, Trump fired him, an impulsive move that led to Mueller's appointment.

The special counsel worked in secret, and each incremental development in the probe was greeted with breathless headlines. Indictments followed of key figures in TrumpWorld: Paul Manafort, his campaign chairman; Michael Flynn, his first national security adviser; Roger Stone, his longtime political guru. They lied to the feds and paid the price.

Trump's behavior toward Russian president Vladimir Putin was always deferential, as he'd talk about his admiration for the authoritarian regime despite anger from his own party. Was Trump actually in Moscow's employ? Did they have kompromat on him? Or was his behavior fueled by insecurity, fears that if he admitted that Russia had interfered with the election, it would cheapen his victory and chip away at his legitimacy? So he lied, claiming that Russia had not interfered, undermining the very intelligence agencies that worked for him.

Trump's erratic behavior only fueled the whispers that he must have been in Putin's pocket, never more so than during the two leaders' July 2018 summit in Helsinki, Finland. It came at the end of a week in Europe in which Trump had threatened to blow up the NATO alliance and repeatedly undermined some of his nation's most faithful allies. I had covered Trump for three years at this point, three years that were shadowed by questions about Trump's ties to Moscow. This was the moment, as Trump stood with Putin, when it was time to ask.

Throughout the meeting, Trump appeared meek, dominated by his Russian counterpart. And then in the news conference afterward, I asked Trump to plainly state his allegiance.

"Just now President Putin denied having anything to do with the election interference in 2016. Every US intelligence agency has concluded that Russia did," I said to Trump. "My first question for you, sir, is who do you believe? My second question is, would you now with the whole world watching tell President Putin—would you denounce what happened in 2016 and would you warn him to never do it again?"

Trump did not hesitate, immediately denying there was any interference and siding with Putin over American intelligence officials. "I have President Putin," Trump said. "He just said it's not Russia. I will say this. I don't see any reason why it would be."

Fiona Hill, the senior Russia expert on the National Security Council, who was sitting one row in front of me, later told me that she considered doing something, anything—including faking a heart attack—to disrupt the proceedings and get Trump to stop talking. Then, I asked Putin if he possessed any kompromat on Trump or his family. He chuckled darkly at the question and, chillingly, did not break eye contact with me as he answered. Putin said it would be difficult to obtain damaging information on all prominent Americans. But he also didn't deny it.

The president's mood darkened soon after Air Force One raced back to Washington, as he watched Republicans and even Fox News excoriate his performance. He even yelled at Sarah Huckabee Sanders, the White House press secretary who replaced Spicer, for calling on me, a "tough reporter," to ask a question. And desperate to put the summit behind him, Trump pushed the pilot to return to Washington as fast as possible, shaving more than an hour off the aircraft's planned flight time. Aides tried to do some damage control, which Trump undermined days later by publicly floating the idea of having another summit with Putin, this time at the White House. It never happened.

The humiliation in Helsinki only heightened scrutiny of Trump's ties to Russia. And it added to the sense of tumult that gripped the nation and hurt the Republicans' efforts to keep power in the 2018 midterms. Beyond passing a major tax cut, which largely helped the wealthy, Trump's legislative scorecard was fairly empty, independents were turned off, and Democrats were motivated. Though the GOP held the Senate that November, Democrats seized control of the House, restoring Nancy Pelosi as Speaker and giving the party the ability to run scores of congressional investigations into the Trump administration—as well as, notably, impeachment power.

But when Mueller finally delivered his report in March 2019, it did not fulfill many Democrats' dreams. The public's first glimpse of its contents was conveyed via a letter from newly appointed Attorney General William Barr, who whitewashed Mueller's findings. It concluded that Russia actively tried to help Trump and that the Republicans' campaign eagerly accepted the help; however, it did not find sufficient evidence to bring conspiracy charges against Trump or his aides. Mueller also did not reach a conclusion about an obstruction of justice charge against Trump, leaning heavily into a Justice Department recommendation that prohibited federal indictment of a sitting president.

But that ambiguity mattered to Trump not at all. With a roar, he leaped into a victory lap, again declaring the whole investigation a "witch hunt" and falsely claiming that he had received a "total exoneration." When Mueller's congressional appearance months later proved anticlimactic, with the former FBI director faltering at times, the Russia probe finally seemed to be behind Trump.

Emboldened, he picked up the phone.

4

THE DEMOCRATS

The night of November 8, 2016, was meant to be one of historic triumph.

Many women throughout the nation looked forward to it with excitement and anxiety, nervously hoping that a sexist barrier would be destroyed and the first female commander in chief would take office. What was to be the former secretary of state's victory party was held at the Javits Center on Manhattan's West Side, a massive convention center that, unsubtly, featured a massive glass ceiling.

But it didn't break. And Hillary Clinton's loss left Democrats reeling.

Instead, Democrats of both genders were left with tears streaming down their faces. The same was true a few miles away at the impromptu party that had gathered at the intersection of President Street and Clinton Street in Cobble Hill, Brooklyn. Democrats throughout the nation were numb and stunned by the night, as it wasn't just that Clinton lost— it's that she lost to *him*. She lost to the candidate who bragged about sexual harassment and openly mused about grabbing women by their private parts. She lost to the candidate who cavalierly rated women on their looks and discussed sleeping with his friends' wives. She lost to the candidate who complained bitterly about a beauty pageant contestant's weight. And she lost to the candidate who was accused of sexual assault by more than a dozen women. It felt like a repudiation of their values, maybe of an entire gender.

To make matters worse, there wasn't much in the way of roadblocks for Trump, as Republicans in 2016 also claimed both the House and the Senate. The day after the election, Barack Obama made a point of walking through the West Wing to tell teary-eyed, shell-shocked aides that things would eventually be okay, that not everything for which they had worked over the last eight years was lost. But when he addressed staffers—and the nation—from the Rose Garden that after-noon, Joe Biden standing forlornly alongside, it appeared that many of those gathered didn't quite believe him.

Leading Democrats were left grappling with how to handle Trump's bull-in-a-china-shop approach, how to deal with a president who attacked mercilessly and lied brazenly and seemed to suffer no consequences for it. Trump would end up often emerging as his own enemy, damaged by his own arrogance and incompetence, but that was difficult to see during the Democrats' dark winter of 2016. Capitol Hill aides, Obama veterans, party leaders in deep-blue enclaves were racked with worry. Trump, to them, was so deeply offensive, so completely unfit for office, and yet he won. Now he wouldn't just be a candidate with a knack for dominating cable, he'd be the man in charge of both the nation's nuclear codes and its civil liberties.

And the lessons from the campaign felt dire. Trump seemed close to self-immolation so many times, from warring with John McCain to in-sulting a Gold Star family to making the vile remarks revealed in the *Access Hollywood* tape. Yet he could not be beaten; Trump now held the Republican Party firmly in his grasp, with so many of the rank-and-file members—and an increasing number of GOP officials—suddenly willing to believe or go along with anything he said. Democrats felt that they had been delivered a body blow.

But while party leaders were dazed by Clinton's loss and left scrambling, many of their rank-and-file members took to the streets. After that mammoth Women's March, the hashtag resistance came to define their approach, with Democrats taking to the airwaves to condemn Trump's defiance of the office's norms while also trying, as best they could, to slow his agenda.

At first, some Democrats harbored hopes that Trump would be reasonable. Maybe he would mature and grow into the job. Perhaps he would be restrained. Maybe he would learn to compromise. Indeed, many Democratic lawmakers spent four years wondering if the entirety of the Trump presidency might have gone differently if he had reached across the aisle to begin his term with a long-overdue infrastructure plan, a proposal that had bipartisan support and could have brought the temperature down across Washington. Instead, Trump dove in on a rancorous effort to overturn the Affordable Care Act and pushed through a massive, polarizing tax cut, while weaponizing his Twitter account to deliver broadside after broadside at the other party. He played only to his base. There would be no compromise.

Democrats needed to regroup.

They did not hold the House or the Senate and had been systematically wiped out at the state level too, as the Obama team had paid little mind to growing the party beyond Washington. Over Obama's eight years in office, twenty-nine state legislative chambers in nineteen states flipped from Democratic to Republican control. Those changes could lead to gerrymandering in the short term and, though no one knew it yet, would loom large five years later when voting rights were scrutinized on the state level in the aftermath of the 2020 election.

Trump ate up all the oxygen in the room. He was everywhere: on Twitter, on cable, at his continued rallies. It was difficult to break through, to gain any control. Democrats were forced to be reactionary.

The energy and opposition to Trump that some Democrats wanted to see prior to the election emerged during his first days in office, a heartening development for the party. Days after he was inaugurated,

Trump signed a hastily drafted executive order that denied entry to the United States to citizens of Iraq, Iran, Libya, Somalia, Sudan, Syria, and Yemen. The measure, a modified version of the Muslim ban he had proposed during the campaign, triggered immediate outrage from coast to coast, with thousands of people spontaneously rushing to US airports to protest the restriction. A federal judge moved to block the ban, which had been written by Steve Bannon and Stephen Miller with little input from the White House counsel's office or the Department of Justice's legal counsel. A week after it was implemented, it was quickly over, as the Department of Homeland Security announced that it would no longer enforce it.

It was an early victory for Democrats. They remained a minority party with little power. But the initial triumph revealed that they would sometimes receive help from unlikely outside allies: figures in Trump's own White House. The Trump West Wing was often a workplace of dysfunction, with aides undermining one another, basic legislative maneuvers—reaching out to members, clearing bills with counsel—often ignored, and Trump changing his positions on issues based on the input of whomever he spoke to last.

There were some early GOP failures. An initial effort to repeal and replace Obamacare—a talking point at nearly every one of his rallies—collapsed that spring in the GOP-led House of Representatives. His long-promised border wall was slowly and haphazardly built (and easily climbed over).

Moreover, Trump's entrance on the global stage was chaotic. In his first months in office, he threatened to pull out of NATO, the long-standing military alliance formed as a bulwark to Soviet aggression. He offered deeply personal insults to the leaders of the United Kingdom, Canada, Australia, France, and Germany, just to name a few, and strained ties with some of America's closest allies. He seemed far more comfortable with the authoritarian leaders of China, Egypt, Russia, the Philippines, and Saudi Arabia. He met with North Korea's Kim Jong Un—whom he once dubbed "Little Rocket Man" and threatened to eliminate with a nuclear weapon—three separate times in made-for-TV summits, the last of which took place at the heavily militarized DMZ on the border with South Korea. I watched as Trump took a dramatic step into the Hermit Kingdom. He once threw a bunch of Starburst candies at Angela Merkel; he called Justin Trudeau "two-faced" and "a lunatic." During his maiden overseas trip, Trump stood with autocratic leaders of Saudi Arabia and Egypt and awkwardly touched a glowing orb at a summit in Riyadh, for some reason. I was there for that too.

White House press releases were rife with typos, world leaders' names were misspelled, facts were optional, staff turnover was rampant. Trump and much of his senior staff had no experience in government and it showed.

Democrats occasionally benefited from divisions within the Republican ranks, and some in the GOP couldn't stomach working with Trump. Fueled by a revulsion to Trump, Senator McCain's July 2017 decision to cast the vote that sank the Republicans' efforts to defeat Obamacare dealt Trump a humiliating defeat. The GOP effort was one vote away when, long after midnight, an ailing McCain—he would be dead thirteen months later from brain cancer—dramatically stepped onto the Senate floor as the chamber awaited his vote. He paused, building the drama. And then he turned his thumb down, rejecting the Republicans' best chance to overturn the Affordable Care Act since it had been signed into law seven years earlier. The GOP did not mount another serious effort in Trump's term.

That McCain was a war hero did not stop Trump from attacking him; the president at first balked at flying the White House flag at half-staff when the senator died and Trump was barred from his funeral. Trump also trained his fire at times at fellow Republicans who dared defy him, attacking members of his own party, including Senators Jeff Flake of Arizona and Bob Corker of Tennessee, simply for daring to disagree with him. Trump's poll numbers sank to the upper thirties, even though many of his critics within the GOP—including those two senators—grew weary of the attacks and soon announced their retirements. The president was reshaping the party into something Trumpier and more loyal to him.

Trump also had undeniable triumphs.

Few moments infuriated Democrats more than the new president's ability to immediately fill a Supreme Court seat. The spot had been vacant since Antonin Scalia's death in February 2016, with Mitch McConnell refusing to fill it, citing Obama's lame-duck status. That was an outrage, Democrats argued, as Obama still had nearly eleven months left in his term. But McConnell had no qualms about defying decades of tradition, and he would not even schedule a hearing for Obama's pick, DC Circuit Court of Appeals Judge Merrick Garland. After Clinton's loss, Garland became a painful reminder of Democratic defeat, of pure powerlessness. He should have been on the court; the Democrats should have won in 2016.

But he wasn't and they hadn't. Instead, Trump happily benefited from McConnell's phony argument and drew upon one of his more effective campaign tactics; in an effort to prove his conservative bona fides, Trump—who, after all, was once a pro-choice Democrat—teamed up with the Federalist Society to create a list of jurists from which he'd fill a potential Supreme Court vacancy. And while the Trump White House was not known for running like a well-oiled machine, it successfully pulled off a surprise glitzy, prime-time reveal of his pick, Federal Appeals Court Judge Neil Gorsuch. He also used the GOP majorities to push through a significant tax cut, one that disproportionately benefited the wealthy.

Democrats looked for a strategy. There was an effort to reach across the aisle, but Trump wasn't interested, forging forward in that first year as if he had been elected with a sweeping mandate, while happily playing the politics of divisiveness. He aimed his policies directly at his base—

with moves such as rollbacks of environmental regulations and of civil rights protections—and blamed Democrats for any Washington failure. Always eager for a foe, Trump governed as he campaigned, and not just by incessantly reliving his win over Clinton. Trump frequently instigated fights and rarely let a slight go unanswered via his favorite weapon: any pre-inauguration talk of restraining his Twitter usage was soon forgotten. He used the 140-character—and later, up to 280—bursts to target foes, traffic in conspiracy theories, salute the programming on Fox News, rattle Congress, and unnerve world capitals.

He was denounced for dismissing African nations as "shithole countries" when he urged a limit on immigration from that continent. He dismissed Senator Elizabeth Warren, Democrat of Massachusetts, as "Pocahontas," mocking her claims about being part Native American. When he visited Puerto Rico after a devastating hurricane, he tossed paper towels into a desperate crowd like they were basketballs—and later tried to stiff the island of federal aid.

Trump had made the calculation that his best move was to divide, to always be in political combat, to fire up his base and dominate news coverage. His instincts were to fight. More than once, he offered a glimpse into how he viewed the presidency—as catnip for cable. "I'm sure their ratings were fantastic. They always are," he said during one cabinet meeting. Conflict sold—the drama was irresistible, he told aides.

And he did not hesitate to lie in an effort to try to score political points. He claimed that Democratic New York senator Kirsten Gillibrand "would do anything" for a donation, an unsavory insinuation made at the height of the #MeToo movement. The discussion about sexual harassment toppled many powerful men but, when Trump's own accusers resurfaced, the White House never changed its story: it was the women, not the president, who were lying.

Trump's commitment to lying, his dedication to never admitting even the smallest mistake, at times took a turn for the surreal and the bizarre.

*   *   *

It was 12:06 a.m. on May 31, 2017, when the following appeared on @RealDonaldTrump: "Despite the constant negative press covfefe"

Typos were hardly foreign to Trump's Twitter feeds, so those still awake expected that a correction would come soon and a follow-up tweet would soon be posted, likely correcting "covfefe" to "coverage" and then finishing with a rant against the media.

But minutes passed and then hours. No change. Only covfefe. The jokes began in earnest, with late-night social media ablaze with posts making fun of the president. But another thought took hold: Had something happened to Trump? The White House had gone silent, the vacuum filled by rampant speculation (and more jokes). His Twitter account was viewed as a place for official statements from the most powerful man on earth—it had been used before to announce policy and threaten North Korea—so there was concern about how an erroneous message, even a harmless one, could be left standing for so long.

Finally, at 6:09 a.m., the Twitter account sprang back to life with this: "Who can figure out the true meaning of 'covfefe' ??? Enjoy!" For once, it seemed like Trump was in on the joke. Perhaps he had fallen asleep and was now up for sharing in the fun. But when pressed at the White House news briefing later that day, the Trump administration again made clear that there was nothing too ridiculous to lie about.

Reporter: "Do you think people should be concerned that the president posted somewhat of an incoherent tweet last night, and that it then stayed up for hours?"

Sean Spicer: "Uh, no."

Reporter: "Why did it stay up so long after? Is no one watching this?"

Spicer: "No, I think the president and a small group of people knew exactly what he meant."

No one believed Spicer. But it didn't matter. The White House would cede no ground, they would fight for this lie. Trump, in a later tweet, claimed that "covfefe" had a "deep meaning."

Was it a small thing? Yes. But it was telling. It was around this time that New York senator Chuck Schumer started repeatedly telling people, "How can we work with this guy? How dishonest can one man be?"

Democrats, so badly on their heels for much of that year, began to find their footing. They started to lean into Trump's lies and erratic behavior. They discovered that his ego, and his unwavering loyalty to his base, would become his weaknesses. And with the national party reeling after 2016, they needed someone to become the face of their opposition, someone who could galvanize their dispirited ranks.

They found her in Nancy Pelosi.

* * *

After the Democrats lost four straight special elections, there were whispers as to whether it was time for fresh blood, time to remove the then seventy-eight-year-old Pelosi as minority leader. She preached patience and defended her record, declaring, "I'm a master legislator. I am a strategic, politically astute leader. My leadership is recognized by many around the country, and that is why I'm able to attract the support that I do."

Humble, it was not. But she was right that while she was a lightning rod for many Republican attacks, she had also proven adept at getting under Trump's skin. She was famed as a relentless negotiator on Capitol Hill, with remarkable attention to detail and expert understanding of the back-and-forth dance needed to land a deal among the competing members of her own caucus. She was tough.

The Democrats hardened their opposition to the White House.

They hit on immigration; they said the tax cut was a giveaway to the rich; they painted his efforts to repeal Obamacare as an attempt to take health care away from the people who needed it most. They embraced efforts by the porn star Stormy Daniels, who accused Trump's former fixer Michael Cohen of paying for her silence. Cohen eventually flipped on Trump. And Pelosi and Schumer, who was then Senate minority leader, placed the ongoing Russia probe at the center of their public messaging. They hammered Trump's possible ties to Moscow and accused Republicans of impeding the special counsel investigation.

Representative Adam Schiff led the charge, with a chorus of lawmakers and MSNBC and CNN pundits quick to act as an echo chamber. They were so desperate to get Trump, so convinced that he had betrayed his country to work with a foreign power, that they celebrated the most incremental developments in the case, seizing on evidence—no matter how circumstantial—as proof of the president's guilt. Democratic voters around the country tuned in religiously to watch Joe Scarborough or Nicolle Wallace or Anderson Cooper or Rachel Maddow or Don Lemon or Brian Williams deliver the latest updates in the probe, while also glued to their smartphones to watch for the latest push alerts from the *New York Times* or *Washington Post* or Associated Press to inform them of Trump's newest surely treasonous development.

And as they put their faith in Robert Mueller, Democrats also moved to recruit a slate of candidates—and motivate voters—to try to win back the House in the 2018 midterms.

Fearful of being painted as too liberal, the Democrats recruited a series of more moderate candidates to win in the very districts that Trump had turned red two years before. They leaned into the suburban districts that either had gone soft for Trump in 2016 or had outright rejected him. They recognized that historical trends favored them: most of the time, the party that controls the White House tends to lose seats in the off-year election. Even popular presidents had taken defeats. And Trump, with scandals swirling around him, did not seem at all popular outside of his loyal base of supporters. His approval rating remained stubbornly stuck in the upper thirties and low forties. But even though Trump loomed over the election, Democrats had traditionally not fared as well in the midterms as Republicans. Many of their voters, including the young and people of color, had a far better record of turning out for presidential elections than midterms. But this year seemed different.

But Trump wasn't going to admit it might be his fault. In a wide-ranging Oval Office interview with me and two of my Associated Press colleagues in October 2018, just weeks before the election, Trump said he wouldn't accept the blame if his party lost control of the House, arguing that his campaigning and endorsements had, in fact, helped Republican candidates. He dismissed suggestions that he might take responsibility, as Obama famously did for the "shellacking" that Democrats took in 2010, for any midterm losses.

"No, I think I'm helping people," said Trump, before he went on to claim that at his campaign rallies "many people . . . have said, 'Sir, I will never ever go and vote in the midterms because you're not running and I don't think you like Congress.'

"Well, I do like Congress . . . and when I say 'Congress,'" he continued, "I like the Republicans that support me in Congress."

And he assessed the influence he thought he had on the GOP's chances that November: "I don't believe anybody's ever had this kind of an impact."

He had an impact all right. His presence led to record fundraising for an off-year election, allowing Democrats to utilize well-financed efforts to reach voters who don't normally turn out for the midterms. And they painted Trump as a fundamental threat, one who stoked racial and gender divides and could roll back liberties for people of color and women. They won. Bigly.

Democrats picked up forty-one seats from where they were after the 2016 elections, their largest gain of House seats since the post-Watergate 1974 elections. Though the GOP maintained control of the

Senate, the House had gone blue, and Pelosi now had the Speaker's gavel. Moreover, she now had the power of the subpoena—and Democrats could open investigations into the Trump White House. It was open season.

The Democratic House launched a slew of probes in the first few weeks of taking control. The investigations included whether Trump had obstructed justice in the Russia probes, whether his businesses inflated their assets, how his daughter and son-in-law obtained their security clearances, how his actions might have slowed aid to Puerto Rico, and conflict-of-interest allegations involving cabinet members. The Trump White House's strategy in response was basically three words: just say no. It refused to cooperate with nearly all the probes, defying requests for documents and testimony. And while the Democrats' ability to enforce cooperation was limited, the steady drumbeat of bad headlines for Trump snarled his agenda and further dragged down his approval ratings.

And as Trump's reelection campaign loomed, Democrats had learned how to best him at his own game, to exploit one of his biggest weaknesses: his insatiable need to show strength, especially on camera. And in two memorable and defining White House confrontations, they did just that.

* * *

The first was in December 2018, when the GOP-controlled Senate unanimously passed a routine appropriations bill, one that looked certain to get the support of their Republican colleagues in the House and Trump. The bill did not include the $5.7 billion in federal funds Trump wanted to build his signature border wall, but his aides had said that the risks of not signing the bill—which would trigger a partial federal government shutdown—were too great, and counseled the president to vie for more border security funds down the road. Trump begrudgingly agreed.

But then the howls began in the conservative media. Laura Ingraham, Rush Limbaugh, Ann Coulter, and others accused Trump of going back on his word and being soft on illegal immigration. Trump stewed. "Build the wall" was one of the loudest nightly chants at his rallies, he told allies. He couldn't back down.

To the horror of some of his aides and many Republicans on Capitol Hill, Trump abruptly announced that he would not sign any appropriations bill that did not fund construction of the wall. The House went ahead and passed a stopgap bill with funding for the wall, but it was blocked in the Senate by the threat of a Democratic filibuster. For the third time in two years under unified Republican rule, the federal government shut down. About 380,000 workers were sent home and not paid, according to the Senate Appropriations Committee. Another 420,000 considered too essential to be furloughed—among them Border Patrol officers—would be forced to work without pay.

But for Republicans, it was worse than that: the president had been outmaneuvered and the Democrats had finally found their footing in Trump's chaotic Washington.

Schumer and Pelosi met in the Speaker's ornate Capitol office the night of December 10, 2018, to discuss who would say what when they met with Trump in the Oval Office the next day. They had a feeling they knew what to expect.

Trump, a man who preferred one-page memos to briefing books, would likely be out of his depth when it came to details of the negotiations, and would aim to get by with bluster and sheer force of personality. Both Pelosi and Schumer had complained to their own aides about how difficult it was to negotiate with Trump, who changed his mind on a whim, switching sides multiple times within minutes and then seemingly agreeing to something during a meeting only to walk it back on

Twitter a short time later. The lawmakers knew that the shutdown was an opening, a chance to further wound Trump just weeks before their party officially claimed control of the House when the calendar flipped to 2019.

They then got word that Trump also was planning to use the meeting to seize control of the narrative surrounding the shutdown. Late that night, the White House sent along word that Vice President Mike Pence would be joining the meeting as well. And the next day, as Pelosi and Schumer entered the West Wing, they were alerted that Trump had changed plans and invited the press pool into the Oval Office to watch. The president couldn't resist: he wanted to play for the cameras. Trump and Pence sat in the chairs near the center of the room, flanked by Pelosi on one couch, Schumer on another.

The next seventeen minutes captivated Washington.

Trump had been handed talking points that matched language GOP House leaders were using. Trump's top congressional liaison, Shahira Knight, met with the president right before the meeting for a "legislative pre-brief." But he ignored all that, focusing instead on trying to make Pelosi and Schumer look weak on what he felt was his base's top issue, border security. But instead of letting Trump perform a monologue in his own house, the Democrats spoke back, changing tactics and showing a more aggressive posture that reflected a renewed confidence in their ability to help shape media coverage.

Pelosi and Schumer shot him down again and again.

"It's called funding the government, Mr. President," Schumer hit at the top of the meeting when Trump began to riff about the border wall. And Pelosi calmly repeated over and over that Trump didn't have enough votes among House Republicans to pay for the border wall. Growing visibly irritated, Trump insisted that they did have the votes—nope, he did not—and challenged Pelosi's hold on her own caucus, to which Schumer responded by alluding to the new power dynamics in Washington that would come with the arrival of a House Democratic majority in a few weeks.

"Elections have consequences, Mr. President," Schumer chided.

All three leaders—Trump, Pelosi, and Schumer—looked uncomfortable at times during the excruciating exchanges. Schumer and Pelosi frequently stared straight ahead, not making eye contact with the president as they disputed him, and then urging him to dismiss the cameras so they could negotiate in private. Pence didn't speak at all.

And when Trump made questionable claims about the wall, Pelosi called out his lies: "We have to have an evidence-based conversation. Let us have a conversation where we don't have to contradict in public the statistics that you put forth." In short: you're lying and we're done with it.

The goading worked. Just before the cameras left the room, Trump turned to Schumer and gave the Democrats a gift bigger than they could have imagined.

"I am proud to shut down the government for border security, Chuck. Because the people in this country don't want criminals and people that have lots of problems and drugs pouring into our country," Trump said. "So I will take the mantle. I will be the one to shut it down. I'm not gonna blame you for it. The last time, you shut it down. It didn't work. I will take the mantle of shutting it down. I'm going to shut it down for border security."

Schumer couldn't resist a little fist pump. Trump had taken ownership of a government shutdown; he had provided a sound bite that could be played over and over. He would be the face of a moment that would cost workers' paychecks and hinder Americans' ability to get vital services. Some White House aides tried to spin that the Republican base would value the strong stance on the border, but Trump's poll numbers fell. And the defining image that day would be Pelosi, in an orange coat and oversize sunglasses, strutting out of the White House. The Democrats had more than just a meme—they had some swagger back.

The battle, at times petty, continued for a few more weeks as the government remained shut. In one negotiating session in early January, Trump warned that he might keep the government closed for "months or years." In another, he bluntly asked Pelosi: "Will you agree to my wall?" When she said she would not, he stormed out. The House Democrats rescinded Trump's invitation to deliver the State of the Union address; Trump revoked military transportation for overseas congressional trips. And so on.

Eventually, Trump blinked. On February 15, he announced he'd sign a spending bill to open the government. The border wall remained mostly unbuilt. The Democrats had bested his lies.

And when Trump finally delivered his delayed State of the Union later that month, a moment from the night was immortalized in a famed photograph: Pelosi, in her position behind Trump, standing and smirking as she gave the weakened president a sarcastic, sideways clap.

Another moment of defying Trump had become another indelible image—with Pelosi, again, becoming the face of the Democrats while her party began the race to replace Trump.

* * *

As Trump's first term drew to a close, Democrats were finally seizing on the momentum of discrediting him. Investigations swirled. Trump was undermining the United States' global position. And the Democrats were able to rally around their interim leader yet again, in a second White House confrontation.

A bipartisan delegation of House members and senators had visited the executive mansion on October 17, 2019, to talk about Trump's widely opposed pullout of US forces from northern Syria, which cleared the way for Turkey's bloody attack on the region. The House had already delivered a rebuke to the president's plans, and Pelosi, in the meeting, pressed the president as to why, by pulling out the troops, he was supporting the interests of Vladimir Putin, who wanted more Russian control for that region.

Pelosi stood up. Most of the heads in the room were bowed, eyes lowered.

Most of the men around the table—and to be clear, most of them were men—seemingly couldn't bring themselves to look at Pelosi. Joint Chiefs of Staff chairman General Mark Milley and House Republican Whip Steve Scalise stared straight down. House GOP Leader Kevin McCarthy's eyes were closed. Senate Republican Leader Mitch McConnell gazed off into space.

But Trump looked right at her, his mouth open, ready to respond.

The photo released by the official White House photographer quickly became iconic. Pelosi had risen from her seat around the conference table in the White House Cabinet Room. Democrats, including Schumer and House Majority Leader Steny Hoyer, were on her side of the table. Trump, the Republican leader, and military officials were seated on the other.

Pelosi was the only one standing. And she was pointing at the president.

Trump blustered that he was simply trying to keep Americans safe. Pelosi swatted that away, declaring it a goal, not a plan. The Turks were moving in and slaughtering the United States' Kurdish allies; European leaders were aghast that America was not honoring its commitments. The nation's global standing was once more taking a hit. Again, Pelosi asked, why is it that so many of your decisions seem to be ordered from Moscow?

Trump snarled at her. Pelosi stood, saying she'd had enough and was leaving. And, leveling her finger at the president, she coldly declared, "All roads lead to Putin."

The moment quickly became a Rorschach test for politics. McCarthy said Pelosi had been rude to Trump; Schumer said the president had insulted the Speaker. Trump then tweeted out the photo, declaring

"Nervous Nancy's unhinged meltdown!" But Pelosi simply took the image and made it her Twitter banner photo, embracing the confrontation with the president. Even on Trump's favorite medium, the Democrats were now able to hold their own.

Wielding the threat of impeachment, Pelosi had become the face of the Democratic opposition to Trump. After a slow start, her party had found ways to slow him down; Pelosi had bridged the gap between the Obama/Clinton era of the Democratic Party and what was to come next. The party needed to find someone to take on Trump in 2020. There seemed to be no shortage of candidates.

Bernie Sanders, the self-proclaimed Vermont socialist who had finished a surprising second in the 2016 primary, said he would run again, bringing with him a sizable base of supporters, including young voters, to this campaign. Another liberal lion of the Senate, Elizabeth Warren of Massachusetts, also said she would run. Others from the Capitol's upper chamber did so as well: Senators Cory Booker of New Jersey, Amy Klobuchar of Minnesota, Michael Bennet of Colorado, and Kamala Harris of California all jumped in. So did some unexpected names: Pete Buttigieg, the mayor of the small Indiana city of South Bend, as well as tech executive Andrew Yang and new age author Marianne Williamson.

In their desperation to beat Trump, the Democrats cast about for anyone to take on the president. Would Michelle Obama take a shot at claiming her husband's former seat? What about a billionaire, like Michael Bloomberg? Some even considered Hillary Clinton, but the party's most recent nominee, though eager to stay involved in politics, signaled that she would not run again. There would be no rematch with Trump.

Few wondered about a former vice president who had quietly returned home to Delaware.

5

CONSERVATIVE REINFORCEMENTS

Rupert Murdoch ambled on the sloping Scottish driveway, steadying himself against a gust of wind that afternoon. It was June 2016.

He slowly moved to his seat on a waiting golf cart. His wife, model and actress Jerry Hall, stepped inside. Murdoch, the then eighty-five-year-old founder of News Corporation, ran a global conservative media empire, including the most influential voice in American cable news, Fox News. He drove the right-leaning coverage that swayed millions of viewers across the United States, helping deeply polarize the politics of an increasingly divided nation.

But Murdoch wasn't at the steering wheel this day. He was sitting in the rear, riding backward. The golf cart suddenly lurched forward, after the driver slammed the gas without warning. Murdoch nearly fell off, a frantic grab for a safety rail the only thing preventing the aged media mogul from tumbling to the hard pavement below.

The driver was Donald Trump, the presumptive Republican nominee for president, and he didn't slow down. The cart careened recklessly along the path with Murdoch just trying to hang on. And that moment displayed a dynamic that would dominate the next five years.

The image of the golf cart offered a telling preview of Trump's power over the conservative media, an entity that had helped create him but was powerless under his direction and forced to follow wherever he would take them. This dynamic began during that campaign and only intensified during his time in office. Trump bent the conservative media and much of the Republican Party to his will, becoming such a dominant force that lawmakers and pundits alike rarely dared to break with him. Instead, they rushed to his defense, attacking his critics and muddying the waters about his faults. They took his falsehoods and ran with them, acting as reinforcements when Trump faced the gravest crises of his presidency, including the COVID-19 pandemic, Robert Mueller's Russia investigation, and his impeachment over threatening to withhold military aid from Ukraine.

And the conservative media and nearly all Republicans would be well trained to have Trump's back when he began to tell the Big Lie.

* * *

Trump had invited the world's media to Scotland, where he took a bizarre break from the campaign trail to showcase his newly purchased golf course just outside of Turnberry. The course, former host of the British Open, was undeniably beautiful, nestled along Scotland's craggy west coast. The promotional blitz was a precursor to how Trump would mingle his politics with his business, as he took advantage of his status as the presumptive Republican nominee to draw the political press to write about the course. His son Eric, who oversaw the renovation, offered a few reporters private tours.

Trump held a news conference at one hole's tee box, the Irish Sea shimmering behind him on a rare sunny day. The next day, at another course on the Aberdeenshire coast, he would hold one long, roving news conference, moving from hole to hole as I and other reporters chased him and took in the views. The press availability in Turnberry was briefly interrupted by a protester who tossed a bunch of golf balls emblazoned with Nazi symbols. Trump's subsequent freewheeling remarks also featured an improbable victory lap about Brexit, which had passed the night before. Scotland, a "Remain" stronghold, was numb from the stunning result, yet Trump—who didn't even know what Brexit meant a few weeks prior—was crowing about the win and linking it to the populist movement that he was leading on the other side of the Atlantic.

Murdoch's News Corp.'s entities in both the United States and the United Kingdom bolstered the "Leave" moment, as did, it would emerge later, the same shadowy Russian forces that quietly backed Trump. At the time, Fox News was in charge of shaping the United States' conservative political coverage, its hosts GOP kingmakers. The 2016 candidates all vied for its attention and approval, and Trump, for a while, didn't seem like its favored choice. After what he deemed unfair coverage of the first Republican debate that cycle, the celebrity developer viciously turned on the network and the debate moderator Megyn Kelly, who he insinuated was having her period. Murdoch was one of the Manhattan elites who looked down upon Trump's gauche ways, and he strongly disagreed with the reality TV star's views on immigration and disapproved of his treatment of John McCain.

"When is Donald Trump going to stop embarrassing his friends, let alone the whole country?" Murdoch had tweeted early in the campaign.

But another voice at News Corp.—one of the few employees allowed to operate outside of Murdoch's influence—was more inclined to bolster Trump. Roger Ailes, a former Richard Nixon adviser turned media consultant, had run CNBC, founded what became MSNBC, and then taken over fledgling Fox News in 1996 and turned it into the most dominant force on Republican politics. The United States' TV news institutions had traditionally been objective, with little in the way of obvious outward bias, but Ailes set out to change that. Brandishing the slogan "Fair & Balanced," Fox News gave voice to conservatives who felt drowned out by the so-called mainstream media that so many on the Right felt implicitly favored the liberal politics supported by the nation's elites in New York, Washington, and Hollywood. Ailes fed into baseless speculation about Barack Obama's birthplace and stoked the rage that accompanied the Tea Party movement. Pugnacious and provocative, Ailes saw something in Trump that resonated with the blue-collar audience he was trying to attract to the network. He spearheaded Trump's regular appearances on the morning show *Fox & Friends*, and his understanding of the self-proclaimed billionaire's surprising appeal helped hone the network's grievance-oriented rhetoric that became a perfect venue for the future president.

Once Trump became the Republican nominee, Fox News had no choice but to go along for the ride. The Republican National Convention was held in Cleveland a few weeks after the Scotland excursion, and the meld between network and candidate was complete. Fox News relentlessly bashed Hillary Clinton, seizing upon her use of a private email account while secretary of state and not subtly playing into sexist tropes about her health and stamina. Moreover, it provided air cover for Trump, whitewashing his scandals and eagerly offering a platform for his views. Fox News repeatedly and strenuously denied slanting its coverage for Trump or any Republican, steadfastly declaring that they were providing "fair and balanced" coverage of the news. But at times, it felt like he was a Fox News contributor as well as a presidential candidate.

Other conservative media heavyweights followed suit. Rush Limbaugh, long the king of conservative talk radio, became a friendly platform and would frequently have Trump on. Glenn Beck initially opposed Trump but later bowed to him once his media company began to lose money as MAGA fans turned on him. And a few other conservative news organizations soon moved to Fox News' right, sensing that some of the Trump fan base had rebelled against the cable giant's minimal nod to objective news. Newsmax and One America News Network (OAN) would, at times, be completely detached from reality, openly musing about conspiracy theories that even Fox News wouldn't touch. Trump would occasionally shower them with praise when he was annoyed at the Fox News coverage; early in his administration, he would particularly flash his ire at some of the network's weekend anchors, who tended to play the news straighter than the more opinionated week-night hosts. Fox News hosts largely supported him while a number at CNN and MSNBC attacked him. Ratings soared across the board. An-chors and contributors all got paid. Some of the loudest voices attacking Trump were filling their bank accounts because of him.

It was the golden age of cable TV.

*　*　*

Kellyanne Conway was frustrated. A senior adviser to the president, she was having a difficult time getting through to Trump on a passion proj-ect of hers, a task force to combat the nation's opioid crisis. He didn't read the memos. He ignored her in meetings. Once, she thought she had convinced him during an Oval Office meeting, but she lost him when he got distracted by another aide. She needed a way to get Trump to pay attention and to move him on the issue.

So she went on Fox News.

It became a standard practice among Trump aides and outside al-lies. The best way to get the president to pay attention, embrace a new policy, or retreat from a catastrophe was to make the appeal on cable. Aides, including Conway, often found it far more effective to make the case via Fox News than even in the Oval Office. Getting an adminis-tration official to come on air was, traditionally, a significant coup for a cable booker. But at times during the Trump years, bookers at Fox News had to turn down one White House aide from coming on a show because another had already called offering an appearance in order to make a pitch to the president.

The TV was always on in the White House. Trump started his day around 6:00 a.m. and, before leaving his bedroom, would turn on cable news. *Fox & Friends* was his favorite, but he'd often flip to *Morning Joe*, which, most of the time, he would hate-watch. Though he used to be a guest on the show, the hosts consistently blasted him, condemning his racism and disruption of presidential norms and global alliances. Sometimes he'd watch Fox live and catch up on the MSNBC juggernaut via DVR later in the day, which would explain some curiously timed tweets. With some frequency in the *Morning Joe* 7:00 a.m. hour, Trump would suddenly unleash a tweet attacking something the show's panel had discussed a solid hour earlier. As a frequent guest, sometimes I'd be called upon to read Trump's blistering tweets on air. The show's chyron, when Trump attacked, would playfully change in response: "Morning Joe Thanks Faithful Viewer."

Trump was obsessed with TV: he'd talk about ratings and slam hosts he didn't like or who were being critical of him. He told advisers that a good way to measure a guest's on-air talent was to watch with the TV on mute and see if that person was still compelling to watch; to their surprise, many found that Trump was right. Aides who had scheduled morning meetings found themselves at times waiting an hour or more for the president, who could not tear himself away from the television. Tired of Trump being late even to meetings with senior lawmakers or to calls with heads of state, White House aides eventually adopted a policy of giving the president some unstructured "executive time" in the mornings, which everyone took to mean time watching television and working the phones about what he had just seen.

The TV would stay on in a private dining room just off the Oval Office, which would eventually play a role on the most consequential day of Trump's presidency. But most days, it became just another spot for him to keep an eye on cable at lunch and in between meetings. Ever the host, Trump would invite awestruck guests to pose for photos in the Oval Office and then, excitedly, whisk them into the dining room for a demonstration of his "Super TiVo," a souped-up television recording/watching device. At night, more TV. Unlike many of his predecessors, Trump was not one to sample Washington's cultural or culinary options; in fact, the only restaurant where he ever dined in DC was in his own hotel down the street. Most nights, you could find him just where you could find many seventysomething men: in front of the television. And his channel of choice was the Fox News prime-time lineup.

The cable critic in chief, he fixated on individual reporters and hosts. Joe Scarborough and Mika Brzezinski, the married *Morning Joe* anchors, drew particular ire, as did their colleague "Sleepy Eyed" Chuck Todd and CNN's Don Lemon and Jim Acosta. On the print side, the *New York Times'* Maggie Haberman was his primary obsession; if she was in the press pool traveling on Air Force One, it was all but guaranteed that the president would take questions. He singled out others too, whom he tried to impress or win over, hearkening back to his long-held desire to be liked and respected by institutions or people he felt mattered. He would, at times, pass along notes to me via his press secretary, sometimes slipped to me on Air Force One, criticizing my coverage or trying to convince me of his popularity.

Trump cared desperately about his press coverage and frequently complained about it. And to be fair, every president has had a litany of gripes about the fourth estate. But no one placed the media at the center of his presidency like Trump. And no one else declared it the "enemy of the people."

* * *

Republican politicians love to point out what they say is liberal bias in the mainstream media and then position themselves against it. Trump was certainly not the first conservative to use the *New York Times* or MSNBC as a foil. But from early on in his campaign, he took the anti-media rhetoric to new, more dangerous places. Those who saw him night after night at his rallies recognized the routine: at some point during his stem-winder, he'd point to the back of the hall where the bank of TV cameras was set up. He'd declare that, as he was attacking Clinton, "the red lights" on the cameras were going off, meaning the liberal-controlled networks were cutting away from their coverage.

None of that was true. In fact, Trump enjoyed outsize media coverage, dwarfing what was received by his Republican rivals or Clinton. His rallies were outrageous and generated big ratings, with people watching in both delight and horror. He was such a draw that, infamously, CNN once kept up a steady shot of Trump's empty podium, waiting for the candidate to appear. Even the possibility of Trump speaking at some point actually seemed like better television than watching his rivals.

But the anger Trump ginned up led to threats graver than the loud chants of "CNN sucks" that became a nightly staple at his rallies. Individual reporters became targets. Acosta was frequently harassed while trying to do on-air hits. NBC's Katy Tur had to travel with security after Trump singled her out from the stage. Haberman and others received harassing emails and tweets. Suspicious packages were mailed to newsrooms and individual anchors' homes. Many in Trump's crowd were friendly: asking for selfies with reporters just moments before (somewhat) good-naturedly booing them. But other times, the crowd surged the barricades and some loose cannons spewed hateful words at reporters just trying to do their jobs.

The old saying in politics is "never pick a fight with someone who buys ink by the barrel," meaning that it rarely was a winning proposition for an outgunned candidate to brawl with the mass media. But Trump had his own megaphone, with tens of millions of followers on Twitter and Facebook, and a conservative media that uncritically amplified his message. He deemed the press the "opposition party," trying to foster the belief that the media was doing the bidding of the Democratic Party. And in moments of criticism, Trump began to use the phrase "enemy of the people" to describe the press, a phrase born of Henrik Ibsen's famous play and used, perhaps most infamously, with the Soviet Union under Joseph Stalin, where being labeled an enemy of the people was akin to a death sentence. Hardly a historian, Trump may not have known those specific references, but he was an expert in labeling his opponents as "Other" or something less intrinsically worthy than he and his allies. The label was inflammatory and dangerous, prompting a surge in threats against members of the media.

"The FAKE NEWS . . . media is not my enemy, it is the enemy of the American People. SICK!" he wrote in the early days of Robert Mueller's Russia investigation.

But not all the media.

* * *

Trump's relationship with Fox News only got cozier the longer he was in office. He'd grant its anchors frequent interviews, largely spurning other media outlets. His staff would frequently fan out on its airwaves, knowing that they could offer largely unchallenged talking points. Stephanie Grisham, Trump's third press secretary, never gave a press briefing but would frequently give interviews to Fox News. Later, she would say that aides would go on Fox News and Fox Business because "that's just where we went to get what we wanted out" and not be pushed with any tough lines of questioning. Trump aides were speaking to their base and could count on laudatory coverage because, as Grisham said in an example, "Lou Dobbs would do all the talking about how great everything was and I would just nod and say, 'Yes.'"

Many times, when Trump would call in to *Fox & Friends*, the hosts would dutifully try to keep him on track by getting him to focus on the issue of the day—like a strong jobs report—instead of a tangent like Hillary Clinton's emails. They'd clean up his mistakes, give him a second chance to say things, and, at times, gently nudge him to end the interview and get back to work. But Trump usually missed the subtle cues; he was the most powerful man on the planet, but his job felt secondary to time he could spend talking on his favorite morning cable show.

More than once, but most famously before the 2018 midterms, Fox would suddenly seize upon an issue that would excite its viewers and, perhaps not coincidentally, help Trump and Republicans. Ahead of those elections, the network began warning of a "caravan" of migrants heading toward the United States' southern border, all but labeling them a threat to life, liberty, and the pursuit of happiness. During the campaign, and again when the border was in the news, Trump took to reciting "The Snake," a thundering spoken-word performance of the dark song—written by social activist Oscar Brown Jr. in 1963 and made famous by singer Al Wilson five years later—as an allegory of what he saw as the dangers of illegal immigrants and refugees allowed into the United States.

"Take me in, oh tender woman, sighed the vicious snake!" Trump would roar, before concluding the poem by channeling the snake in declaring that the woman "knew" all along the danger she had let in as the serpent injected her with poison. Fox would carry the whole performance. At times, the lines blurred: Was Fox News taking its cues from the White House or was the Trump administration picking its political fights based on what it was watching on cable?

And the Fox personalities were more than just images on a screen.

Sean Hannity, Tucker Carlson, Laura Ingraham, Lou Dobbs, Jeanine Pirro. They all would grow used to their phones lighting up soon after their show went off the air, with the president on the other side of the call praising how they had defended him or gone after his enemies. He'd preview attack lines, review the quality of guests, suggest better lighting. And it became a two-way street: the hosts would lobby Trump as well, with Dobbs, in particular, pushing the president to build his border wall and ramp up his anti-immigration diatribes. But the hosts weren't always in lockstep: in January 2020, viewers witnessed a marked difference in approach to Iran from Tucker Carlson in the 8:00 p.m. hour and Sean Hannity in the 9:00 p.m. hour. Carlson slammed Trump's decision to authorize the killing of top Iranian general Qasem Soleimani, while Hannity praised the move. Both men also made their cases privately to Trump on the phone.

When the COVID-19 pandemic hit, the network and the White

House became more intertwined. Carlson, who would supplant Hannity as the network's top host, visited Trump at Mar-a-Lago to warn him that the virus could cost him the election. Ingraham, in April 2020, visited the White House to push hydroxychloroquine, a drug that many on the Right touted as a cure for COVID. There was no evidence to support such a claim, and it was later deemed ineffective to use. But Trump himself took the medication, and the constant hype around it on Fox left it scarce for patients, including people with lupus and other autoimmune disorders, who truly needed it.

And even more pervasive—and dangerous—on the network's airwaves was skepticism over masks and then the vaccine, misinformation that undoubtedly cost American lives. Trump voters, per polling, were far less likely to take the vaccine than Biden voters.

* * *

First, Donald Trump said that Ted Cruz's wife was ugly. Then, Trump said Cruz's father helped assassinate President John F. Kennedy.

How did Ted Cruz get back at Trump?

By becoming one of his most faithful and fierce defenders.

Cruz's calculated capitulation to Trump, a move made largely out of fear of Trump's supporters, served as a perfect microcosm of how Trump bent the Republican Party to his will. For a time in the 2016 campaign, Cruz was Trump's most potent rival in the GOP, his Texas persona and Ivy League debate club pedigree making him a shrewd politician, even if he was also one of the most disliked people on Capitol Hill. He was savvy but smarmy, and a number of Democrats and Republicans alike made no secret that they believed he was a phony. But Cruz's well-organized ground game won several states—including Iowa and Wisconsin—and his delegate operation outmaneuvered the Trump team to keep the contest alive for months.

Trump dubbed him "Lyin' Ted" and offered a nightly routine at rallies when he'd declare that "Lyin' Ted holds the Bible high, puts the Bible down, and then he lies." He also had fun noting that the Texan was actually born in Calgary. And for a time, Cruz fought back. Right as his campaign drew to a close that spring, the Texas senator unleashed a diatribe on Trump, calling him a "pathological liar," "utterly amoral," and "a narcissist at a level I don't think this country's ever seen." And at that party's convention in Cleveland that summer, Cruz was given a prime speaking spot but declined to offer a full-throated endorsement, instead urging the delegates to "vote their conscience." The speech was stunning and explosive and a betrayal. It was a rare moment of surprise, a real piece of political drama at a political convention, which in recent decades had turned into tightly scripted and often boring set pieces. The crowd booed loudly. Trump, flanked by his family, emerged from a skybox and glared down at the senator.

The moment was electric. It also marked the end of Ted Cruz's political courage.

The backlash was immediate and vicious. The audience was deafening in their boos, and Cruz and his family got jeered as they were whisked out of the downtown arena. Fox News, which usually gave Cruz a friendly home, turned on him immediately and denounced what he did. Other Republicans declared that Cruz had shattered efforts at party unity. Donors threatened to withhold their checks. Cruz was up for reelection, and there was immediate talk of a GOP challenge. Cruz was stunned, telling aides that he did not realize that Trump's takeover was so immediate and thorough.

Only two months after Cruz declared that his principles would not allow him to endorse Trump, the senator officially backed the GOP nominee. He later privately apologized to Trump and began to be one of his loudest supporters in the Senate. And his transformation was mirrored, if less dramatically, by other Republicans. There were a few exceptions—John McCain, Mitt Romney, Bob Corker—but for the most part, GOP lawmakers fell in line behind Trump. Some, like

Representative Jim Jordan of Ohio and Representative Devin Nunes of California, were true believers, enthralled by Trump's policies and personalities. Others, like Cruz, supported him out of fear. Their own future success, they reasoned, would happen only if they lashed themselves closely to Trump, staying out of his Twitter crosshairs and avoiding the wrath of his supporters and his favorite cable channel.

Mostly through intimidation, Trump had consolidated power. Both the conservative media and the Republican Party followed his whims—and they rushed to his defense during two of the biggest challenges of his presidency, setting the stage for what was to come.

The first was named Robert Mueller.

*　*　*

The special counsel worked in the shadows.

He had served as FBI director for more than a decade under presidents both Republican and Democrat, receiving bipartisan acclaim for his toughness, fairness, and relentlessness. Once he left his post in 2013, he quietly settled into private life, moving away from the bright Beltway spotlight. But in the first months of 2017, Attorney General Jeff Sessions recused himself from the early stages of the Russia investigation, citing his own questionable contacts with Moscow's ambassador. And then, in a fit of rage over the probe, Trump fired James Comey. Deputy Attorney General Rod Rosenstein, now atop the case with Sessions sidelined, appointed a special counsel to oversee the investigation that was threatening to overwhelm the Trump White House.

He picked Mueller.

Trump was devastated by the appointment, slumping over when he heard the news and moaning to the aides present that "my presidency is over." Mueller's credentials were impeccable, earning compliments from both sides of the aisle. He staffed up with some of the nation's top investigators. For a time, even the White House pledged some co-operation, and negotiations began for Trump to give an interview with investigators.

Mueller's team moved swiftly, examining any and all contacts between the Trump campaign and Russians—and there seemed to be a shocking number of them—and zeroing in on some key figures in the president's inner circle. One focus: a June 2016 meeting at Trump Tower of Jared Kushner, Donald Trump Jr., and then–campaign manager Paul Manafort with a Kremlin-connected lawyer. Roger Stone came under scrutiny for his ties to WikiLeaks and the hacker who was releasing Clinton's emails during the campaign. And beyond the Russia interference, Mueller opened an investigation into whether Trump had obstructed justice in the early stages of the probe, including by firing Comey.

The breadth of the probe was breathtaking, and it happened in silence. Immediately, the edict came down from Mueller to his team: they would not talk. With remarkable discipline, the special counsel's office did not speak to the press; it did not leak. The quiet added to the air of mystery around the probe, filled by breathless speculation on the cable news shows and relentless, award-winning journalism by outlets like the *New York Times, Washington Post,* and *Wall Street Journal.* The White House was under siege, enshrouded in a scandal that felt like Watergate in scope.

But Mueller's silence left a vacuum. And Trump and his allies seized the opportunity to fill it and shape the story.

The White House was initially caught off guard by the sweep of Mueller's probe—the investigation was called "Crossfire Hurricane"—and the president's aides' initial responses were faltering. Trump, briefly, held his tongue, for fear that attacks on the popular special counsel could backfire. But soon, his reticence faded, and he went on the offensive, declaring the Russia probe "a witch hunt," the phrase that would come to dominate his defense to Mueller's investigation.

Always desperate to be defended on TV, he drafted former New York City mayor Rudy Giuliani to be the public face of his legal team, as other lawyers toiled behind the scenes. Just a decade and a half earlier, Giuliani had been hailed as "America's Mayor" for his stoic defiance after the September 11 terror attacks, becoming the face of American resolve. But times had changed.

Giuliani had drifted ever rightward, first for his ill-fated 2008 presidential run and then in an effort to stay relevant on the conservative media circuit. His consulting firm picked up some unsavory international clients, and Giuliani's personal life became a fixture in the tabloids. Still, he had been a useful surrogate for Trump on the campaign trail, as well as a subject of the candidate's mockery, usually for drinking too much and falling asleep on the plane. When Trump won office, Giuliani had asked to be secretary of state. Trump had said no.

Giuliani was therefore eager to get back in the game and took on the dirty work. His media performances were scattershot, compelling, and at times incoherent. Sometimes, there was a method to his apparent madness: more than once, he'd get out ahead of an unflattering story to defuse the bad headlines, such as when he revealed to Hannity that Trump did, in fact, reimburse his fixer Michael Cohen the $130,000 that was paid to keep porn star Stormy Daniels from talking about their affair. Other times, well, he just plain messed up. But, writ large, his tactics proved surprisingly effective: he spewed such nonsense every day, and floated such outlandish conspiracy theories—wait, Hillary was the one colluding with Russia?—that it got too confusing for many average Americans to follow. What was real and what was the lie? It all became noise. And both Giuliani and Trump eventually unleashed a fusillade of attacks on Mueller, ignoring his sterling reputation and record as a Vietnam War hero to suggest that the man investigating the president's possible ties to Moscow was actually the treasonous one.

They had help. Other Republicans, leery at first of attacking the special counsel, began to join in, with Representative Jim Jordan declaring that "the public trust in this whole thing is gone," and others insinuating that previous donations to Democrats made by members of Mueller's team undermined their integrity. Fox News did the same, with its prime-time hosts bemoaning the probe's time and expense while painting it as a Democratic plot to bring down a GOP president. The media ran with two of the president's more outlandish claims: that Mueller had once begged him for his old FBI job back and that the special counsel had once quit one of Trump's country clubs in a rage. Neither of those was true.

It was night after night, attack after attack, lie after lie. Trump's falsehoods filled the space and his right-wing allies both in Congress and in TV studios were happy to regurgitate them. To be sure, they didn't distract the methodical, quiet nature of Mueller's work: the special counsel's team indicted or got guilty pleas from thirty-four people and three companies during their lengthy investigation. Among those convicted or pleading guilty were some of Trump's closest allies: Paul Manafort, Michael Flynn, and Roger Stone.

But the attacks dragged down the perception of Mueller in the public eye. The special counsel remained silent, but the withering broadsides that filled that void sent the special counsel's approval rating falling. That, in turn, emboldened more Republicans to denounce the probe, making Trump's impeachment and removal from office unlikely. A sitting president couldn't be charged with a crime, according to a Justice Department guideline that the special counsel seemed committed to following; so the probe would likely end with a political outcome, and Trump's allies—as they would after the 2020 election—went along with whatever falsehood he claimed if it meant keeping him in office and maintaining their own access to power.

Washington's wait for Mueller's report lasted nearly two years.

Finally, in March 2019, the special counsel turned in his findings to the Department of Justice. William Barr had become attorney general not long before and had the first look at the findings, which he then summarized in a letter to Congress released two days later.

Barr wrote that Mueller was unequivocal in his conclusion that Russia did try to interfere with the election, both by online disinformation and by hacking and releasing Clinton's emails. But he quoted the report as saying, "Although the investigation established that the Russian government perceived it would benefit from a Trump presidency and worked to secure that outcome, and that the Campaign expected it would benefit electorally from information stolen and released through Russian efforts, the investigation did not establish that members of the Trump Campaign conspired or coordinated with the Russian government in its election interference activities." And then Barr took it upon himself to color how he presented the rest of the findings, writing that Mueller had reached no conclusion on the question of obstruction of justice and noting that the special counsel wrote, "While this report does not conclude that the President committed a crime, it also does not exonerate him."

Trump's response was immediate: "No Collusion, No Obstruction, Complete and Total EXONERATION. KEEP AMERICA GREAT!"

That, of course, was not true: Trump was not exonerated. And in reality, the findings were more damaging to the president. Once a redacted version of the report was released the following month, it became clearer that Mueller had uncovered plenty of evidence of obstruction. But at that point, the nation had largely moved on. Barr had established the narrative, the final piece of Trump's enablers' lengthy campaign to help the president. In what would be a moment of stark foreshadowing, a powerful government official stepped beyond his usual role to assist Trump.

After years of being convinced that the Russia probe would bring Trump down, the Left was disheartened. And its last embers of hope were extinguished when Mueller turned in a shaky performance in a congressional hearing on the matter that July 24, at times seeming uncertain about the findings of the investigation that bore his name.

Trump had won. His allies in the media and the Republican Party had helped. And a playbook had been written.

* * *

Just one day after Mueller's shaky showing, Trump called Ukraine's new president, Volodymyr Zelenskyy. Zelenskyy, a former actor and comedian, was under extraordinary pressure due to the threat posed by Russian troops along his border and was eager for a show of support from Washington.

Trump had other ideas. He pushed the new Ukrainian president to get his country's prosecutor to open an investigation into Joe Biden, at the time perceived as the Democratic front-runner for the 2020 election, and his younger son, Hunter Biden. Trump and his allies had seen a potential opening for an attack: when he was vice president, Biden had pushed the Ukrainian government in 2015 to fire its top prosecutor, Viktor Shokin, who was widely seen as an obstacle to reform because he failed to bring corruption cases. At the time, Hunter Biden sat on the board of a Ukrainian energy company, Burisma Holdings Limited, which was the subject of an investigation that Shokin's office had essentially abandoned.

Trump was holding back hundreds of millions of dollars in military assistance that Congress had appropriated to help Ukraine fend off Russian aggression. And when he mentioned the aid, and the possible investigation into the Bidens, he asked Zelenskyy for a "favor."

A whistleblower soon sounded the alarm and furor quickly followed. Democrats were outraged as they connected the dots: Trump had threatened to withhold US military aid to an ally in need unless that foreign government investigated his domestic political rival. And once more, he seemed to be doing Vladimir Putin's bidding.

Trump had declared war on the wheels of American governance, from the diplomatic corps to the intelligence community to Congress. In an effort to bend Zelenskyy to his will, the president ousted the American ambassador to Ukraine, froze congressionally approved military aid, shut out foreign-policy experts in the National Security Council, and sidestepped the State Department to set up a back channel to Kyiv with Giuliani, his personal lawyer. After the whistleblower flagged the call, and key members of Congress objected to withholding the aid, the White House released it and Zelenskyy—who would return to the global spotlight a few years later—abandoned a promise to investigate the Bidens. But word of the whistleblower report leaked late that September. The Democrats swiftly began an impeachment inquiry in the House.

Once more, the president and his allies raced to his defense. Trump denied any wrongdoing, deeming his conversation with Zelenskyy a "perfect call." He and Giuliani railed against the whistleblower, calling him a spy. Others who flagged the president's inappropriate behavior, like Lieutenant Colonel Alexander Vindman, feared for their lives. Those who tried to report on the episode were vilified in the conservative media; Tucker Carlson called the whole proceedings "a flimsy scandal."

A number of key Republicans—including House Minority Leader Kevin McCarthy and Representative Trey Gowdy—deemed the investigations into the call "a sham." Lindsey Graham went further: though he chaired the Senate Judiciary Committee and would have to swear an oath to uphold his sacred duty as a potential impeachment juror, Graham immediately denounced the proceedings and suggested he had no intention of being impartial.

"I am trying to give a pretty clear signal I have made up my mind. I'm not trying to pretend to be a fair juror here," Graham said. "I will do everything I can to make [the impeachment trial] die quickly."

The Democrats held the House and had the votes: Trump was impeached. But the GOP-controlled Senate stayed in lockstep: only one

Republican, Mitt Romney, voted to remove Trump from office. The rest voted to acquit. Trump remained president.

Trump was stung: he was only the third president to be impeached, and this would be (so he thought) the first line of his political obituary. But he also, once again, proved indestructible. Using their now-familiar scorched-earth playbook, the president's allies had done their job: Trump's approval rating went up during the impeachment trial. In early February, he hovered just below 50 percent, his highest mark yet in the Gallup daily tracking poll. And the day after his acquittal, he strolled into the White House's elegant East Room. It was time to gloat and settle scores.

"It was evil," Trump said of the attempt to end his presidency. "It was corrupt. It was dirty cops. It was leakers and liars."

His rambling, angry, sixty-two-minute remarks were meant to air out grievances and unofficially launch his reelection bid—with the crucible of impeachment behind him, his so-so approval ratings unharmed, Republicans unified, and the economy roaring. The president's advisers also watched, relieved that the shadow of impeachment was now behind them, letting them focus on the reelection battle ahead. Trump had won again.

But there was something else stirring. The Russia and Ukraine probes had used the same script: he and his allies created a smokescreen, tossing out false accusations and exaggerated claims to impugn Mueller's integrity or that of the Democrats running the Ukraine investigation. While most of the claims were laughable on the surface, many got traction in the conservative media and, therefore, were taken as gospel by many Trump supporters. Polling suggested stark divides, with Republicans believing blatant falsehoods put forth by the president in his own defense.

Angry tribalism was growing. And it created a template for the year—and the election—on the horizon.

6

2020

Donald Trump couldn't sleep.

Moments later, Larry Kudlow's cell phone buzzed. He recognized the number.

It was afternoon in Washington; it was the middle of the night where the call was coming from. But that didn't matter to Kudlow, a former CNBC presence now working as a White House economic adviser, for this wasn't the first call he'd received from the same man halfway around the globe.

The sun would not rise for several hours in India, but the president of the United States hadn't slept, pacing in his palatial New Delhi hotel suite. He was battling some jet lag, to be sure, but he wasn't awake because of that, or because he was still charged up from the 125,000-person rally he had held at the world's largest cricket stadium or the majestic tour he had received of the Taj Mahal.

The president didn't know it yet, but he was embarking on one of the most consequential weeks of his term. At the beginning of the week, he had believed that he would be running for reelection on the back of a strong economy while facing a socialist. By the end of that week, neither was true.

And in the months to come, it would become clear that for the first time in his political life, Trump's lies weren't going to save him. And it just so happened to be in an election year.

Trump's whirlwind trip to India in the final days of February 2020 was meant to be pure celebration. Short on policy but long on pageantry, the president was to be feted by Prime Minister Narendra Modi, the head of the self-proclaimed world's largest democracy, whose rule had tilted menacingly to the right, leading to open discrimination and violence against the nation's Muslim minority. It was meant to be a trip of the grand: the biggest Trump rally ever; a photo op at arguably the world's most famous building; a visit to the home of one of history's most revered men, Mahatma Gandhi.

The spectacles were as massive as expected, fit for a president whose demands were always for things to be bigger and better. But, upon reflection, a small, unassuming event tucked into the presidential schedule carried by far the greatest import.

The event was a quick talk to business leaders, held at the US ambassador's residence in New Delhi and slated for just a few minutes. But this was where Trump felt compelled to address the coronavirus, which had begun rattling the foundation of his argument for another four years in office: the economy.

"We lost almost a thousand points yesterday on the market, and that's something," Trump told the two dozen or so gathered. "Things like that happen where—and you have it in your business all the time—it had nothing to do with you; it's an outside source that nobody would have ever predicted."

The virus was "a problem that's going to go away," he said with bravado. "And I think I can speak for our country, for—our country is under control."

But his public confidence was undermined by his private worry. Trump had been up the night before, repeatedly calling Kudlow and other economic advisers. He asked Kudlow what he had heard, what the titans of business were saying, and if he would go on cable TV—always the most important part of a Trump public relations overture—to defend the president's precious economy. Trump was nervous about the first significant stock market slide caused by COVID-19, the mysterious new virus that had stealthily emerged in China two months prior and was beginning to race around the globe. There was suddenly talk of lockdowns, travel bans, and mass death, and the stock market—so bullish for most of the Trump era, it had become an idealized symbol in his mind for economic prosperity—was shaken.

Trump had known for a while that COVID-19 was poised to spark a pandemic unlike the globe had seen in a hundred years. After he and other top aides, among them Mike Pence and Health and Human Services Secretary Alex Azar, initially downplayed warnings coming from elsewhere in the administration—including from national security aide Matt Pottinger and trade adviser Peter Navarro—the president had grown convinced of the danger posed by what he often dubbed "the plague." He confided to journalist Bob Woodward as far back as February 7 that he knew the virus was deadly.

But publicly, Trump lied.

He lied at the gathering of the world's elite in Davos, Switzerland, on January 22, saying, "It's one person coming in from China. We have it under control. It's going to be just fine." He lied days later in Iowa, declaring that "everything's going to be great" and falsely claiming, "We pretty much shut it down coming in from China." He later said the virus was going to have "a very good ending for it." And with an eye toward Wall Street, he lied to the entrepreneurs in India, declaring, "As far as what we're doing with the new virus, I think that we're doing a great job."

But the markets fell again that day, creating their biggest two-day slide in four years. When Trump boarded Air Force One well after sundown in India, he was in a rage about the virus and his inability to slow the market tumble with reassuring words, according to the officials. Trump barely slept on the plane as it hurtled back to Washington overnight, landing early in the morning of February 26 after more than a dozen hours in the air, creating the effect of one endless day. He then quickly tore into aides about Nancy Messonnier, director of the National Center for Immunization and Respiratory Diseases, who had just publicly predicted that the virus's impact would be severe.

The president returned to the West Wing to watch the market tumble yet again and, in something akin to a panic, told aides that later that day he would take the podium and preside over the coronavirus task force briefing.

The virus was on the nation's doorstep, poised to claim hundreds of thousands of lives, alter the very norms of society, and define Trump's final year in office.

But that was not the only event in February's final days that sealed Trump's political fate and helped shape the nation's future.

* * *

Joe Biden was a lion of Washington. He had served for thirty-six years in the Senate, representing his home state of Delaware, rising through the ranks to, at various points, chair two of its most powerful committees, Judiciary and Foreign Relations. He was well liked among his colleagues, occasionally reached across the aisle to work with Republicans, and gained the spotlight—for better or worse—in Supreme Court confirmation hearings. He also liked to talk. He never, his friends said, wasted a chance to turn a one-minute story into five minutes, gaffes often included.

His life was also touched by immense tragedy. A 1972 car crash killed his first wife and one-year-old daughter and put his two young sons in the hospital. Decades later, one of those sons, Beau, who was Delaware's attorney general, a military veteran, and a rising political star, died of brain cancer. Once more, Biden was burying one of his children.

Beau's death, in 2015, seemed to put an end to his father's lifelong dream of living in the White House. He had run twice before and neither attempt got much beyond the launching pad: his 1988 campaign was doomed by a plagiarism scandal and a series of other missteps, and then his 2008 bid didn't survive past Iowa. But that year he did impress Barack Obama, the young Illinois senator who turned the political world upside down yet needed Biden's gravitas and foreign-policy experience to help address doubts about his own youth and experience. Moreover, a candid calculation was made: an older white senator might offset some voters' anxieties about a youthful Black candidate. Biden was reluctant at first but later relented, exacting a promise to be the last person in the room any time Obama made a key decision.

Their partnership wasn't flawless, but it was undeniably effective. Amid the 2008 financial crisis, Biden was tasked with steering the auto industry bailout and much of the recovery act and played a key role in getting the Affordable Care Act passed (he declared the adoption of Obamacare "a big fucking deal"). He also came out in favor of gay marriage before the president and took the lead in the White House's negotiations with Congress in massive budget deals.

Moreover, a true friendship was born between Obama and Biden, with the president offering to pay Biden's mortgage when Beau's medical bills mounted. Biden was wrecked by Beau's death, later saying that he believed his son would have been elected president. Biden's friends saw him buckle under the weight of his grief.

Obama also telegraphed that he favored his successor to be another trailblazer to follow his own history-making election, suggesting that his former secretary of state Hillary Clinton be the party's next standard-bearer. Biden passed on the presidential run and watched in horror with fellow Democrats when Trump was elected. His political career seemed over. Until Charlottesville.

Clad in khakis and carrying tiki torches, more than two hundred white supremacists marched through the Virginia college town in August

2017 to protest the planned removal of a statue of the Confederate hero Robert E. Lee. The chilling images were emblematic of the rise in hate, as those who had kept silent before were emboldened to emerge from the darkness upon Trump's election. The next day, during a counterprotest to the march, the violence was worse, and a car driven by one of the white supremacists struck and killed Heather Heyer, a thirty-two-year-old anti-racist demonstrator.

Trump pinned the responsibility on "both sides."

That was the turning point for Biden. In that moment, he felt the nation tear at the seams. It tore again in Helsinki when Trump sided with Putin over his own intelligence community; and once more when children were held in cages at the southern border. The very "soul of America" was at stake, Biden kept telling people, as he slowly, inexorably moved toward declaring a third presidential campaign. He proved a successful surrogate for Democrats during the 2018 midterms and began to be considered a possible candidate again, even if a seemingly uninspiring one. Few people had tried to be president longer than Joe Biden had. He consulted his family, he pulled the trigger, he was in, he was making one final attempt. He declared his candidacy in April 2019.

At first it didn't go all that well.

Armed with unparalleled name recognition, Biden entered the race in the pole position. But as 2019 turned to 2020, his campaign seemed sluggish and listless, and it struggled to raise money. He had jumped in the race late and missed the chance to hire some of the top staff talent in the party. And though he was a beloved former vice president, Democrats weren't clearing the field for him. Biden was overpowered by enthusiasm on the Left (Senators Bernie Sanders and Elizabeth Warren) and eclipsed by a fresh face in the center (Mayor Pete Buttigieg of South Bend, Indiana). And to make matters worse, Mike Bloomberg and his billions eventually entered the race, offering another moderate option for Democrats, one who could potentially spend Trump into oblivion.

Iowa had not been kind to Biden. His 1988 campaign had never even reached the first caucus state, imploding before any votes were cast. And in 2008, Biden finished fifth, winning less than 1 percent of the vote. He abandoned his campaign just a few days later. This time around, it wasn't much better, with Biden drawing far smaller crowds than his rivals and finishing fourth, at just over 16 percent.

Iowa was bad. New Hampshire was worse.

In a moment that became the sort of metaphor that political writers can only dream about, one of Biden's campaign buses broke down alongside a wintry New Hampshire road in the primary's final days. The cash-strapped campaign appeared stalled as well. In a primary week appearance on *Morning Joe* filmed at a Manchester, New Hampshire, restaurant, Biden confided off camera to the panel that he was bracing for the worst. Trump, who held a counterprogramming rally in the state just before the primary, reveled in Biden's failing. Things were so grim that Biden left the state before the polls closed. He finished a shockingly poor fifth. His political obituaries were being written again.

But Biden wasn't dead yet. The voters of South Carolina, and one man in particular, offered him a lifeline and helped change the course of American political history.

Representative Jim Clyburn, the then seventy-nine-year-old House minority whip, had known Biden for decades. He and his late wife, Emily, who had passed away the year before, had grown close to the former vice president's family. Clyburn's endorsement was heavily coveted, with every candidate making an appearance at his famed fish fry in an effort to secure his support. The primary, the first of the season in which Black voters—a key part of the Democratic base—would play a sizable role, was on February 29. Four days before the primary, the Democratic field gathered for what for many of them was a make-or-break debate, and Clyburn, one of the party's most influential Black voices, hustled backstage during a late commercial break.

He grabbed Biden and reminded him of a promise the candidate had made a few days earlier: that he would use the debate to unveil a commitment to name a Black woman to the Supreme Court. Biden had missed out on several opportunities to do so during the debate and Clyburn was afraid he was running out of time, both in the debate and as a candidate.

Biden, eventually, awkwardly, got it out.

"The fact is, what we should be doing—we talked about the Supreme Court," he said. "I'm looking forward to making sure there's a Black woman on the Supreme Court, to make sure we in fact get every representation."

Clyburn had pledged to make his endorsement after the debate. The SCOTUS promise, and his longtime friendship with Biden, was enough. He backed Biden, who already had an enormous reservoir of goodwill among Black voters after loyally serving the nation's first African American president for eight years.

A Biden victory in the South Carolina primary wasn't surprising. But he didn't just win. He romped, reaching almost 49 percent of the vote, while Sanders finished a distant second at just under 20 percent.

The race was turned on its head. Once the contest moved past the demographically homogeneous Iowa and New Hampshire, Biden suddenly appeared to be the only candidate who could win with the minority voters who made up the core of the electorate Democrats needed that November. The very next day, even though Biden had won only one state, the other major moderate candidates—Buttigieg and Minnesota senator Amy Klobuchar—both dropped out and endorsed the former vice president. Beto O'Rourke, another moderate who briefly sizzled in the race, also threw his support behind Biden. They consolidated their portion of the party under the premise that Biden was the one Democrat who could win in November, and the pressure was on Warren and Sanders to bow out too.

Biden, given up for dead just days earlier, was suddenly the prohibitive favorite. He racked up more wins on Super Tuesday and the race was his. The country was increasingly rattled by the virus, and Biden had begun the improbable comeback journey that would lead him to become the Democratic nominee. As a moderate choice with decades of experience, Biden reassured a public that found stability appealing as it grappled with a once-in-a-century pandemic.

* * *

It would be two more weeks before the world stopped. On the night of March 11, in a matter of hours, the NBA suspended its season, Tom Hanks announced that he had contracted the coronavirus, and the United States hurriedly moved to ban travelers from Europe.

But the final days of February were when the year began to slip away from Trump. He had thought he was going to campaign on the back of a strong economy; that was now destroyed by the virus. And he had been expecting to run against a scary socialist; now he was going to face a less threatening moderate in Joe Biden.

Riding high off his impeachment acquittal, Trump had been telling confidants that he could foresee a walk to reelection. He was in disbelief that this had changed. To that point in his political career, he had been able to bend Washington to his will, using sheer force of personality—including an extraordinary shamelessness—to dominate the media and his fellow Republicans.

With the ground under his feet suddenly unsteady, Trump once more tried to exert control by force of will. But for the first time, that method didn't work. A shaky Oval Office address did little to reassure a jittery nation. And his blustery social media posts didn't move the needle either.

The virus, after all, didn't have a Twitter account.

The COVID-19 task force had been led by Azar, then Pence; now Trump was taking over to become the leading voice of the nation's pandemic response. Even in the early days of the pandemic, when it was too soon to predict just how many Americans would die and how the very norms of society would be reshaped, some White House aides warned the president that he should take a step back. Defer to the scientists, the aides said, as a matter of both good policy and good politics, as they urged him not to be the face of something that was not guaranteed to end well.

But Trump couldn't resist. He couldn't stay away from the TV cameras, couldn't accept not being center stage. The briefings would, for a time, become must-see TV for a panicked nation. Trump would brag about the ratings and try to schedule appearances each day around 6:00 p.m., just ahead of the nightly evening news. They were a daily ritual for Trump to try to enforce his belief that the virus was under control, even as infections surged and the death toll mounted. Only a handful of times did Trump strike a more somber tone from the podium; most of the time it was pure gaslighting with claims that the virus was on the run.

But these lies didn't work. COVID-19 was immune to his force of personality.

It was already too late to pretend otherwise, not that Trump stopped trying. Warning signs had been missed. The Centers for Disease Control and Prevention failed in an early attempt at a coronavirus test. Trump refused to turn up the pressure on China for fear of alienating Xi Jinping and scuttling a trade deal. Schools shut down. Businesses closed. There were runs on hand sanitizer and, inexplicably, toilet paper, and millions of Americans tried to figure out how to use Zoom.

There was so much fear and so little known. Images of refrigerator trucks parked outside a New York City hospital, just a few miles from the Queens neighborhood where Trump grew up, shook the president. But even within those terrifying first weeks of the pandemic, Trump saw the frozen economy as the gravest threat to his reelection chances and began pushing for society to reopen far sooner than his public health experts advised.

He reflexively rejected measures that made the nation—or himself—

look weak. When scientists coalesced around the idea that masks offered protection against the airborne virus, Trump refused to wear one, even though a president modeling the behavior could have had a far-reaching impact, particularly when that president inspired such devotion from his supporters. Aides urged him to do so, and some later wondered if the choice to not wear one helped cost him the election. Trump thought that wearing a mask made him look like "a pussy," he told aides, and it hurt the image of strength he always tried to project.

"I just don't want to be doing—I don't know, somehow sitting in the Oval Office behind that beautiful Resolute Desk, the great Resolute Desk," he said in early April. "I think wearing a face mask as I greet presidents, prime ministers, dictators, kings, queens—I don't know, somehow I don't see it for myself. I just, I just don't."

Even more dangerously, he lied and claimed on national television that a CDC study shows that "85 percent of the people wearing masks catch" the virus.

He mocked aides who showed up at the White House in masks and talked down to reporters who wore them to his briefings. Advisers tried repeatedly to get him to wear one—even flattering him by dubbing him the "Lone Ranger" when he did, as required, wear one to visit wounded troops at Walter Reed medical center—but Trump resisted, even when it was explained to him that he was putting his own voters' lives in jeopardy, since they would follow his lead.

To Trump's credit, he invested heavily in the development of COVID-19 vaccines, in part fueled by the hope that their emergence before the election could be an "October surprise" that would propel him to victory. But his management of the pandemic was otherwise disastrous, primarily due to his efforts to repeatedly downplay the severity of the virus in a misguided attempt to return the country to normal ahead of November.

The lies were constant.

"It's going to disappear. One day—it's like a miracle—it will disappear."

"Many of those cases are young people that would heal in a day. They have the sniffles, and we put it down as a test."

The pandemic is "fading away. It's going to fade away." America is "rounding the corner" and "rounding the final turn" of the pandemic.

They were all lies. And with each lie, more people died.

The country was soon divided: with GOP governors eager to please the president, the Trump-friendly states imposed far fewer virus restrictions and subsequently experienced more deaths. Trump's poll numbers saw a slight uptick in the early weeks of the pandemic; though nowhere close to the surge George W. Bush saw after 9/11, there was still, even in a sharply divided country, an instinct to rally around the flag. But the bump faded with each Trump misstep, including his suggestion at one COVID briefing that health experts study the impact of injecting bleach into a human body. After that, much to some of his aides' relief, the daily coronavirus briefings were suspended for a while.

The more the country saw of Trump, the less they trusted his pandemic response. He would keep declaring that the nation was through the worst of the virus, and the death count would keep proving otherwise. His Democratic opponent took a different angle. As COVID-19 swept across the nation, Biden quickly pledged that his administration would follow the science, respect health guidelines, and take an approach opposite the cavalier mentality demonstrated by Trump's team. Biden told aides repeatedly that he didn't understand why Trump wouldn't don a mask and presciently feared that the White House itself could be a site of a virus outbreak at some point.

The pandemic also provided a silver lining for Biden. With travel deemed too dangerous, Biden hunkered down at his Delaware home, with aides converting a spare room at his Wilmington estate into an ad hoc studio for TV appearances and virtual campaign appearances. Everything became remote: speeches, fundraisers, policy releases. The shift allowed the then seventy-seven-year-old Biden, who moved notice-ably more slowly than he had even four years earlier, as vice president, to avoid the rigors of the road. And the remote campaign allowed his events to be far more closely managed by staff, cutting down on the off-the-cuff gaffes for which Biden was known and that could dominate a news cycle.

That drove Trump—who had been banking on Biden self-destructing—mad. He and his allies began to take shots at the former vice president for hiding, brazenly suggesting that the Democrat was a mere puppet controlled by staff or more liberal members of the party—like Nancy Pelosi or Alexandria Ocasio-Cortez—and that he didn't have the mental capacity for the job. While members of the Trump base ate up the conspiratorial talk and spread it on social media, the lies, like his foolhardy COVID reassurances, didn't resonate with the general public.

And, though simplistic, one of Trump's great strengths was his abil-ity to deliver a cutting nickname and, through the power of repetition via Twitter or the rally stage, effectively brand an opponent. Crooked Hillary. Low-Energy Jeb. Lyin' Ted. Lil' Marco. The nicknames were savage, and they stuck. But Sleepy Joe, his moniker for Biden, didn't quite land. The Democrats' poll numbers kept going up the deeper the nation fell into the pandemic.

The president told aides he knew what was wrong. He looked weak, he said, largely stuck at the White House. He needed the energy of the crowds, and he complained to aides during the first half of 2020 that he was in withdrawal. He wanted to draw the contrast to stuck-at-home Biden, he needed to reassure his base that he was out there fighting for them, and he felt it was time to deliver a sign that America was back and unafraid. It was time for a campaign rally.

* * *

Trump rallies were a singular, undeniable political phenomenon. On one hand, they were a throwback to the door-to-door barnstorming of campaigns past, a break from the high-tech, data-driven operations of recent years. But the rallies were more sophisticated than they appeared, as they enabled the Trump campaign to gather data from attendees so they could target them later. And, of course, they allowed Trump to connect with his supporters, some of whom followed him from city to city like groupies following a band on tour. One of his true talents was his ability to read a room, and he'd road test material, using the feedback from the crowds to calibrate new attack lines. Many of those lines, of course, would be lies.

The country was still on fire from the virus when Trump wanted back out on the road. So his choices were limited. He had fought repeatedly with Democratic governors throughout the pandemic—with New York governor Andrew Cuomo, his most consistent foil, emerging as a darling of the Left for his no-nonsense briefings that stood in stark contrast to what Trump was offering.

But Trump also encountered resistance from the Democratic leaders of key swing states like Pennsylvania, Wisconsin, and Michigan, and those states would not bend local health regulations to allow a large gathering like a rally. The governor of Michigan, Gretchen Whitmer, frequently clashed with Trump and became a target for right-wing extremists. Their plan to kidnap her, an ominous hint of future violence inspired by Trump, was thwarted by the FBI.

The next thought was Florida, now officially Trump's home state and a key battleground, but Governor Ron DeSantis impressed upon the campaign that the virus was simply too rampant there. Pence then pointed out that Oklahoma had both lower case levels and lax regulations, and its GOP governor was willing to play ball. No one would mistake deep-red Oklahoma for a swing state, so the internal strategy shifted: instead of being portrayed as a comeback rally in a key battleground, it would be a show of force in a Republican stronghold.

The goal was to go big, really big, to show that the virus was on the run and both Trump and America were back. Campaign manager

Brad Parscale, the team's digital guru in 2016 who now had the big job thanks to ties to Jared Kushner, was happy to feed into that notion, and took to bragging on Twitter about receiving more than a million ticket requests. Trump wouldn't just fill the indoor arena: plans were in the works for him to speak at one, and maybe two, overflow outdoor stages too.

But the rally, it would soon become clear, was doomed by outside forces too big for Trump to browbeat into submission.

The campaign had unknowingly originally scheduled the rally for the night of Juneteenth, a holiday celebrated annually on June 19 that honors the end of slavery in the United States. Nor did they appear to realize that Tulsa had been the site of one of the country's bloodiest outbreaks of racist violence nearly a century before. The moment, instead of offering a glide path back to the campaign trail, underscored how out of touch Trump was when it came to Black Americans. And it wasn't the only one that month.

George Floyd was a forty-six-year-old Black man who was stopped by Minneapolis police after a convenience store employee called 911 and said that he had bought cigarettes with a counterfeit twenty-dollar bill. What happened next would soon ricochet around the world, as Darnella Frazier, a seventeen-year-old bystander, filmed the officers taking down Floyd. One of them, Derek Chauvin, kept his knee on Floyd's neck for well more than eight minutes.

Floyd yelled, "I can't breathe," and called for his mother. The knee never budged. Floyd died.

Protests soon swept the nation, the vast majority peaceful. Already in the grips of a pandemic, America was in the middle of a new reckoning on police violence and race—all while being led by a man who had not subtly winked at white supremacists from his perch in the White House.

One protest took hold at Lafayette Square, just steps from the White House. A small fire was ignited at nearby St. John's Episcopal Church—

long known as "the church of the presidents"—and the protests grew so intense that the Secret Service rushed Trump and his family down to an emergency bunker under the executive mansion—a move that, when leaked to the press, caused Trump to explode with anger for fear that it made him look weak.

Aides later recalled that they perhaps had never seen the president in such a rage. Two of them described Trump, his face red and veins popping, screaming, "Find me the fucking leakers," and ordering an investigation to find out who had told the media that he had been taken to the bunker. Though always upset about unflattering stories, this one pushed him to another level, the aides thought. No leaker was ever publicly identified.

Still livid, Trump wanted to push back, to project strength. A plan was hatched for the military and federal police to clear Lafayette Park so Trump could cross it to hold a photo op in front of the damaged church. Outside of that first night, the protests in Washington were largely peaceful. But Trump lied in order to justify his actions, deeming the protesters "thugs" and endorsing violence by declaring "when the looting starts, the shooting starts." In what would become a template for the events of that fall and winter, Trump used a lie as the basis for abusing the powers of the presidency for his political gain.

The scenes that unfolded horrified much of the nation.

Peaceful protesters were forcibly pushed from the park by federal officers, who deployed tear gas and clubs to clear out the nonviolent demonstrators. Flash-bangs and the wails of sirens could be heard in the Rose Garden, where the press had gathered to hear Trump speak. And the president led much of his cabinet and senior staff on a fateful walk through a park.

They strode to the church, with Ivanka Trump handing her father a Bible from her bag. He held it awkwardly near his head, as if he weren't sure what to do. When asked by a reporter if it was his Bible, Trump didn't answer. He stood there, camera shutters clicking. He believed he had put together an unforgettable American image, a tableau of the triumph of law and order and presidential power.

Some of those who walked with Trump realized a mistake had been made. Joint Chiefs Chairman Mark Milley, wearing his general's uniform, broke away from the pack to make a point of talking to officers on duty. He was joined by Defense Secretary Mark Esper, who also tried to distance himself from the scene, which they both feared was a gross overreach of the use of the military on American soil. Milley offered an apology for his presence a few days later, triggering Trump's ire.

"Why did you apologize?" Trump asked him. "That's weak."

"Not where I come from," said Milley in a scene first recounted in Michael C. Bender's book *Frankly, We Did Win This Election*. "It had nothing to do with you. It had to do with me and the uniform and the apolitical tradition of the United States military."

"I don't understand that," Trump said. "It sounds like you're ashamed of your president."

The stunt backfired, with polling suggesting that a majority of Americans were, in fact, ashamed of the display and the president who ordered it. With the nation already roiled by racial tension, Trump had thrown gasoline on the flame. Two crises had engulfed the United States: the virus and the racial reckoning.

Against that backdrop, Trump went to Tulsa. And it was there that he was presented with a stinging visual reminder that 2020 was not 2016: a sea of empty seats.

The ticket requests for the rally, though sizable, were inflated, thanks to a wave of TikTok pranksters who registered for seats but had no intention of going. Some Trump fans also stayed away, turned off by the conservative media's breathless warnings of violent protests or racial clashes that never materialized. And still others, despite the president's relentless minimization of the threats posed by the virus, were leery of attending a packed indoor rally where few would be masked. One supporter who did attend, former GOP presidential candidate Herman Cain, died of COVID-19 a few weeks after the rally.

The outdoor overflow stages were quickly pulled down, and Trump erupted in fury when footage of the sparse crowd appeared on Air Force One's televisions as the presidential plane descended into Tulsa.

He lashed out at Parscale, who soon found himself demoted. He raged at aides who had promised him a triumph and had delivered a humiliation. He still gave a game performance for those who had gathered inside the arena—attendance, all told, topped out at about six thousand people—and went into a long rant about how he had urged his staff to test fewer people for the coronavirus because, the thinking went, the more you test, the more positive cases you'll find, and those numbers were bad for Trump.

That declaration was the lasting sound bite from the rally. The enduring image came a few hours later, well after midnight back in Washington, as Trump trudged from Marine One across the White House lawn. His tie was loosened, his face drooping and fatigued. For a president whose appearance meant everything to him, he looked beaten. He looked like a candidate who, try as he might, may have encountered the first crisis that he could not gaslight his way past.

Trump bowed to reality and tabled rallies for nearly two months, though any talk of him being humbled by Tulsa was dashed by his grandiose appearance on July 4 at Mount Rushmore—including posing so it looked like his visage was the fifth on the famed South Dakota mountain. He amped up the culture war rhetoric and the violent imagery, lying about Biden's Senate record and claiming he was in the clutches of socialism. Biden's polls didn't drop. A dystopic Republican National Convention, in part held at the White House in violation of federal guidelines, also didn't move the needle.

But another large event at the White House, held on September 26, was the final twist of the campaign, one both stunning and inevitable, and yet one more 2020 moment during which the powers that had worked for Trump up to that point failed him when he needed them most.

After Justice Ruth Bader Ginsburg died just six weeks before Election Day, Trump and Senate Majority Leader Mitch McConnell rushed to seat a new Supreme Court justice. Democrats howled hypocrisy, since there was far less time left in Trump's term than there had been in Obama's back in 2016 when McConnell had refused to even give a hearing to the Democrat's nominee, Merrick Garland. It didn't matter: Amy Coney Barrett soon took her place on the bench.

Trump hosted a celebration for his pick at the White House, drawing her family, Republican senators, and dozens of GOP allies. But there was also another, uninvited guest: the coronavirus. Within days, nearly two dozen people—including GOP senators and senior White House staff—tested positive for the virus. Some, including former New Jersey governor Chris Christie, became so ill they had to be hospitalized.

Trump got sick that week. When he first tested positive remains a matter of some dispute, but his own chief of staff, Mark Meadows, said it was before he shared a Cleveland stage with Biden on September 29 for their first debate. Trump's family defied venue regulations by remaining maskless while the president blew off the required predebate test. Trump was erratic and angry that night, constantly interrupting both the moderator, Fox News' Chris Wallace, and his Democratic opponent, who at one point exclaimed, "Will you shut up, man?" The president was all over the place, giving comments that seemed to support the Proud Boys white supremacist group and berating his staff after he stepped off the stage.

For nearly a year, Trump had flouted the rules. He had refused to wear a mask; he held packed events; he was convinced that even if he caught the virus, he was strong enough to easily defeat it. He was wrong. At a rally in Minnesota the night after the debate, Trump seemed low energy and cut his speech short. One of his top aides, Hope Hicks, fell ill and isolated on Air Force One on the flight back to Washington. The next day, Trump still went ahead to a maskless fundraiser at his New Jersey golf club. He tested again when he returned to the White House and called in to Hannity's show while waiting for the result.

"I just went out with the test . . . and the first lady just went out with a test also," Trump told his longtime confidant. "So whether we quarantine, or whether we have it, I don't know."

Across Washington and New York, newsrooms slowing down for the night sprang back to life. Speculation grew. Guests on late newscasts like *The 11th Hour* on MSNBC were asked to hang around as the shows blew through commercial breaks and stayed on the air for hours past their normal time. At 12:54 a.m., the president tweeted the official confirmation: he and the first lady had COVID-19.

It felt like the world quaked. The leader of the free world, just a month before he was to stand before voters at the end of a tumultuous term, was ill with a deadly disease. The markets were rattled; global capitals watched with worry. The Biden campaign was livid that their candidate may have been exposed to the virus at the debate. It was the biggest story in the world, but there was little in the way of news from the White House. And when updates did emerge, they quickly proved untrustworthy.

Aides told reporters the next morning at the White House that the president was resting and in good health. That afternoon, a quiet update was given to the reporters in the presidential pool that Trump would travel to Walter Reed for a checkup and that he'd likely return to the White House in a few hours. A short time later, we were told it would be a few days. His condition had worsened.

When my colleagues and I in the pool gathered on the South Lawn a short time later, we came to a quick agreement: Trump, contagious with the virus, wouldn't be allowed to come over and talk to us unless he was at a safe distance. It became a moot point, as the president, this time wearing a mask, only waved at the press as he slowly walked to the helicopter waiting to take him to the hospital. His condition had deteriorated rapidly, and his alarmed staff told him that, if he wanted to walk out under his own power, he had to get on Marine One right then, or, if he waited, he would likely need to be taken out in a wheelchair as he fell more ill.

More lies came the next day. With the world watching, the president's medical team, led by Dr. Sean Conley, held a news conference for the pool outside Walter Reed. I pressed the doctor over and over as to the vital questions of the moment: What was Trump's oxygen level and had he received supplemental oxygen? But Conley repeatedly answered disingenuously, parsing his language and obfuscating his answers. His performance was so unhelpful that Meadows, hardly a paragon of truth, approached the pool after the news conference to confirm that Trump had, in fact, needed oxygen and was in far worse shape than publicly believed.

Pumped full of state-of-the-art treatments not available to the general public, Trump recovered. To demonstrate his vitality, the White House put out a photo of him in the hospital's presidential suite. The next day, fueled by the medication and his ever-present need to not look weak, he demanded to visit the crowd of supporters who had gathered across the street from Walter Reed. It was a scene reminiscent of the weekend of the *Access Hollywood* tape, back in October 2016, when he exited his isolation at Trump Tower to see his adoring fans. Like then, this was a decisively low moment, and Trump needed to hear the cheers, it seemed, to keep going. But this time, Trump was full of virus, and he put the Secret Service agents in his vehicle—wearing protective suits—in grave danger.

He pushed for a discharge, and Marine One returned to the White House at dusk on October 5. He had been hospitalized for three days. The lighting just so, Trump strode back across the lawn and up the steps to the Truman Balcony. And though still highly contagious, he tore off his mask before stepping inside. Reporters on the lawn, though, noticed something odd: Trump immediately backtracked out to the balcony again before returning inside, as if re-creating his entrance. And that's what he did: he was using the moment to film a video marking his so-called triumph over COVID.

"Don't be afraid of COVID. Don't let it dominate your life," Trump said.

Trump, though having required emergency hospitalization, was once more downplaying the virus. More than two hundred thousand Americans already had died. And as much as the president was trying to project strength, to convey the impression that he was impervious and could bully and trick his latest and greatest foe into submission, a careful watch of the video depicting him ripping the mask from his face showed a different story.

Trump was gasping for air.

7

THE ELECTION

"Hail to the Chief" played loudly.

Some in the East Room of the White House winced at the sudden noise, but their brief surprise was quickly overwhelmed by loud, somewhat drunken cheering and applause. The well-dressed and well-lubricated crowd was geared up for a celebration, a night to revel in their candidate once again defying the odds and proving the polls and pundits wrong. For hours, it looked like a repeat of four years before, with Donald Trump showing surprising strength in key battlegrounds like Florida and seizing early leads in the trio of Great Lakes states—Michigan, Wisconsin, and Pennsylvania—that he won in 2016 and needed again this time. But things had taken a turn. The president looked poised to lose.

President Trump strode to the lectern wearing a dark-blue suit, a blue silk tie, and a flag lapel pin. Standing in front of a wall of American flags, he was flanked by Vice President Mike Pence and First Lady Melania Trump. It was still Election Night, though the clocks had long ago raced past midnight and it was now nearly 2:30 a.m. on November 4.

The world was watching as the Big Lie was born.

"This is a fraud on the American public," Trump said. "This is an embarrassment to our country. We were getting ready to win this election.

"Frankly, we did win this election."

What followed from Election Night was a two-month assault on the vote, in which Trump and his allies exhausted every avenue to overturn the will of the people—a sustained effort in which he was aided by Republicans and that led to an unthinkable attack on the nation's very capital.

But Trump, of course, had taken the first steps to this moment more than four years before, with accusations against his own party during the 2016 Iowa caucus and then the full-throated conspiracy theories about election fraud that he first unveiled in an otherwise routine Ohio rally that summer. He spent his entire term moving further down that path, brazenly lying without consequence, knowing that his supporters would follow him and his fellow Republicans would back him. He had steadfastly assaulted the pillars of government and its institutions, attacking their credibility, so when the moment came—when it was time for a lie bigger than an altered hurricane map, time for one about the central tenant of the nation's democracy—enough of the public would believe him.

There had never been widespread voter fraud throughout the history of American democracy. Like clockwork, after nearly every major recent election, some in the GOP would grab a single irregularity here or there to claim that voting laws needed to be tightened, that access to the ballot needed to be restricted. The trends, both electoral and demographic, had been clear for decades: the more people voted, the better it was for Democrats, and more new voters tended to be Democrats. But that was a trend that Trump defied: his presence on the ballot in both 2016 and 2020—as well as his looming presence in the 2018 midterms—inspired huge turnout from both parties. The examples of fraud were so few—and often laughable—that GOP efforts to use them to slash voting rights never went anywhere. Yet history had never before seen such a steady, methodical, consistent effort by a national figure, and certainly not an incumbent president, to undermine the country's faith in the outcome of free and fairly conducted elections.

Having laid the groundwork for years, Trump accelerated his attacks on the election during the spring of 2020 as the virus swirled around him.

All campaign, he ranted and raved to aides behind the scenes that the election would be stolen, that Democratic governors and the federal bureaucracy—which he had long distrusted and that Steve Bannon has long wished to dismantle—were out to get him. And as the pandemic gripped the nation, forcing states to consider how to safely conduct elections when people were afraid of gathering in crowds or standing in lines, Trump saw a potential threat—and a potential opportunity to sow distrust.

The mail.

As the COVID-19 pandemic spread in early 2020, states holding primaries and special elections began widening opportunities to vote by mail. Trump went into a rage on Twitter in May, threatening to withhold federal funding from Michigan because its secretary of state had sent absentee-ballot applications to all registered voters. He went further against California, when he falsely claimed that the state was "sending Ballots to millions of people, anyone . . . no matter who they are or how they got there." That, of course, wasn't true, as the ballots went only to registered voters. But the falsehood was so blatant and so dangerous—undermining faith in both the civic process and the public's health—that Twitter for the very first time moved against its most famous user. It took down two of the president's tweets that maligned mail-in ballots in the nation's largest state.

Even before the coronavirus emerged as a global threat, Democrats had generally favored ways to expand access to voting by mail. Some Republicans had long argued against voting by mail and in favor of tightening voter identification and registration requirements. But there was no evidence of fraud, despite GOP claims. A number of White House aides tried to dissuade Trump from arguing against mail-in ballots, nervously noting that Republican voters tended to skew older and that senior citizens, the population most vulnerable to the coronavirus, might be more apt to mail in their votes as opposed to taking a risk by standing in line at a polling station.

Moreover, the facts weren't on Trump's side: before the pandemic, a handful of states, including the GOP stronghold of Utah, already conducted their elections almost entirely by mail and reported very little fraud. But that fell on deaf ears with the president.

"Mail ballots, they cheat," Trump said that September. "Mail ballots are very dangerous for this country because of cheaters. They go collect them. They are fraudulent in many cases. They have to vote. They should have voter ID, by the way."

Trump's goal was clear: by asserting that voting by mail, which was to be used at record levels that fall, was highly vulnerable to fraud, he was aiming to fabricate a justification for contesting election results in any state he lost. Following his lead, a number of Republican officials began to also advise their voters against mailing their ballots and to instead, despite the pandemic, show up at the polls on Election Day. Conversely, Democrats were already doing far less door-to-door canvassing than their GOP rivals, and their leaders advocated widespread use of mail-in ballots. They also raised concerns that Trump, via a slew of budget cuts and crony appointments, was trying to undermine the postal service as a means to strip down its ability to process mail-in ballots.

It was an assault on the integrity of the election. And the president's Democratic opponent was frantically trying to get ready to defend it.

Election security first became an issue for the Biden team in early March, right after it was clear that he was going to be the Democratic nominee. Bob Bauer, the former White House counsel who also ran Barack Obama's election protection program in 2008 and 2012, soon began telling others on the campaign that this would be a far tougher vote to safeguard because this time the Democrats were facing a Republican Party and president who no longer played by any rules.

And then COVID complicated things that much further.

The primary in Wisconsin was an early test. The state considered moving its April 7 election date, and it did end up extending its window for absentee votes to be counted. Voters didn't know where to cast their ballots, and some showed up at the wrong polling places. Some election workers—many of them elderly volunteers—didn't show up, for fear of contracting the virus, and it was a struggle to find adequate staffing. Bauer and others on the team—Democratic powerhouses like Anita Dunn and Jen O'Malley Dillon—saw Wisconsin as a moment from which to draw lessons on the upcoming election. As they watched Trump rail against the sanctity of the ballots, the Democrats knew they had to work on a public messaging campaign to make sure voters would believe in the integrity of the election.

Bauer created a team of former solicitors general to fight the legal battles ahead while the campaign veterans began to focus on mail-in balloting and the importance of ballot drop boxes. Private fundraising was directed toward election supplies to keep workers and volunteers safe: masks, goggles, Plexiglas partitions, hand sanitizer. And internally, strategy sessions were held, with tabletop exercises to game out what could happen during the campaign and its aftermath. Led by Dunn and Ron Klain, they tried to project scenarios both mundane and far-fetched. What if Trump refused to leave office? What if Trump considered calling in the military?

The ideas were rejected as absurd and unrealistic.

* * *

As Election Day approached, the polls were not encouraging for the president.

Joe Biden's lead, though not massive, remained consistent as the campaign's pace quickened dramatically that October, once Trump got out of the hospital and back on the road. The second debate with Biden was canceled after Trump refused to hold it remotely due to his own

COVID diagnosis. The third one was marked by Trump's efforts to re-create the stunt he had pulled with Bill Clinton's accusers; this time the surprise guest was a former business partner of Hunter Biden. But it fell flat and the debate failed to change the race.

As the backlash to Trump's handling of the pandemic grew, Republicans also looked likely to suffer significant losses across the board, including in the Senate and House, which made the president's frequent prediction of a "red wave" mystifying. He declared night after night that the GOP would defy the polls and roll to massive wins up and down the ballot. Many GOP pollsters thought Election Night might prove to be a defeat, and Trump aides worried that the president's public projections of overconfidence would keep some Republicans home at a time when the party couldn't afford to lose any votes.

But what truly loomed ominously over the election was not Trump's boast of a "red wave." It was what might happen were there to be a "red mirage."

As mid-October arrived, Biden campaign aides began circulating memos to senior staff, other Democrats, and news organizations. The memos carried an urgent warning that Trump might try to prematurely declare victory in order to shape news coverage and, more worrisomely, fuel claims of election fraud that could cause him to refuse to concede and provoke his supporters to violence.

There is no federal system of elections in the United States; instead, each of the fifty states conducts its own process. And in many states, mail-in ballots and early votes begin to be counted only on Election Day itself or, in some cases, after polls close that day. Therefore, because Democrats prioritized mail-in balloting during the pandemic, a lot of their votes—including in some key swing states—would not be counted until later in the day or days later. And because Trump had pushed Republicans to vote on Election Day itself, those votes would likely be counted first, giving the illusion that Trump was ahead early. The fear: that at some point on Election Night, Trump would point to the votes that were already counted and declare victory, even though thousands upon thousands of legal mail-in ballots would not yet have been counted.

The newscasts were encouraged to begin calling it "Election Week," rather than "Election Day." And reporters and government groups were urged to begin conditioning the public to expect that, due to the pandemic and the close nature of the race, this election would be different from previous years. The nation might not go to bed on Tuesday, November 3, knowing the winner, no matter what Trump said.

"MILLIONS OF MAIL-IN BALLOTS WILL BE PRINTED BY FOREIGN COUNTRIES, AND OTHERS. IT WILL BE THE SCANDAL OF OUR TIMES!" Trump had tweeted earlier in the campaign.

The campaign's final push was frenetic. Biden finally adopted an aggressive schedule, crisscrossing the country to hold small, socially distanced, outdoor events. His high-profile surrogates did too, including Obama, who seemed to be having the most fun of anyone as he held a few drive-in rallies, bounded up the stage to U2, cracked some jokes, and reveled at the drivers honking their horns in approval of his blistering attacks on Trump.

The Biden team also worked quietly behind the scenes to prepare for the inevitable fusillade of attacks on the integrity of the election. In an effort led by Bauer and O'Malley Dillon, their game plan emerged: they would fight lies with transparency. A war room went state by state in the most granular detail: What time do polls close? Which counties count fast or slow? Where should the votes stand once they are counted? How many absentee ballots would be out and when would they be tallied? Every data point was saved and examined. The Biden campaign needed to have all the information for legal challenges, but it also ramped up an unprecedented education campaign for its voters to reinstall confidence in the election and ensure that its supporters could safely cast their ballot amid the pandemic.

But on the Republican side, you'd barely know there was a virus.

Yes, most of Trump's rallies were outdoors—though a few, like one just outside Las Vegas, were held inside and later found to be home to virus outbreaks—but they were packed and few masks were spotted other than those on the faces of the reporters covering the events. The rallies followed a standard playbook: people would gather at the site, often an airport tarmac; Air Force One would arrive; Trump would spend an hour or so lying about Democrats and the pandemic—"we're rounding the corner," he'd say night after night; and then he'd goofily dance to "YMCA" before departing again.

He also forcefully returned to his most dangerous stance from four years before: once again, Trump would not commit to adhering to American democratic traditions and refused to pledge to ensure a peaceful transfer of power. But this time he was already president, with the levers of government and world's most powerful military at his disposal.

During an appearance in the White House briefing room in late September, Trump was asked whether he would "commit here today for a peaceful transferral of power after the election." Trump demurred, passing on a chance to call for a calm and orderly election process. He then once again made a baseless attack against the integrity of mail-in ballots.

"Get rid of the ballots and you'll have a very peaceful—there won't be a transfer, frankly. There will be a continuation," he said.

Trump's refusal to endorse the most fundamental tenet of American democracy, breaking from the behavior of any of his predecessors, caused grave uncertainty around the November election and its aftermath. He said it over and over, casting doubt on the election results. Democrats were increasingly alarmed as Trump repeatedly questioned the integrity of the vote and suggested that he might not accept the results if he were to lose. Biden's team began to strategize as to how to handle it if Trump prematurely declared victory, while Nancy Pelosi, who long questioned Trump's mental stability, was blunt in her private assessments to allies. "He's going to try to steal it," she warned over and over.

Some Republicans were worried too, but they kept those thoughts private for fear of antagonizing Trump. Mitch McConnell was no fan of Trump the man—he found him arrogant and incurious—but also told fellow Republicans that "We had a hell of a good four years," as he pointed to accomplishments like tax reform, a humming economy, and the appointments of scores of federal judges. He talked to William Barr a lot, both men resigned to a Trump loss and concerned as to how the president might lash out in defeat.

And since he had witnessed the measures Trump was willing to take during the George Floyd protests and at Lafayette Square, Mark Milley was deeply concerned about how the president might act were he to lose. He maintained a back channel to his Chinese counterpart to reassure Beijing that the United States did not want war. And Milley told his chiefs that a dangerous period was on the horizon, between Election Day and the January 6 certification of the results. There were hints of a coming furor: the Trump campaign embraced military-style rhetoric and language that leaned on baseless assertions of voter fraud and corruption. "Stop the steal" became a rallying cry.

"We need you to join ARMY FOR TRUMP's election security operation!" read one Trump campaign post, with the president's eldest son declaring that "every able-bodied man, woman" should enlist. "Don't let them steal it," Donald Trump Jr. wrote in one posting.

Milley was deeply worried and offered a sobering—and prescient—prediction in one meeting: "If President Trump wins, then the street's going to explode with riots and civil unrest. If President Trump loses, there's going to be significant issues there about a contested election."

In the campaign's final days, polls showed a tightening race in the battleground states that would decide the election. Republicans felt increasingly confident about Florida and North Carolina, but alarms were flashing about highly motivated Democrats making inroads in two longtime GOP strongholds: Arizona and Georgia. Still, in the campaign's final stretch, Trump made only one visit each to the two states.

His focus instead was on the trio of Michigan, Wisconsin, and Pennsylvania. Seemingly indefatigable, he showed no sign that he had been hospitalized for COVID less than a month earlier. The crowds were big and getting bigger, and the energy had picked up. People were tired of COVID, Trump told aides; they wanted a chance to go back to their lives. And they didn't want radical socialist Democrats telling them how to live. Even some Trump campaign aides who had been deeply pessimistic about the president's chances, believing he had dug himself too much of a hole with his scattershot response to COVID and racial justice, found themselves starting to believe once more. Maybe, just maybe, he could defy the odds again.

Forever superstitious, Trump ended his 2020 campaign the same way he'd wrapped up 2016, with a late-night rally in Grand Rapids, Michigan. In his closing remarks, he veered toward the nostalgic and the optimistic, capping off a dark speech with a ray of light.

"With your help," Trump said, "your devotion and your drive, we are going to keep on working. We are going to keep on fighting and we are going to keep on winning, winning, winning."

Twenty-four hours later, he was losing. And he couldn't believe it.

Election Night had started promisingly, with those early leads on the board across the Midwest. Florida did end up in Trump's column fairly early, giving him a huge victory and one that revealed surprising Republican strength among Latino voters, some of whom had experiences in their ancestral countries that made them particularly receptive to warnings about socialism. Victory was in the air.

And then the night turned, and news of a loss in a Republican stronghold came from an unlikely source. Shortly before 11:30 p.m., the decision desk at Fox News called Arizona for Biden, giving the Democrat a win in what was traditionally a deep-red state and dramatically narrowing Trump's paths to victory. The Map Room, where Franklin D. Roosevelt had tracked the progress of World War II, had been turned into an Election Night command center, and news of Fox's call ignited outrage.

"They betrayed me! Betrayed me!" Trump yelled. He pushed his aides, including Jared Kushner, to call Fox News, to call Rupert Murdoch, and get them to rescind the call. Fox would not take it back, and the Associated Press—the gold standard of election calls, one whose lead was followed by major newspapers and treated by both parties as the final word—followed with its own call of Arizona for Biden a short time later. Though the decision desks at both Fox News and the AP privately sweated out the call in the days that followed, they stood by it. And while none of the other networks immediately followed suit by awarding Arizona to Biden, the perception of the night had changed. Trump was on the run.

When Biden appeared before a crowd of supporters parked in their cars outside a Wilmington convention center, his deficits in Michigan, Wisconsin, and Pennsylvania had all shrunk and the votes left to be counted were coming from heavily Democratic counties in each state. But Biden did not declare victory, instead urging patience for the mail-in vote to be tallied.

Trump did nothing of the sort when he took the small White House podium hours later and unleashed his angry speech. No one had called the race—and the networks continued cautioning viewers that it could be several days before they would—but the vote count trends were bad for the incumbent. Trump was in trouble, and he railed to aides against what he saw, declaring that the only way he could have lost would be if the election were stolen.

But off camera, he took a slightly different tone, even wondering aloud to Kellyanne Conway how he could "lose to fucking Joe Biden," in what she took as a sign that he understood, deep down, that he had been defeated, even if he was not ready to say so publicly. She thought, as did some other Republicans, that Trump needed to perform, that he needed to vent publicly and exhaust all potential legal options.

In the first days after the election, a lot of Republicans were okay with taking results to court: the race was close, they reasoned, and a Democrat in the same position would look at the same legal options. This was a tough campaign and a narrow defeat and it would take some time to get over that; they all knew how much Trump hated losing. Plus, they assumed, Trump couldn't be seen as quitting on his fervent base, since he needed to keep them ginned up in order to maintain their support—including financial—down the road. One Republican even infamously mused to the *Washington Post* for a story that ran on November 9:

"What is the downside for humoring him for this little bit of time? No one seriously thinks the results will change."

The downside would become evident soon enough. But there were warning signs almost immediately. Soon after Election Day, Donald Trump Jr. sent a text to Mark Meadows outlining paths to declaring victory for his father no matter the vote tally. And the president's Twitter account over the next forty-eight hours became completely unhinged.

"We are up BIG, but they are trying to STEAL the Election. We will never let them do it. Votes cannot be cast after the Polls are closed!"

"Last night I was leading, often solidly, in many key States, in almost all instances Democrat run & controlled. Then, one by one, they started to magically disappear as surprise ballot dumps were counted. VERY STRANGE, and the pollsters got it completely & historically wrong!"

"They are finding Biden votes all over the place—in Pennsylvania, Wisconsin, and Michigan. So bad for our Country!"

There wasn't a need to fact-check the first sentence of that last tweet; Biden votes were indeed being counted in Pennsylvania, Wisconsin, and Michigan from ballots that were legally cast early or absentee. The prophecy of the "red mirage" had come true: the votes counted first showed Trump ahead, but he was on the verge of being surpassed by Biden in the states still tallying ballots. And despite the president's claims, it was perfectly acceptable for states to keep counting votes postmarked by Election Day—it just was going to take longer than usual due to the sheer volume of pandemic-related mail-in ballots. That didn't sit well at 1600 Pennsylvania Avenue.

"STOP THE COUNT!" Trump tweeted. And then: "ANY VOTE THAT CAME IN AFTER ELECTION DAY WILL NOT BE COUNTED!"

This was not a misunderstanding of a fundamental principle of American election law. This was something more insidious. This was Trump trying to wildly toss out accusations of misconduct in order to explain away his loss and to paint his defeat as less than legitimate. On that Saturday, November 7, four days after Election Day, the Associated Press called Pennsylvania for Biden, which put the former vice president over the 270 Electoral College vote threshold to make him president-elect. I wrote the story that announced Biden's win to audiences around the world. The networks quickly followed suit, including Fox News.

Biden's quest was complete. He had returned Pennsylvania, Michigan, and Wisconsin to the Democrats' column, his victories there due to both a surge in Black voters and his ability to win back some of the blue-collar workers who had defected to Trump four years earlier. He also won Arizona and, in the coming days, would be awarded Georgia, grabbing another GOP stronghold. He finished the race with 306 electoral votes to Trump's 232. At home in Wilmington, Biden blinked back tears as he thought about all his loved ones whom he had leaned on to make it there. He thought of his parents. He thought of Beau. That night, he took the stage and made a pledge to heal the bitter national divides that had only grown during the heated campaign.

"It's time to put away the harsh rhetoric. To lower the temperature. To see each other again. To listen to each other again," Biden said. "To make progress, we must stop treating our opponents as our enemy.

"We are not enemies," the new president-elect continued. "We are Americans."

Trump, meanwhile, was at his golf course in suburban Virginia that afternoon, when the announcement came that he soon would no longer be the most powerful, or most talked about, man on the planet. When his motorcade wound its way back to the White House a few hours later, it encountered thousands of revelers. They had descended on the area next to the executive mansion, congregating at the newly dubbed Black Lives Matter Plaza just to the north of the park that Trump had used the military to clear during the George Floyd protests five months before. They danced, they hugged, they pulled their masks down to pose for photos as they flipped off the White House. Some had been there forty-six months earlier, wearing pink pussy hats, as they marched across the capital in the wake of Trump's inauguration. That day, they were outwardly defiant but inwardly despondent. This time, they were simply exultant. Trump had lost.

At nearly the precise moment that the race was called for Biden, an undeniably pathetic spectacle was unfolding, an event that would soon become an infamous shorthand for the ineptitude displayed after the election by the Trump legal team.

The tweet from the president had sounded impressive: "Lawyers Press Conference at Four Seasons, Philadelphia. 11:00 am." That made sense: the Trump legal team had fanned out across the battleground states checking for voter irregularity and weighing their legal options. So a luxury hotel in a key swing state's largest city seemed like an appropriately grand setting for the elite team of lawyers representing the president of the United States in the nation's most pressing legal matter.

Not quite.

The second Trump tweet made the painful correction: the news conference was actually to be held at Four Seasons Total Landscaping, a rare GOP-friendly business in a deep-blue city that had the added bonus of being right off a major highway in case the lawyers needed to make a quick escape. It was a strange spectacle. The event was just Rudy Giuliani at a landscaping business down the street from a porn shop named Fantasy Island. The setting quickly became a national punch line, with DIY T-shirts sold online by day's end. And the claims of fraud Giuliani pushed that day were almost as laughable. Giuliani was midsentence at his news conference when word came down that the AP had called the race and Biden was now president-elect. It seemed like a perfectly ignominious end to the Trump campaign.

But while that moment was a farce, something far more serious was going on behind the scenes.

In the first few days after the election, Trump had privately seemed to resign himself to defeat. But the vacuum between Election Day and when the race was called a few days later was soon filled by other, shadowy voices. A contributing factor: the White House was the site of yet another COVID outbreak, this one traced to the gathering on Election Night. Staffers and advisers were testing positive or had been exposed to someone who had come down with the virus. Aides were staying home; some, like communications director Alyssa Farah, never came back.

And in that hollowed-out West Wing, there was space for others to gain a foothold. Some were staffers, like Mark Meadows, Stephen Miller, and Peter Navarro, who seemed to believe that there must have been rampant voter fraud. Others needed the gray White House visitor's badge, like Michael Flynn, the disgraced national security adviser who had flirted with the QAnon group of conspiracy theorists (among its theories: suggesting that some Democrats were pedophiles and that Trump was a near-mythical figure meant to redeem America). Sidney Powell, a former federal prosecutor, also stepped into the breach to push her increasingly far-fetched theories. Some of the president's fiercest allies in Congress—like Representatives Jim Jordan of Ohio and Mo Brooks of Alabama—appeared on Fox News and other conservative media outlets to reach Trump that way, to urge him not to give up. Conspiracy-loving Mike Lindell, the CEO of MyPillow, the bedding company that ran frequent ads on conservative outlets, was a Trump backer who suddenly found himself with easy Oval Office access. And there was Giuliani, the former mayor of New York City who led that wounded city so admirably after the September 11 terror attacks. He told Trump that he was hearing from loyalists across the country who knew of stories—crazy stories, sir!—about fraud and corruption and how the results in Pennsylvania and Michigan and Wisconsin and Georgia and Arizona all couldn't be trusted.

Trump stopped telling people he lost. He gave Giuliani and the others permission to investigate, and the ex-mayor, who had not worked as a lawyer in a courtroom in decades, swaggered into both the White House and the campaign's Arlington, Virginia, headquarters. He seized control of the proceedings, claiming he had dozens of affidavits from Michigan alone that proved fraud. He pushed aside the campaign lawyers and told the president that the case could end up at the conservative-leaning Supreme Court, where the justices, three of whom were appointed by Trump, would surely rule in his favor.

No one stepped in to stop the growing movement in its infancy. No one dared tell Trump he lost.

Hope Hicks, one of Trump's longest-serving and most loyal aides, met with Kushner and other top campaign aides the day the race was called for Biden. She asked who would tell Trump that it was over. Kushner, according to those present, said in a soft voice: "There is a time for a doctor and a time for a priest." He suggested that the aides could play doctor and tell Trump that it didn't look great. But he made clear that the plug was not to be pulled, that the president should be allowed to fight for a while. Last political rites, he said, would be the duty of the family. And it wasn't time yet.

McConnell, too, wasn't ready to pull the plug. He told confidants that he believed Trump lost—and, candidly, he was fine with that—but he wanted to keep the president involved and focused on the up-coming two Senate runoff races in Georgia. McConnell needed at least one win to keep Republicans in the majority—and McConnell as majority leader. He refused to tell Trump to concede, nor would he place a congratulatory call to Biden, a longtime Senate colleague, for fear of word getting out and infuriating the president.

There were a few lonely voices in the GOP who congratulated Biden privately or publicly acknowledged his election, including Nebraska senator Ben Sasse, Alaska senator Lisa Murkowski, and Illinois representative Adam Kinzinger. But these were the familiar faces, the usual small allotment of Republicans who would on occasion defy Trump. Their voices were dismissed by those left in the West Wing as same old, same old, the usual crew of bitter losers. No Republican with any real juice, no surprise voice, no powerful presence that could have made a difference—that could have shaken some sense into Trump's inner circle, if not the president himself—dared speak up.

They had been conditioned. They had spent five years watching Trump's popularity with the Republican base. They had spent five years living in fear of the president's tweets that could turn his supporters—whose votes they all needed too—against them. Trump's bullying, over matters big and small, had paid off. He had dominated his adopted party so thoroughly that, in the most perilous moment of his presidency, few dared cross him.

Even Senator Lindsey Graham, though he spoke to Biden, declined to nudge Trump to concede. In a series of private calls, he did urge the president to be mindful of his legacy, to not embark on a polarizing legal battle. But he never called on the president to step aside. Trump ignored him anyway. He also ignored Hicks, who suggested finishing his term with a series of events that reinforced his accomplishments. Her tenure at his side ended with a quiet resignation.

In the aftermath of the Four Seasons (Total Landscaping) debacle, Trump was angry at Giuliani, who he felt was humiliated by the low-rent performance. He wanted the former mayor's fighting spirit on the team but asked David Bossie, a sharp-elbowed Republican strategist who had worked on Trump's 2016 campaign, to keep the trains running on time. But the sigh of relief some felt about the possibility of Giuliani taking a back seat quickly vanished when Bossie tested positive for COVID and was sidelined. Giuliani and Powell were running the show.

And, for another week or so, it mostly resembled a clown show. The two, as well as lawyer Jenna Ellis, held a news conference on November 19, at the Republican National Committee headquarters in Washington, DC. Despite the raging pandemic, the room was packed, few were wearing masks, and it was warm. As Giuliani ranted and raved about fraud across the Midwest, as well as working in a reference to the movie *My Cousin Vinny* as a legal precedent, streaks of hair dye began running down his face. He was a mess. Powell went further. She insisted that voting machines made by Dominion Voting Systems, which was headquartered in Denver and Toronto, were part of a global communist conspiracy. Somehow Venezuela, Cuba, and China were all part of a worldwide plot to deny Trump the second term he'd rightfully won. The news conference was, in a word, ridiculous.

Later, Dominion filed a $1.3 billion defamation suit against Fox News, Giuliani, and Powell. Powell's defense? That her allegations were—wait for it—too ridiculous to be believed.

* * *

It might have looked like amateur hour. But this was no joke. What unfurled over the next eight weeks was a carefully coordinated effort to overturn the will of the people, to deny Biden his victory, and to keep Trump in power. Every move, from the farcical to the deadly serious, added up and came far closer to succeeding than most Americans realized.

It began in court and seemed, to most, to be harmless enough. The Trump legal team's record was woeful: it brought sixty-two federal and state lawsuits and all but one—a minor win on technical grounds in Pennsylvania—were defeated. The sheer number of lawsuits was seemingly absurd, and a waste of time and resources, but there wasn't much of an uproar to stop them. Trump was allowed to exhaust his legal avenues, the thinking went, even though it was transparent how thin his cases were. Time after time, Giuliani would deliver incendiary and baseless accusations in front of news cameras on courthouse steps—only to backtrack inside the courtroom for fear of drawing a judge's wrath for not presenting evidence for his claims. Two cases that made it before the Supreme Court—one challenging the legality of mail-in ballots, the other about state legislatures' powers—were also swiftly shot down.

The Trump campaign also pushed for recounts in several battle-ground states, believing that a careful tallying would reveal widespread fraud and push at least one of the states—maybe more!—into the president's column. They targeted three states in particular: Wisconsin, Arizona, and Georgia. None of them went as the Trump campaign hoped.

Wisconsin's recount wasn't cheap: the Trump campaign shelled out $3 million for it. And, in the end, the margin did change. By eighty-seven votes. In favor of Biden.

Georgia recounted three times, once by hand, between Election Day and May 2021. All three times, the result remained unchanged: Biden won narrowly, but clearly. Yet each recount seemed to grow distrust in the result, as did a partial fourth recount in the summer of 2021 of some of the absentee ballots. Though it had no chance of changing the outcome, it did lay the groundwork—once irregularities were found—to give Republicans a reason to claim even more oversight over elections in that state.

And then there was Arizona. A five-month-long audit by the state senate Republicans awarded Biden a few more votes than before. But what set this one apart was that it was fueled by conspiracy theories, and Cyber Ninjas, a small Florida-based data firm, was hired to find irregularities. It was a curious choice: the company had no election recount experience and its CEO, Doug Logan, had touted widespread election fraud claims on social media. Election experts also warned that the $150,000 cost was too low to do it successfully. And, well, a review of its review, however, found that seventy-six out of its seventy-seven claims were false; citing a $2 million debt from its work in Arizona, Cyber Ninjas went out of business not long after completing its recount.

As expected, none of the recounts changed the outcome of a state. But they all gave Trump more ammunition to sow distrust in the nation's election system.

As the counts were launched in distant states, Giuliani and Powell remained the faces of the effort in Washington, while other supporters, including Flynn and Lindell, each took moments to advocate Trump enacting martial law. That option was never seriously considered, nor was a plan to have the National Security Agency sift through raw electronic intelligence to prove that foreign powers were trying to sway the election for Biden. But there were other, quieter efforts led by Steve Bannon and Trump himself to push state officials and pull the levers of government to stop the certification of Biden's win.

The president and some of his top aides pushed Republican legislators in battleground states won by Biden to dispute the results before they could be certified. But despite some private presidential pressure, the efforts went nowhere, and all fifty states and the District of Columbia certified their election returns by December 9. The president's campaign also convened unauthorized "Trump electors" in the close states won by Biden on the same day the real electors voted. Documents were drawn up, memos circulated. Giuliani and others seized on it, and groups of fake electors were convened in states like Arizona. But this effort went nowhere and five days later the real presidential electors cast their ballots to make Biden the president-elect.

That was finally enough for McConnell. He was still deeply worried about the Georgia races, but Trump's rally there earlier in December was a chaotic mess. The president had whined openly about his electoral fate and cast doubt on the integrity of the upcoming January 5 special election—which, the Republican leader feared, might depress

GOP turnout, since Trump loyalists might opt to stay home if they felt the proceedings were not on the up-and-up. On December 15, the day after the Electoral College vote, McConnell called Meadows with the heads-up that he was going to recognize Biden's win on the Senate floor.

Moments after McConnell publicly said the magic words, "President-elect Joe Biden," Trump called in a fury. He screamed at McConnell, calling him disloyal and weak.

"The Electoral College has spoken," McConnell replied. "You lost the election."

He hung up and called Biden to congratulate him.

* * *

There weren't many Republicans calling the president-elect. And those who did make calls did so quietly and urged Biden to give Trump some space, to let him sulk on his way out. No one in the Biden inner circle believed Trump would concede or attend the inauguration, and that was fine. They chose to ignore him, to go ahead with their transition.

Meanwhile, Trump was also pursuing other avenues, trying to find other powers of the government he could exploit. He leaned on Barr to declare that there had been major election fraud, which the attorney general refused to do. Barr told the president that the Justice Department would of course look into credible allegations, but there had been nothing substantial. Nervous that Trump was sinking deeper into the conspiracy fever swamps and was surrounded by lawyers putting nonsense in his head, Barr summoned Michael Balsamo, the Associated Press's justice reporter, for lunch on December 1 and delivered this on-the-record assessment: "To date, we have not seen fraud on a scale that could have effected a different outcome of the election."

It was cold water on Trump's theories. Within hours, Barr found himself in front of apoplectic Trump, who chewed him out for not supporting his lies.

"You must have said that because you hate Trump, you must really hate Trump," the president screamed, an account first reported in *Peril* by Bob Woodward and Robert Costa. Barr assured him that he did not but stressed that there was no sign of widespread fraud and warned Trump that he was listening to crackpots. Two weeks later, Barr resigned.

Trump moved to have others at the Department of Justice help, finding a sympathetic ear in Acting Assistant Attorney General Jeffrey Clark, who penned a series of draft letters that falsely claimed that the Justice Department was investigating claims of election fraud in several states—including Georgia, Michigan, Pennsylvania, and Wisconsin—and called for each state to convene its own investigation. The attempt, aimed to cast more doubt on the sanctity of the election, was blocked by Acting Attorney General Jeffrey Rosen and Acting Deputy Attorney General Richard Donoghue, who both refused to go along. The letters were never sent.

Despite that failure, Trump maintained a particular fixation on two longtime Republican states that Biden had embarrassingly swiped from his column. Both of them—Arizona and Georgia—had GOP governors. Trump pushed especially hard in early December on Georgia, calling Governor Brian Kemp, who had long been an ally. But when the president asked him to convene the state legislature to overturn the results and appoint a pro-Trump set of electors, Kemp refused. Trump grew enraged and attacked Kemp. And Trump's sense of betrayal ahead of the governor's reelection race was so overwhelming that he threw his support not just behind a possible GOP primary opponent, David Perdue, but also to—wait for it—the Democratic gubernatorial favorite, Stacey Abrams.

A few weeks later, Trump went so far as to call Frances Watson, a staffer who investigated elections for the state, to find fault with mail ballots to justify his victory, telling her that he won the state "by hundreds of thousands of votes. It wasn't close." And then, on January 2, he called Georgia's secretary of state, Brad Raffensperger, and made it clear what he wanted: some way, somehow, for precisely enough votes to turn up to overcome his deficit to Biden and flip the state.

"So look. All I want to do is this," said Trump in a recording later obtained by the *Washington Post*. "I just want to find 11,780 votes, which is one more than we have. Because we won the state."

He went on with what appeared to be a threat: "You know what they did and you're not reporting it. You know, that's a criminal—that's a criminal offense. And you know, you can't let that happen. That's a big risk to you and to Ryan, your lawyer. That's a big risk."

It was brazen and galling. A push to disregard vote totals to quite literally change the outcome of an election, all caught on tape. It was also quite possibly illegal. Raffensperger refused. But the effort to pressure and bully elected officials in his own party—which later attracted attention from Georgia prosecutors—was a stunning act by a defeated president, a move to crash through legal and ethical boundaries as he desperately tried to cling to power. At every moment, he was goaded on by a small group of loyalists who believed that there was a chance to maintain the White House or delegitimize Biden so significantly that he would be unable to govern and be ripe for defeat by a Trump return in 2024.

Steve Bannon declared it was their moment "to kill the Biden presidency in its crib."

Bannon was the right's wild-haired provocateur, a navy graduate who worked at Goldman Sachs and had grown rich from his piece, of all things, of the *Seinfeld* syndication deal. He went on to run Breitbart News, the influential right-wing news site that frequently trolled in racism and became a thorn in the side of Democrats, particularly Hillary Clinton. He joined Trump's 2016 campaign in its final stretch, amped up the "America First" national messaging, and had the candidate lean in hard on a populist appeal. After Trump won, Bannon became a White House chief strategist known for undercutting colleagues—he loathed Kushner—as much as for his bomb-throwing populism. In a few months, he was drummed out of his post and later ostracized after trashing the president's family in a bestselling book, Michael Wolff's *Fire and Fury.*

Carrying himself as a roguish intellectual who wore a comical amount of shirts at once, Bannon supported similarly nationalist candidates in Europe. Ensconced in a Capitol Hill town house a few steps from the Supreme Court, he worked on the behalf of Trumpist causes. He was later indicted for trying to scam Trump supporters who thought they were helping build the president's promised wall along the US–Mexico border, though Trump eventually pardoned him. But as the election approached and Trump grew desperate, he began quietly talking again to Bannon, who he privately acknowledged understood his base better than just about anyone.

Bannon had warned the president that the race was slipping away from him, but he really sprang into action after Election Day. He saw an opportunity to stop the transfer of power on a date in early January when Biden's Electoral College victory would be certified by the House of Representatives. It was an obscure date, known only by a few political junkies. Bannon soon promised the date would be "known the world over."

He was not wrong.

That event became the target. In a series of meetings at the White House, the nearby Trump Hotel, and the Willard hotel down the street from the executive mansion, the group gathered: Bannon, Giuliani, Flynn, Lindell, the former New York City police commissioner Bernie Kerik, and the lawyer John Eastman. Separately, Senator Ted Cruz, a Harvard Law School graduate, consulted with pro-Trump congressman Mo Brooks of Alabama and had his staff research the Electoral Count Act, to see if there was a way to stop the certification of Biden's win.

Trump's allies whirred with unproven claims: People voted twice! Dead people voted! Dead people voted twice! With Giuliani at the helm, they presented their case to Graham, the head of the Judiciary Committee. The senator was sympathetic but demanded evidence. They didn't have any. Eastman then wrote and circulated a memo that claimed that an alternate, pro-Trump set of electors had been convened by seven states. Again, it was greeted with skepticism.

The memo outlined a plan to have the election thrown to Trump during the certification. It might work. But it all hinged on one man. Thankfully, the Trump allies thought, the one man had been perhaps the most loyal to the president of all.

Vice President Mike Pence.

Trump had largely gone into hiding after Biden was named the winner. He held only a handful of public events, even as the coronavirus pummeled the United States that winter. Reporters and photographers stationed at the White House would watch for the marine-posted sentry at the exterior door of the West Wing; if he was there, that meant Trump was in the Oval Office. Night after night, that marine would stand guard until 8:00 p.m., 9:00 p.m., 10:00 p.m. But Trump never showed his face.

The vaccine was ready—too late to give Trump a preelection boost, which he was convinced was a conspiracy—but not widely available. Hospitals filled up; deaths mounted. These were some of the darkest days of the pandemic, a moment when the nation needed leadership, and Trump was largely absent. His government was hollowed out. It was a dereliction of duty.

Pence was still out there, pushing the administration's response and touting its accomplishments of the last four years. But while Trump regularly blasted election conspiracy theories on Twitter, Pence largely avoided the subject in his public remarks. He was torn. He was immensely loyal to Trump, who had plucked him from a likely defeat in his Indiana gubernatorial reelection run in 2016 to be his vice president.

A deeply religious man with ties to the evangelical GOP base, Pence had watched in amazement as Trump connected with Republican rank and file. He and his wife, Karen, may not have cared for Trump's personal conduct. But he firmly believed Trump was good for Republicans, good for the country, and good for his personal political future—including his own run for president in four or eight years.

If a single senator formally objected to certification, all hundred would have to weigh in: all the Republicans would have to go on record as to whether they thought Biden won. They'd have to choose between Trump and the rule of law. Josh Hawley of Missouri was the first to say he would object, followed by Cruz and others. The plan, outlined in a memo Eastman authored, would be for Pence to announce that due to ongoing disputes in the seven contested states, those electors would be tossed out. That would leave forty-three states: and the electors from those would tally 232 votes for Trump and 222 for Biden. And then Pence was to gavel in Trump as reelected.

Pence knew he couldn't do it. But he gave it some thought; he wanted to be sure; he explored every avenue. He consulted legal scholars, constitutional experts. Around the same time, the vulnerabilities surrounding the Electoral Count Act became apparent to the Biden team. It wasn't as strong as we'd like, Bauer told a nervous team. He was on the phone with Chuck Schumer and Senate aides constantly, and the team's lawyers got ready to walk the legislators through the process step-by-step. But they also wondered aloud: Surely Pence would do the right thing, wouldn't he? Pence talked to Dan Quayle, another former vice president from Indiana and a mentor of sorts. Quayle had been, of course, a widely mocked running mate to George H. W. Bush, but in this moment, he emerged as an unlikely defender of the republic. He told Pence his duty, his obligation, was to the Constitution, not Trump. Pence knew he was right.

The night of January 5, Trump summoned Pence for a meeting. He made the case again: throw Biden's electors out, let the House decide the election. He told him that all his supporters, that Republicans, that tens of millions of GOP voters wanted him to do it. You can do it, Trump said. You can do it.

"I wouldn't want any one person to have that authority," Pence said.

Pence then stressed to Trump that he had talked to scholars, reviewed his options. His job the next day during the certification of the Electoral College vote was simply "to open envelopes." He knew a plot was underway for Trump allies in the Senate and House to object; he knew the next day would be messy. But he wouldn't be a part of it.

Trump was incensed, and he threatened to not be Pence's friend anymore. Pence pushed back, told him to abandon his wild fantasy. You aren't going to be president anymore, he told him. On the twentieth, it will be Biden.

"You've betrayed us. I made you. You were nothing," Trump said. "Your career is over if you do this."

Pence did not budge. Trump did not relent. The campaign put out a statement saying that Pence and Trump were in "total agreement," a complete fabrication. Midnight came and went, and it was the day of the certification. Trump tweeted once more about his plot, declaring that if the vice president "comes through for us, we will win the Presidency."

It was a coup. It was a coup endorsed by the Oval Office.

The nation was in unchartered waters. No president had ever done anything like this before.

And Republicans let him.

* * *

There were a few in the GOP who bowed to the truth and noted Biden's win. Many more acknowledged the Democrat's victory in private but declined to say so publicly for fear of triggering Trump. And then there was a third group: Republicans who were true believers, who believed that Trump, somehow, should still be president beyond Inauguration Day.

But all of them, no matter their own beliefs about the election, had discovered something else.

When lawmakers returned home for visits, including over Christmas, they found widespread talk from neighbors, friends, and family members about the election being stolen. Their offices were inundated with calls, their inboxes overflowing. Trump's power was pervasive: conservative media outlets, Facebook groups, social media postings, text message threads ricocheted around Republican circles, all claiming that the election was rigged, that Biden had improperly taken it.

In the days after the election, the bogus election claims seemed limited to hard-core Trump supporters, QAnon followers, and other conspiracy theorists. But as the weeks ticked by, and Republicans continued to hold their tongues and give Trump freedom to spread his false claims, the dangerous ideas took hold among more rank-and-file Republicans as well. Law enforcement groups picked up more extremist chatter and threats of political violence. Underground online communities grew in size and became more prominent. More and more Republicans believed the election had been stolen.

The nation was splintering, and the trends of the last four years accelerated over those weeks after Election Day. It wasn't just that the parties couldn't agree on policy—they couldn't agree on the same basic set of facts. Two media ecosystems, two dueling narratives, two sets of truths. It was a nation of silos, of two tribes. Tribes that were growing more and more hostile.

More and more everyday Republicans convinced themselves that something was wrong, that something was rigged, that something had to be done. Many of them planned to be in Washington to attend a rally the president was planning in the hours before Biden's Electoral College vote was going to be certified in the Capitol. Some camped out the night before to get a good spot, holding their places as dawn approached. They were loud. There was energy and menace in the air. It was the day they were going to take their country back. The rally was going to be at the Ellipse, a short walk from the White House. Trump had tweeted that it "will be wild!"

The crowds gathered.

They had to stop the steal.

The Big Lie was everywhere.

It was finally the day.

It was January 6.

8

JANUARY 6

The Oval Office is surprisingly small and somewhat disorienting.

It takes its name, of course, from its shape. People are largely accustomed to rooms that are square or rectangle, with a clear point of entry, a gateway to a room that orients everything inside. That's not the case in what is likely the most famous room in the world.

The Resolute Desk, fashioned from the oak timbers of a British Arctic exploration ship and given as a gift from the Crown to President Rutherford B. Hayes in 1880, sits at the southern portion of the room, the large windows behind it looking out onto the White House South Lawn. When the president is at the desk, the Rose Garden is to his right, a pair of couches and other ornate seating directly in front of him, portraits of past presidents on the wall.

It's one of the most consequential places on earth, where history-altering decisions are made. There is no obvious way in or out to the rest of the building, though there is a door out to the Rose Garden. But when the interior doors are closed, the room looks almost smooth, nearly a continuous oval wall. But there are three doors tucked away if you know where to look for them. One leads to the Cabinet Room, where the president gathers his most trusted advisers. Another opens to the Roosevelt Room across a hallway, a smaller place for meetings and press events, with the White House reporters stationed just down the hall in a far more dilapidated section of the West Wing.

But there is one more door, just to the president's left when he sits at the desk. It leads to a small study. And just a few steps beyond that lies a private dining room, featuring a table and a bank of TVs on the wall, a place of refuge to be used only by the person who calls the White House home.

That was where Donald Trump watched one of the darkest days in the nation's history. And he did nothing to stop it.

For hours, the forty-fifth president of the United States stared at a television as a riotous mob of thousands committed heinous acts of violence in his name. The hordes stormed the United States Capitol, assaulted police officers, sat in the seats of power, put lawmakers' lives in jeopardy, and threatened to hang the vice president. A Confederate flag was burnished for what was believed to be the first time in the citadel of the nation's democracy. American flags were used as weapons. A police officer was Tasered with his own device. A gunshot rang out. All told, five people died.

The searing, brutal images from the United States Capitol on January 6, 2021, transfixed a nation and horrified the world. They exhilarated Trump.

His people were fighting for him. They had believed the Big Lie.

The power of Trump's falsehoods was on full display that day, both inside and outside the US Capitol. His lies had come home to roost, the nation's constitutional bonds fraying like they had not since the Civil War. Inside the Capitol, Republican lawmakers bent to the will of the president, defying their oaths of office in an effort to hijack the election results. And outside, a mob tried to do the same, using violence to keep their favored candidate in power. This was happening here. American democracy was in peril.

* * *

In the weeks the president had spent contesting the election, January 6 had been elevated from an obscure date in the federal calendar to a last stand for the MAGA movement. More than a dozen Republican senators and more than a hundred members of the House had indicated they would vote against certification of Joe Biden's win. Trump had tweeted about it several times. As the date approached, thousands of Trump supporters wearing red hats descended on Washington, arriving at the area's airports and populating downtown and the National Mall. The night of January 5, members of extremist groups like the Proud Boys and Oath Keepers became an ominous presence, involved in skirmishes breaking out around the city.

Ali Alexander, the leader of "Stop the Steal," which organized many of the protests against Biden's certification, tweeted at 1:13 a.m., "First official day of the rebellion."

They began converging on the Ellipse.

Soon after the sun was up, Trump was rallying his troops via Twitter, continuing his pressure campaign against Mike Pence. "States want to correct their votes, which they now know were based on irregularities and fraud, plus corrupt process never received legislative approval. All Mike Pence has to do is send them back to the States, AND WE WIN. Do it Mike, this is a time for extreme courage!"

Pence was shown the tweet as he got ready that morning at the vice president's residence, the Naval Observatory. He grimaced. He had told some of his closest aides that he had been unnerved by the president's behavior the night before; Pence grew pale as he talked about it, one aide noticed. But his mind was made up, and he wanted to head off the narrative as best he could, asking staff to draft a letter that he could release before the event at the Capitol so he could try to end speculation that he would do Trump's bidding and deny Biden's win.

"I just want to get this day over with," Pence told one aide.

January 6 had already started poorly for Republicans: the Georgia Senate runoff election was held the night before, with the final result announced on the sixth. Both Democratic candidates, Raphael Warnock and Jon Ossoff, had won. Democrats had surged to the polls, repeating the push that had led Biden to capture the former GOP stronghold two months earlier. Republican turnout was down, in part because Trump had cast so much doubt over the election that some of his supporters stayed away, believing the outcome was rigged. The wins were significant: the two new Georgia senators would now give the Democrats fifty votes in the Senate, and the resulting fifty–fifty divide meant that ties would be broken by the incoming vice president, Kamala Harris. For the first time since 2010, Democrats controlled the presidency and both branches of Congress.

From the White House, Trump could hear the excited crowd gathering a short distance away at the Ellipse. The temperature was in the forties, not too cold. He was handed a note that thirty thousand people were expected at the rally, far more than had been originally anticipated. He effused at how much the crowd "loved" him. Two aides said it was the most energy Trump had displayed in weeks.

The "Save America" rally at the Ellipse had all the trappings of a Trump campaign event: same soundtrack, mostly the same aides, the president standing in front of a phalanx of flags. But there was one difference from a normal rally: in a nod to the uncertainty of the day and the public nature of the Ellipse, Trump would stand behind bulletproof glass. Some advisers wondered if it would be the final time that Donald Trump would step in front of a crowd like this. His family gathered. Ivanka and Jared Kushner came over from the White House; Eric Trump and Lara Trump, a senior campaign aide, were there, as were Donald Trump Jr. and his girlfriend Kimberly Guilfoyle. The crowd was huge and cheered the opening speakers, growing especially loud when Rudy Giuliani called for "trial by combat" to defend the election. There was a sense of danger in the air. The question that hung over the teeming crowd: What would Mike Pence do?

When Trump took the stage to roars right around noon, he kept the heat on. He repeated his false claim that the election was stolen, he tore into his fellow Republicans for not doing enough to support his allegations, he suggested that "no third-world countries would even attempt to do what we caught them doing." And he denounced his vice president repeatedly.

"Republicans are constantly fighting like a boxer with his hands tied behind his back. It's like a boxer. And we want to be so nice. We want to be so respectful of everybody, including bad people. And we're going to have to fight much harder," said Trump as some in the crowd chanted, "Fight, fight."

"And Mike Pence is going to have to come through for us," the president continued, "and if he doesn't, that will be a sad day for our country because you're sworn to uphold our Constitution."

Thousands in the crowd peeled off, beginning their planned march to the Capitol. The chants of "fight for Trump" grew louder. Trump used a variation of the word "fight" more than twenty times in the speech, the crowd getting more and more agitated.

"We fight. We fight like hell. And if you don't fight like hell, you're not going to have a country anymore," Trump said. The crowd felt combustible. And then the president urged the thousands still gathered in front of him to also march to the US Capitol to apply the pressure in person.

"We're going to the Capitol, and we're going to try," Trump said. "The Democrats are hopeless, they're never voting for anything. Not even one vote. But we're going to try and give our Republicans, the weak ones because the strong ones don't need any of our help. We're going to try and give them the kind of pride and boldness that they need to take back our country."

He concluded: "So let's walk down Pennsylvania Avenue."

Despite his exhortation, Trump did not join the crowd, instead returning to the White House, setting up shop in the private dining room off the Oval Office. But about ten thousand people left the rally and marched toward the Capitol, officials later estimated, joining thousands more—including three hundred members of the Proud Boys—who were already there. One Capitol police officer reported seeing a rifle. The crowd pressed up against the temporary security barrier installed outside the famed building. A noose hanging from a gallows was spotted nearby. A new chant had gone up: "Hang Mike Pence."

Just before 1:00 p.m., the first barricade fell.

A sea of protesters surged through the protective fencing put up by US Capitol police on the building's west front, pushing the officers back toward the exterior stairs. The pro-Trump mob, for the time being, remained outside, milling about as more and more joined the assembling masses who were concluding their walk down Pennsylvania Avenue. Seeing the growing crowd, Capitol Police Chief Steven Sund made his first request to have the National Guard deployed to add reinforcements. That call, and four more in the next hour, were all ignored.

But for most people either inside or outside the Capitol, it was not apparent that the moment was on the precipice of crisis. TV coverage was trained on the inside of the people's chamber, waiting for the certification ritual to begin. At 1:00 p.m., Pence and US senators began their walk to the House chamber for the start of the event that would lead to Biden's official election. Pence's office used that moment to release the statement in which he reaffirmed his decision to defy Trump and not interfere with the afternoon's events.

"It is my considered judgment that my oath to support and defend the Constitution constrains me from claiming unilateral authority to determine which electoral votes should be counted and which should not," he wrote.

News alerts about Pence's letter soon flashed across the phone screens of the assembled crowds. The vice president was letting them down; he was letting Trump down. The cries of "traitor" and "hang Mike Pence" grew louder.

Pence was not the one committing the betrayal. The venom toward him was the sole creation of the man whom the vice president had served so loyally for four years. Pence had never broken from Trump publicly, and his effusive praise of the president had bordered on obsequious: he had set the tone for the "Dear Leader" cabinet meetings that had become punch lines; at times he even mimicked Trump's mannerisms. He had done everything that a faithful vice president was supposed to do except this one thing: he would not defy the Constitution.

But that was not enough for the president. Loyalty had always been a one-way street for Trump, and he thought nothing of casting it aside in the service of staying in power. In the service of the Big Lie. And now he was putting his vice president's life in danger.

Just as news of Pence's letter began to ricochet across Washington and dominate cable news chyrons, the flash of blue and red police lights surrounded the areas near the Capitol. A pair of pipe bombs was discovered, one at the headquarters of the Republican National Committee, one at the Democratic National Committee. Vice President–Elect Harris was at the DNC and hustled to safety as the areas were evacuated. As of this writing, no one has been charged with planting them.

Inside, the proceedings continued apace. And, fueled by the false claims of election fraud, the Republicans put their plan in place. At 1:12 p.m., Senator Ted Cruz and Representative Paul Gosar objected to certifying the votes in Arizona. The attempted coup was underway.

By rule, that move separated the joint certification sessions, with lawmakers splitting up to head to the House and Senate chambers to debate the objections. Those separate sessions would be capped at two hours, with each lawmaker given five minutes to speak. But the Republicans were vowing to contest all seven states, requiring two hours of debate for each objection, meaning that the certification would be delayed by half a day or more.

When the session paused, it was only the third time since the adoption of the Electoral Count Act of 1887 that there had been a debate about a state's results. In 1969, there was a brief kerfuffle over a segregationist faithless elector from North Carolina who voted for George Wallace instead of Richard Nixon. The objection to the faithless elector was rejected by both chambers. And then in 2005, one Democratic senator, Barbara Boxer of California, joined Ohio congresswoman Stephanie Tubbs to object to what they said were acts of voter suppression in the battleground state. It too was debated and put aside.

And there had been a brief effort four years earlier, as a few Democratic House members raised objections to Trump's win over concerns about Russia's influence on the 2016 election, but Biden—who was vice president and serving, as Pence was now, as president of the Senate—repeatedly slammed his gavel and rejected the effort because they lacked a Senate sponsor.

"It is over," Biden had said.

Republicans in the chamber applauded. Pence told others he remembered that as a moment when Biden put country before party.

What was happening was not quite unprecedented. But there had never before been such a coordinated effort to question the integrity of the results or to challenge the veracity of so many states. Pence seemed steadfast, but some in Trump's orbit traded texts that early afternoon, wondering if the vice president might cave under the pressure of the GOP lawmakers—some of his closest friends and allies—making a principled stand for the president. Bannon gleefully exclaimed, "He might blink," but reasoned that even if the vice president held firm, the damage done to Biden was incalculable.

"Seventy-five million Americans already think he didn't win," Bannon said. "That number is going to only go up today, there will be more doubt. He'll be crippled."

The pressure was building both inside and outside the chamber. It was a split-screen testament to the power of Trump's hold on his party and its members: there was no evidence of voter fraud, no legal justification for any outcome other than Joe Biden's election being certified.

Yet some of the most important figures in the Republican Party were doing his bidding under the Capitol dome, challenging the results and staking their reputations to his lie.

And outside the crowds were building. Many held Trump flags, others American flags. Some wore tactical gear or carried zip ties. They pushed forward, forcing the Capitol police to retreat up the building's steps. The officers were overwhelmed, some pushed to the ground.

At 1:35 p.m., Mitch McConnell spoke in the Senate deliberations, offering a sharp rebuke to his GOP colleagues and demanding that they set aside their challenges to the election results.

"The voters, the courts, and the states have all spoken. They've all spoken. If we overrule them, it would damage our republic forever," McConnell said. "If this election were overturned by mere allegations from the losing side, our democracy would enter a death spiral. We'd never see the nation accept an election again."

But some of his Senate colleagues looked back, unmoved.

Scenes of the unruly crowd outside the Capitol were flying across social media and now catching the attention of the cable channels. But some of Trump's allies were quick to add to the confusion with their own social media gaslighting, claiming that the mob was fueled by antifa or other left-wing forces looking to carry out a false flag operation to discredit the Republican president and his supporters.

The rioters reached the Capitol walls. Sund's next call for the National Guard to be deployed went unanswered. The senators continued to debate the validity of the Arizona electors. Trump watched from the dining room off the Oval Office.

At 2:11 p.m., a rioter used a plastic shield stolen from an officer to smash a window on the Capitol's northwest side.

At 2:12 p.m., the first rioters entered the Capitol through that broken window.

At 2:13 p.m., the Senate was gaveled into recess and security hastily removed Pence from the Senate chamber.

The rioters were inside. The certification had been stopped. Law-makers ran for safety.

It was an insurrection.

* * *

The United States Capitol was attacked during the War of 1812, long before its famed dome rose over what was then a small city built on swampland. The capital city, which drew its name from the nation's first president and was built on land annexed from Virginia and Maryland in the deal Alexander Hamilton had struck with Thomas Jefferson, was besieged during the conflict. President James Madison was forced to evacuate the White House before both the executive mansion and the Capitol were torched by advancing British soldiers.

During the Civil War, President Abraham Lincoln ordered a fortification of the city—which sat just across the river from Virginia, a slave state, and a mere hundred miles from Richmond, the capital of the Confederacy—but the district remained largely free of fighting during the bloody conflict. The Confederates never mounted a serious offensive against Washington, and the Capitol dome, completed in 1863, soon became a symbol of the resolve of the Union. The building remained untouched in the century and a half that followed, standing tall amid the antiaircraft artillery installed nearby during World War II, its dome barely visible during the occasional blackout meant to reduce the risk of bombing from the German Luftwaffe.

The building remained a target, but was never fired upon, during the Cold War, in which the United States and Soviet Union aimed enough nuclear missiles at each other to destroy the world several times over. Officials have long suspected that the Al Qaeda hijackers who seized control of Flight 93 on September 11, 2001, may have planned to slam the plane into the Capitol, but a heroic rebellion from the passengers on-board sent it crashing into an empty field in rural Pennsylvania instead.

Despite the threats from foreign foes, the Capitol had stood impregnable for more than two centuries. On this January day, it was breached by its own citizens.

They carried Trump flags and American flags. Some had hockey sticks and other clubs. A few wore masks—not to prevent the spread of coronavirus but to obscure their identities. The rioters poured in through the broken windows, while a few climbed exterior scaffolding to gain entrance to the building's second floor. And then it happened: the rioters who had gained entry swung the ornate front doors wide open. The others could now storm in.

"It's open!" one man screamed as the crowd surged by.

They pushed over and through the Capitol police. The behavior of some officers, who appeared to be sympathetic to the pro-Trump crowds, would come under harsh scrutiny in the weeks that followed the insurrection. But the vast majority of police behaved heroically. Video shows the mob chasing a lone officer up a flight of stairs. Officer Eugene Goodman confronted one group of rioters who had an otherwise unimpeded path to the Senate chamber with lawmakers still inside. Goodman shoved one rioter, drawing the group's attention, and then proceeded to lure them away from the chamber. He had willingly put himself in harm's way—he became the mob's bait—and diverted their attention, buying precious time for the senators to escape.

Later, a video would capture Goodman racing Senator Mitt Romney—a likely target of the mob, since he was the lone Republican who had voted to convict Trump during his impeachment trial—away from the crowd and to a secure location. Other rioters reached a hallway less than a minute after Pence was hustled through it to a safe room; had the rioters reached the grand space just a little earlier, they could have overwhelmed the vice president's security detail and set upon the man whom the president had all but labeled a traitor.

The rioters were in the building and yet the lie that brought them there—that the election was stolen from Trump—was still being spun on the House floor. As Representative Gosar continued his challenge to the certification of the Arizona results, House Speaker Nancy Pelosi was hustled from the chamber. Representative Dean Phillips, Democrat of Minnesota, yelled, "This is because of you!" toward the Republican side of the chamber. The House was gaveled into recess.

For those in the House chamber, the sounds of tumult in the hallways grew as the mob advanced. Lawmakers hid behind chairs, some clutching hands and praying, some texting loved ones. A few with military experience, like Representative Jason Crow, Democrat of Colorado, took the lead, checking on others' safety and making sure that they fastened the gas masks left under their seats. The scent of tear gas was suddenly in the air, followed by the unmistakable sound of glass shattering. The rioters were at the door, breaking a pane of glass in an attempt to get in. Officers on the inside of the chamber barricaded that door, their guns drawn, screaming at the rioters to step away.

On the other end of Pennsylvania Avenue, the president tweeted.

"Mike Pence didn't have the courage to do what should have been done to protect our Country and our Constitution, giving States a chance to certify a corrected set of facts, not the fraudulent or inaccurate ones which they were asked to previously certify. USA demands the truth!"

Members of Congress, including Trump's fellow Republicans, were running for their lives. But his only concern was the Big Lie.

Minutes later, Trump tried to call Alabama senator Tommy Tuberville, one of the senators who had announced his intention to object to Biden's win. But Trump mistakenly called Senator Mike Lee of Utah, who then handed the phone to Tuberville. The two senators were hustling from the chamber, and Lee told Trump that Pence had been rushed to safety.

But Trump seemed not to hear him, Tuberville recounted later. Or simply didn't care.

The rioters flooded the Capitol. A Confederate flag, which is believed to have never penetrated the Capitol during the War between the States, was held aloft in Statuary Hall. A man commandeered Pelosi's office, putting his feet up on her desk. A self-proclaimed shaman wearing a Viking headdress stood behind the lectern in the Senate chamber as someone bellowed, "Where's Pence? Show yourself!"

Rioters looted the building; at least one defecated in a trash can. Law enforcement officers were viciously beaten by the surging crowd; one pleaded with rioters that he had children. Michael Fanone was Tasered by his own weapon and suffered a heart attack as he was pummeled by the crowd. He later said he feared he would be shot to death with his own gun. Officer Brian Sicknick was sprayed with a chemical substance—believed to be bear spray—and collapsed. He died the next day after suffering two strokes.

Lawmakers texted one another, expressing fears of being kidnapped. Some representatives, mostly Democrats, were leery of trusting and following the officers and instead barricaded themselves in their offices. Representative Alexandria Ocasio-Cortez, Democrat of New York, later said she felt specifically targeted by some of the rioters and feared she would be raped and killed. Two men clad in all black were spotted holding zip ties, which could have been used to bind the arms and legs of a possible hostage. Law enforcement officials, in the aftermath of the attacks, privately said that their greatest fear was that a prominent Democrat would be executed on a livestream.

But Democrats were not the only ones in danger. As Sund once more requested the National Guard, and was again denied, some GOP lawmakers began calling the White House for help. Pence, who along with his family was moved to another secure location within the Capitol complex, checked with aides and implored Mark Meadows to bolster security. And Kevin McCarthy, the GOP House leader and close Trump ally, called the president's cell phone and screamed at him to put out a public statement asking his supporters to leave the Capitol.

Trump refused, snapping that it was clear that the rioters loved their country—and their president—more than McCarthy did.

Despite McCarthy's plea, Trump made no attempt to ask his supporters to leave. That's because Trump didn't want them to go. He was transfixed.

The president, after returning from the Ellipse, walked back into the Oval Office and ambled through the door that led to the private dining room. It was there, sealed off from most of the White House, that he watched the Republican lawmakers object to Biden's win and, now, the rioters storm the citadel of democracy in his name. There were few people around to disturb him: at this point, with only two weeks left in his term and COVID surging, the White House was nearly empty. Meadows, who had free rein of the Oval Office, darted in a few times, nervously pointing out to Trump that things were getting violent.

"This is going to hurt your cause and not help it, sir," Meadows told Trump.

The president ignored him, his eyes glued to the televisions. They were full of images of chaos, rising smoke, and waving Trump flags. "They love me," the president breathed.

At 2:38 p.m., Trump tweeted a second time since the insurrection began, making his first mention of the disturbance at the Capitol.

"Please support our Capitol Police and Law Enforcement. They are truly on the side of our Country. Stay peaceful!"

Minutes later, a shot rang out.

* * *

Ashli Babbitt was not the same person she used to be. She had served more than twelve years in the military, settled near San Diego, had trouble keeping in business a pool service and supply company she ran with her husband. She found solace online, in the social media of the like-minded. She delved into QAnon, embraced its conspiracy theories, believed that Trump was being unfairly ousted from power. For weeks, she had January 6 circled on her calendar, believing it to be the day the nation would begin to win again. The night before, she tweeted: "Nothing can stop us. . . . they can try and try but the storm is here and it is descending upon DC in less than 24 hours. . . . dark to light. . . ."

She had fallen under Trump's spell, believed his lies. And it cost Babbitt her life.

Babbitt worked her way toward the front of a surging crowd of rioters who were pressed up against the door to the Speaker's lobby, adjacent to the House chamber. They pushed against the door, which buckled but held. A chant went up: "Fuck the blue!" Lawmakers on the other side of the door were being hurried to safety, with officers fearing that the situation could deteriorate at any moment. Three of the officers stepped back, away from the door.

A rioter, later identified as Zachary Jordan Alam, smashed a window in the door to the Speaker's lobby. The officers, with the guns raised, screamed at the rioters to stay back, to not breach the door.

Babbitt didn't listen. She attempted to climb through the broken glass, perhaps reasoning that her small frame could squeeze through and then she could open the door from the inside to let the others in.

The officers yelled again. Babbitt kept climbing. One of the officers pulled his gun's trigger.

The video of Babbitt's death was everywhere within hours. Investigators would later declare that the Capitol was the most documented crime scene in history, with journalists and the rioters themselves all using cameras and phones to snap photos and take videos. Several of the cell phone videos show the bullet drop Babbitt, her body instantly lifeless. She died that afternoon.

The rioters kept coming.

Ivanka Trump, the president's daughter and senior adviser, was long perceived as the person to whom her father listened the most. She was one of the few people, White House aides believed, who could get him to change his mind, or at least temper his instincts, smooth his rough edges. She was now in the private dining room off the Oval Office, urging her father to do something. She made the appeal that those in danger were police officers, so many of whom had backed him in the last election. He relented, but still did not call for the rioters to leave. He still thought they were helping his cause.

"I am asking for everyone at the U.S. Capitol to remain peaceful. No violence!" Trump tweeted. "Remember, WE are the Party of Law & Order—respect the Law and our great men and women in Blue. Thank you!"

But that was as far as Trump would go. Only a few aides—including Deputy National Security Advisor Matt Pottinger and Keith Kellogg, Pence's national security adviser—moved in and out of the Oval Office during the afternoon. Other allies reached Trump by phone. Some were stunned by his demeanor, others horrified. The president seemed unfazed by the scenes of violence and chaos that were on full display on the television that held his attention. At times, he smiled. He was getting what he prized above all else: people fighting for him on television.

The pleas kept coming in, including from some of Trump's closest allies, those who had supported him on cable for years. Many couldn't get through to Trump directly, but pleaded with Meadows to make the president do something. Among those who made the desperate pleas were the same conservative media heavyweights who had spent four years defending Trump—and, in recent months, propping up his Big Lie—but now were afraid that their own reputations would be damaged.

"Mark, the president needs to tell people in the Capitol to go home," Laura Ingraham wrote in a text later released by the House committee investigating the riot. "This is hurting all of us. He is destroying his legacy."

"Please, get him on TV. Destroying everything you have accomplished," texted Brian Kilmeade of *Fox & Friends*.

"Can he make a statement? Ask people to leave the Capitol," texted Hannity.

Others demanded answers as to why the rioters were still allowed to roam the Capitol. Lawmakers of both parties huddled in secure rooms, with Democrats furious at Republicans for not wearing masks in confined spaces and accusing them of inspiring and even aiding the rioters. The National Guard had still not arrived by three o'clock. Chuck Schumer called top Pentagon officials and urged them to demand that Trump tweet that everyone should leave. Hunkered in a secure room, Pence reached Acting Defense Secretary Christopher Miller, who took over once Esper was fired after Election Day, and made clear that the Capitol was not secure and a military presence was needed.

"Clear the Capitol," Pence demanded.

The order to mobilize the National Guard had been slow to come, with military leaders anxious about the public perception of sending troops to break up a civilian protest. Many in the Pentagon had been stung by the condemnation they received in June, when those in uniform were called in to help Trump clear Lafayette Park of the George Floyd protesters. That had been a mistake, many said privately. They had been used as political pawns and didn't want that to happen again. In other words: Trump's lie in June slowed down the response seven months later and put lives in danger.

Images of political rebellion that Americans had associated with other nations, those run by despots and dictators, had come home. Offices were ransacked, flags used as weapons, cell phones held aloft to record videos of vandalism. Tear gas filled the air outside the Capitol's steps, illuminated by the bright lights of flash grenades. As the skies began to darken, the scene was harrowing and eerily beautiful.

Biden had been in a great mood celebrating the Georgia wins. He had plans to speak that afternoon about the economy, which had been devastated by the pandemic. Those plans changed as he and his team watched the scenes from the Capitol, his rage growing. A number of his staffers had just convened a Zoom meeting to discuss inauguration prep when someone shouted: "Oh my God, they are attacking the Capitol!" Anita Dunn felt her mouth open in shock. Quickly, Mike Donilon and other aides scrambled to write something for the president-elect. Biden took the stage at the theater in Wilmington that his transition team had turned into an event space, screens displaying the words "Office of the President Elect" behind him. He began to speak in a quiet voice not much louder than a whisper.

"At this hour, our democracy is under unprecedented assault, unlike anything we've seen in modern times. An assault on the citadel of liberty, the Capitol itself."

His voice rising, he declared, "This is not dissent, it's disorder. It's chaos. It borders on sedition."

Nearly barking his words, he urged Trump to go on television and make a statement demanding the mob retreat. He dismissed the idea that his own safety could be in danger at the inauguration, saying, "The American people are going to stand up," and concluding, in answering a question from a reporter, by declaring, "Enough is enough is enough."

Some of the aides at the White House saw the clear distinction between Biden's forceful denunciation and Trump's earlier tweet, which included no push for the rioters to go home. They were dismayed and embarrassed. But the idea of a live, in-person statement was dismissed, for fear of what Trump might say off-the-cuff either on camera or to a pool reporter. When Trump was at last persuaded to intervene, the decision was made to record a video from the Rose Garden. But in his first two takes, he dwelled almost solely on his false claims of election fraud; in one, he didn't make any mention at all of a need for the rioters to depart.

Eventually, he said this: "I know your pain, I know you're hurt. We had an election that was stolen from us. It was a landslide election and everyone knows it, especially the other side. But you have to go home now. We have to have peace. We have to have law and order. We have to respect our great people in law and order. We don't want anybody hurt. It's a very tough period of time. There's never been a time like this where such a thing happened where they could take it away from all of us—from me, from you, from our country. This was a fraudulent election, but we can't play into the hands of these people. We have to have peace. So go home. We love you. You're very special. You've seen what happens. You see the way others are treated that are so bad and so evil. I know how you feel, but go home, and go home in peace."

Trump tweeted it out at 4:17 p.m., more than two hours after the rioters first set foot inside the Capitol. It was rife with lies, claims of a stolen election. In the months after the riot, as those who participated were arrested and stood trial, dozens of them said their violent actions were directly motivated by Trump's words. And here, amid an insurrection he inspired, Trump would not relinquish his lie.

An hour after Trump's tweet, the first few hundred National Guard troops, all clad in riot gear, arrived at the Capitol. The rioters who were still there, unable to reach lawmakers, were dispersed, many running from the possibility of arrest. A short time later, word was sent that Congress would not head home, but remain in session to finish the certification of the vote. Lawmakers who had left the Capitol complex were urged to return. Pence made clear that he would stay to preside. Trump was furious and tried to shift blame elsewhere for the day's violence.

"These are the things and events that happen when a sacred landslide election victory is so unceremoniously & viciously stripped away from great patriots who have been badly & unfairly treated for so long," he tweeted again at 6:01 p.m. "Go home with love & in peace. Remember this day forever!"

All told, nearly 800 people have been arrested across the country for crimes related to the insurrection. That includes over 165 individuals charged with assaulting or impeding law enforcement. Of those, more than 50 have been charged with using a deadly or dangerous weapon or causing serious injury to an officer.

The investigation is continuing.

* * *

As the rioters slowly left the Capitol the evening of January 6, a question hung in the air: Would the Republican senators continue to object to the election?

Many eyes turned to Josh Hawley. Weeks before, he had been the first senator to say that he would challenge the results of some of the contested states. And earlier on January 6, before the violence, the brash forty-one-year-old was photographed raising a fist in solidarity to some of the pro-Trump protesters who had assembled near the Capitol. He was urging them on, suggesting that he endorsed their fight. Hours later, some of the people he saluted would breach the Capitol and threaten the lives of all inside.

McConnell was resolute that the Senate finish the certification job before heading home, convinced that even a postponement would hand a win to the rioters outside. He wanted to go fast, to speed things along. Democrats were furious, demanding their GOP counterparts abandon their plan. Some Republicans wanted to do the same; Georgia senator Kelly Loeffler, fresh off her defeat, told her colleagues that she was changing her position and would drop her protest. She wanted to go home.

But Hawley would not. He would continue his objections to Arizona and Pennsylvania. He would remain in lockstep with Trump.

How the next hours played out on the Senate floor appeared to provide a preview of the politics within the Republican Party in the post-Trump era. Trump had lost, and the certification would continue. Most Republicans, including McConnell and the rest of the leadership, were pushing the party to move on. Some of the president's most loyal supporters, including Lindsey Graham, turned on him. And the few allies who remained stalwart, like Hawley and Cruz, were vilified and, briefly, appeared to be pushed to the margins of the party, their fates certain to sink with the outgoing president.

For a moment, the Republican Party looked largely ready to stop believing the Big Lie.

Just after 7:00 p.m., in an unprecedented step, both Facebook and Twitter removed some of Trump's incendiary tweets from that day, citing their contribution to the violence. Twitter then suspended the president from its platform for twelve hours, Facebook doing so for twenty-four. Trump's megaphone was turned off and, since he refused to face reporters, he was silenced as Congress reconvened to make his defeat official. For the first time in five years, he was unable to intimidate Republicans into obeying him.

When the Senate reconvened, the Capitol resembled a war zone. Windows were broken, offices vandalized, floors bloody. National Guard troops in full uniform were stationed throughout the complex, meaning that the democratic ritual would happen under armed guard. The anger in the chamber was palpable when Hawley registered his objections to Arizona, and then to Pennsylvania. Senator Mitt Romney glared at the junior senator from Missouri, only his eyes visible behind his double mask, and the image of his death stare quickly went viral. Mike Lee, Republican of Arkansas, stared at his GOP colleagues and told them that his own exhaustive legal research had led him to an undeniable conclusion: "Our job is to convene, to open the ballots and to count them. That's it."

And Graham, arguably Trump's closest confidant in the Senate, took to the floor to give an emotional speech reflective, many Republicans hoped, of the mood of their party.

"Trump and I, we've had a hell of a journey. I hate it to end this way. Oh my God, I hate it," Graham said. "All I can say is 'Count me out.' Enough is enough."

The objections to both Arizona and Pennsylvania were roundly defeated in the House. At just after 3:40 a.m. on January 7, nearly fifteen terrifying hours after the proceedings began, Pence announced that Biden had been certified the winner. It was over.

* * *

The nation woke up the next morning to find news of Biden's certification and to gaze in horror at the images of the previous day. Washington was a blizzard of talk about forcing Trump from office, by either impeachment or the Twenty-Fifth Amendment, which would have required a majority of the cabinet and Pence to find that the president was "unable to discharge the powers and duties of his office." Pence was furious at Trump, who never apologized for his role in endangering the vice president's life. But he quickly scuttled talk of the Twenty-Fifth Amendment and refused to engage Pelosi and Schumer in discussions of the topic.

Trump's grip on power was precarious.

He soon lost his primary ability to spread his misinformation and to keep Republicans in line. Two days after the insurrection, Twitter permanently banned Trump from its platform, citing his ongoing efforts to incite violence. Trump had 88.7 million followers, and his account was his central means to rally his fans and intimidate others in his party. Now it was gone. Facebook soon followed suit with its own ban. Trump was silenced. It was devastating. In those first few days after the ban, Trump frequently reached for his phone or shouted for Dan Scavino, his social media guru, to post something—only to unleash a storm of four-letter words when he remembered that he could not.

Several cabinet members—including Education Secretary Betsy

DeVos and Transportation Secretary Elaine Chao, who is married to Mitch McConnell—handed in their resignations. Several senior staffers quit. And while Pence would not entertain discussion of the Twenty-Fifth Amendment, House Democrats made clear that they planned to impeach Trump again, and there were real questions as to whether enough Republicans would go along with the move to forcibly remove the president from office.

In an effort to quell that talk, Trump gave in to pressure from his few remaining aides and recorded a video to send out the afternoon of January 7.

"Now Congress has certified the results. A new administration will be inaugurated on January 20," Trump said. "My focus now turns to ensuring a smooth, orderly, and seamless transition of power. This moment calls for healing and reconciliation."

For the first time, Trump acknowledged that he would no longer be president after Inauguration Day. But he stopped short of admitting he had lost, nor did he concede the election to Biden. A week after the insurrection, with growing chatter that Senate Republicans might join in an effort to convict him, he released another video, with a stronger condemnation of the Capitol riot.

"I want to be very clear: I unequivocally condemn the violence that we saw last week. Violence and vandalism have absolutely no place in our country and no placc in our movement.

"Like all of you," he continued, "I was shocked and deeply saddened by the calamity at the Capitol last week."

It was, of course, another lie. But Trump needed to change the political momentum that was seemingly hurtling toward removing him from office. He desperately didn't want that: the first impeachment was tough enough on his ego, even though it ended up galvanizing his supporters and would have propelled him to reelection, he believed, had it not been for the pandemic. There was little he could do to stop the Democratic-controlled House from impeaching him again: he was

going to have to live with being the first president to have been impeached twice. It would be part of his entry in the history books.

But Trump told confidants he didn't want to be the first president
convicted and removed from office, even though the punishment
would largely be symbolic since the trial itself wouldn't happen until
after Biden called the White House home. Why did Trump care? Because were he convicted, he would likely be barred from running for
federal office again—including another bid at the presidency.

To keep that hope alive, Trump needed to keep his head down, he
grudgingly admitted to a few select aides. He saw Pence in the Oval
Office a week after the insurrection and offered no apology but kept
things civil. He bent to his aides' wishes and upheld a presidential tradition by leaving a note for Biden. He never said publicly what he wrote
in longhand the night of January 19, his last in the White House. But
Trump did break with another tradition: he announced that he would
be the first modern president to skip the inauguration of his successor.
Pence would go in his stead.

Donald John Trump stepped out of the White House for the final
time as president just after 8:00 a.m. the morning of January 20. He
and First Lady Melania Trump stopped to thank those who worked
in the executive mansion and then strolled slowly across the lawn to
board Marine One a final time. He seemed to be taking it in, realizing what he once had and now had lost. After the short flight to Joint
Base Andrews, a farewell reception was held and Trump delivered brief
remarks. There, in his final hours as president, he finally did what his
aides had wanted since the moment the race was called for Biden: he
touted his own accomplishments; he extended good wishes to the new
administration; he made no mention of contesting the election.

A few minutes later, Air Force One lifted off for its final flight with
Trump aboard as commander in chief.

Ten miles away, Biden was fulfilling a moment he had dreamed
about most of his life, yet in a manner he could never have imagined.

With America's tradition of peaceful transfers of power never appearing more fragile, the inauguration ceremony unfolded in front of a US Capitol that still bore the wounds of the insurrection just two weeks earlier. Biden became the nation's forty-sixth president within a circle of security forces evocative of a war zone and devoid of crowds because of the coronavirus pandemic.

He placed his hand on a thick Bible and took the oath of office, his family alongside him, but a spot empty in his heart without Beau. Denouncing a national "uncivil war," Biden gazed out on a cold Washington morning dotted with snow flurries to see over two hundred thousand American flags planted on the National Mall to symbolize those who could not attend in person.

"The will of the people has been heard, and the will of the people has been heeded. We've learned again that democracy is precious. Democracy is fragile. At this hour, my friends, democracy has prevailed," Biden declared in his speech. "Through a crucible for the ages America has been tested anew and America has risen to the challenge. Today, we celebrate the triumph not of a candidate, but of a cause, the cause of democracy.

"This is America's day. This is democracy's day," Biden continued. "A day of history and hope, of renewal and resolve."

As inscribed in the Constitution, Biden officially became president at noon. But because the ceremony ran ahead of schedule, he actually took the oath at 11:48 a.m., yet did not officially become president for twelve more minutes, at which point he was midway through delivering his speech.

Therefore, Trump was still president as his motorcade passed the cheering crowds along the roads leading from Palm Beach International Airport, over Lake Worth Lagoon, and onto the gilded enclave of Palm Beach. The cars then turned into Mar-a-Lago's driveway, disappearing behind the well-manicured hedges.

Just before noon, Trump was seen walking into his residence at the estate, having only a few more minutes as the most powerful man in the world and the undeniable center of global attention. At 12:01 p.m., the Secret Service began reducing its assets on the property. The military aide who carried the nuclear football stepped away. Agents and officers began getting in their vehicles to drive off. The transfer of power, more tumultuous than ever before, was complete.

Trump was alone.

9

THE GRIP TIGHTENS

Mitch McConnell adjusted his glasses.

He peered around the well of the Senate, the place he had called home for more than three decades. Staring back at him on February 13, 2021, was a wall of faces, evenly divided between Republicans and Democrats. Both sides gazed at him with anticipation, mixed with some dread. Not even a month ago, McConnell was the Senate majority leader, but now he had been reduced to leading the minority, a position he despised.

He also hated the man who put him there.

McConnell had privately disliked Donald Trump for years but was willing to make "a deal with the devil," as he put it with some grim mirth to a handful of select aides and influential Republicans. Trump had been good for the party, the Kentucky senator reasoned, and had paved the way to stack the federal judiciary, not to mention the Supreme Court, with conservative justices. But Trump had overstayed his welcome. McConnell had, without question, hoped that the president would be reelected, yet he expressed some degree of private relief when Trump lost. He knew Joe Biden, a longtime colleague in the Senate. He could work with Joe Biden. He might not have agreed with him on much, but Joe Biden was rational and predictable and they could find some degree of common ground. He could live with Joe Biden being president.

He could not live with losing the Senate. And he blamed Trump for that.

Once the presidential race had been called for Biden, Trump had stopped actively leading the Republican Party. He had vanished into a hole of self-pity and conspiracy theories, surrounding himself with lunatics who claimed the election had been stolen from him, McConnell told confidants. McConnell himself had been willing to indulge Trump for a short time, a move he told others he now regretted, in order to keep Trump motivated to help with Georgia. But the lame-duck president held only one rally in the formerly deep-red state and delivered a lackluster performance mostly centered on his own feeling of grievance. And his constant claims of election fraud, it appeared, motivated some Georgia Republicans to stay home, either out of solidarity with Trump or out of a belief that their votes wouldn't be counted in what the president had declared would be a sham election. McConnell went on to recognize President-Elect Biden's victory when the Electoral College met in mid-December.

Stunningly, the Republicans lost both Georgia races. The Senate would be fifty–fifty and, since Vice President Kamala Harris would break any tie vote, it flipped to Democratic control. McConnell was suddenly on his way out of power when the two races were called early on January 6. And hours later, McConnell was being hustled to safety in a secure room at the Capitol when insurrectionists stormed the citadel of democracy to try to keep Trump in power. The violence was a black mark on the nation, and McConnell was a loud voice that night to push the Senate to continue with the certification of Biden's victory, even though it dragged past 3:00 a.m. "We will not let them win," he told his GOP colleagues in the moments after the riot.

He commanded the spotlight again that day in February, the final day of Trump's second impeachment trial, this one for inciting the insurrection. The world was watching.

"January 6 was a disgrace. American citizens attacked their own government. They used terrorism to try to stop a specific piece of democratic business they did not like," McConnell said. "Fellow Americans beat and bloodied our own police. They stormed the Senate floor. They tried to hunt down the Speaker of the House. They built a gallows and chanted about murdering the vice president."

McConnell continued.

"They did this because they had been fed wild falsehoods by the most powerful man on earth—because he was angry he'd lost an election. Former President Trump's actions preceding the riot were a disgraceful, disgraceful dereliction of duty."

He stared ahead: "There is no question, none, that President Trump is practically and morally responsible for provoking the events of the day."

The chamber was silent. McConnell, though now the Senate minority leader, was poised to be the most powerful Republican in Washington during Biden's presidency, akin to the leadership role that Nancy Pelosi had harnessed for Democrats the previous four years. And now he was denouncing Trump, holding him responsible, urging the Republican Party to turn the page on the man who for four years had bent it to his whim.

Of course, none of these words really meant anything. Because a few minutes earlier, McConnell had voted to acquit Trump.

The minority leader cited a narrow reason to not convict Trump: an ex-president could not be removed from an office he no longer held. But in reality, McConnell read his caucus: only seven GOP votes were cast to convict the former president while forty-three were for an acquittal. The measure ended fifty-seven to forty-three, falling far short of the sixty-seven needed to find Trump guilty. Banished to Mar-a-Lago,

Trump would become the first president to be impeached two times, but the lack of a guilty verdict meant that there would be no prohibition on him seeking federal office—including the White House—yet again.

Even if the measure was doomed to fail, McConnell could have cast his vote for it, giving it more teeth and sending a stronger signal that Trump was not welcome back in Washington. It would have been a total rebuke of the Big Lie that nearly toppled the nation's democracy. But McConnell chose not to do so, instead opting for a halfway measure that would, he believed, allow him to save public face while also retaining the support of the majority of his caucus as he aimed to keep his leadership role with an eye on regaining the majority in 2022.

Still worried about alienating Trump's supporters, McConnell would not fully cast out the former president. He still worked in fear, namely in fear of the ex-president's voters. And then, not even two weeks later, he went a step further when asked in an interview if he would support Trump if he were the party's presidential pick in 2024.

He didn't hesitate.

"The nominee of the party? Absolutely."

In many ways, the effort to ostracize Donald Trump ended right there. In the weeks after the Capitol riot, the moment was there for Republicans to once and for all sever ties with Trump and turn their back on the falsehoods that inspired the insurrection. They chose not to do either. And soon, there were clear signs that Trump's exile would not last long. And that the power of his lies would only grow stronger and would remain the most powerful force in American politics even after Trump left office.

With startling speed, Trump's hold over the Republican Party not only was sustained; it tightened. There were a few rebels, but their insurgency was largely crushed. With the new Biden administration's focus on the dire pandemic, Trump was able to work in the shadows, regaining strength, basking in the unwavering devotion of most rank-and-file

Republicans. And when GOP leaders realized they had no choice but to embrace him, Trump demanded loyalty.

And he demanded loyalty to the Big Lie.

* * *

For a time, Donald Trump did the unthinkable.

He stayed silent.

When he hurriedly left Washington the morning of January 20, he did so under a shadow of disgrace. Some of his closest allies had seemingly abandoned him, denouncing his words that led to violence. Trump returned to the surprisingly modest living quarters at Mar-a-Lago, surrounded by only a small staff and Secret Service detail. Despite the near-universal rebuke he received for what happened on January 6, Trump did not abandon his claim that the election was stolen. His closest advisers were telling me that Trump was ranting behind closed doors about the impeachment trial, but there was nothing he could do about it. Democrats were hell-bent on making him the first president stained with that stigma twice, and Chuck Schumer was telling anyone who would listen that he thought he could snag enough Republican senator votes to convict and ban Trump from ever holding federal office again.

Trump was nervous that his longtime rival might be right. His small smattering of remaining aides told him otherwise; that, yes, there were cracks in the previously rock-solid loyalty that Republicans had shown him, but not enough for a conviction. They didn't know, at that time, what McConnell would do, but even if he turned on Trump, they reasoned, it wouldn't be enough to bring along enough votes to lead to a conviction. But just to be safe, the aides implored Trump to stay quiet. He would survive the vote unless he messed it up. Just be quiet.

For once, he listened. For once, he stayed quiet.

Of course, being off Twitter made that easier. Trump put up a brave face with those to whom he spoke about the social media ban, saying he was "relieved" to not be on it anymore.

"Do you know how many people I'd have to go after?" Trump told one amused visitor. "I'd never get anything else done!"

But privately, he fumed about losing his Twitter account, which he always viewed as the most important way to connect directly with his base. He wasn't president anymore but, for now, because of his impeachment trial, people were still talking about him incessantly. He hated his loss of ability to shape the coverage, to change a cable chyron with one 280-character burst. He also knew that once the trial ended, much of his immediate relevance would be gone.

His life at Mar-a-Lago was, in many ways, idyllic. He went golfing just about every day, sometimes more than once. The club was beautiful in a somewhat garish way, built by socialite Marjorie Merriweather Post and purchased by Trump for about $10 million in 1985. Much to Trump's chagrin, it did not quite have beachfront property on the Atlantic, but it became his winter White House, where he'd retreat on numerous weekends and host world leaders (and make money off all the Secret Service and staff who stayed there). Now, he was feted by his club members, a certain slice of conservatives of Palm Beach society, the club's parking lot filled with expensive cars owned by people with expensive face-lifts. Many evenings, Trump would don a suit or a tux and mingle with guests, often asked to deliver a speech at a microphone that just happened to be there, ready at a moment's notice if the former president wanted to say something that inevitably would be recorded for a club member's Instagram account.

Trump miserably followed the impeachment proceedings from Florida, picking up the phone to call allies about the possible Senate vote. He watched with dismay when his defense attorney Bruce Castor of Pennsylvania gave a long-winded and rambling opening statement, all while wearing an ill-fitting, oversize suit. He raged when Republicans, including longtime rivals Mitt Romney and Susan Collins, voted against him. But he kept his mouth shut. And he was acquitted. Trump breathed a sigh of relief. He was heartened by a statement of support from Republican National Committee chair Ronna McDaniel, who said the GOP "should not go along" with impeachment. It was far from clear at that moment that he would mount another campaign, but he at least wanted to keep alive the possibility so he could maintain his relevance in the Republican Party.

Despite the condemnation he received from some of his closest allies over the insurrection, it soon became clear that the party was still very much his.

* * *

One of the first to come back was Lindsey Graham. Truthfully, he had barely left.

He said he was hopping off the Trump train with an emotional speech in the hours after the Capitol riot but, within days, soon fell back into his usual habit of calling the president. Trump's anger was elsewhere; he didn't hold the speech against Graham. The two men had something of a friendship, forged over golf and Graham's ability to get booked on Fox News. Many in Washington had been puzzled by the relationship; Graham had been close to John McCain, attempting to model his career after the longtime Arizona senator. But as McCain's health failed, Graham had sidled up to Trump, despite his mentor's hatred of the president and Graham's own 2016 campaign condemnations of the celebrity developer. Graham had a penchant for forming deep ties with powerful men, and he took it upon himself to become Trump's liaison with the Republican Senate. He boasted to friends of his proximity to the president, his aides admitted, but was willing to occasionally break with Trump—particularly on matters of foreign policy—and claimed he had talked the commander in chief out of countless bad decisions.

Graham looked at the political landscape in early 2021 and saw both trouble and an opportunity. The Democrats controlled the White House and both houses of Congress, and the Republicans were clearly in disarray in the aftermath of Trump's collapse. But Graham also knew that it would not be easy going for Biden. The pandemic was raging and vaccines had only just come online. The economy was under tremendous strain. Almost half the population didn't even recognize Biden as the president. Though things looked dark for the GOP at the moment, the possibility was there, Graham thought, for Democrats to take the blame if things didn't improve soon—and Republicans could take advantage. But they would need to be unified, he thought. And they would need their leader back.

Graham had given Trump plenty of space to contest the election result. Hell, he told others, he wanted there to be proof of fraud so Trump could stay president. But he didn't think that happened and felt that it was time to turn the page. He tried to tell Trump that, but the former president wasn't having it. His focus was solely on seeking revenge on those Republicans who turned on him—particularly McConnell for his condemnation from the Senate floor. Trump seethed that McConnell had abandoned him; Graham replied, "Mitch thinks you cost him Georgia and the majority."

But Graham knew how to play the game. He went on Fox News that Valentine's Day night, the day after Trump's acquittal, to offer a prediction about the ex-president that he hoped—through the magic of cable—would become a reality.

"He's ready to move on and rebuild the Republican Party," Graham said.

* * *

Trump had been at Mar-a-Lago only a few days when the request came in.

Kevin McCarthy, the Republican House leader, was planning to visit Palm Beach to raise some money and wanted to visit the president on January 28, just a week after Trump had left Washington. Trump had always privately thought McCarthy was "dumb," per aides, and needy to the point of being annoying. Trump had also, on more than one occasion, mistakenly called the GOP leader "Steve." McCarthy never corrected him. The two men had not spoken much since McCarthy called him during the insurrection, with rioters just a few hundred feet away, demanding that the president help, demands that Trump had refused.

But McCarthy needed Trump. Paul Ryan had been House Speaker when Trump first took office, but he had retired before the Democrats took control in 2018. McCarthy had just spent two years leading the minority and was prepared to do two more but looked at the Democrats' margin—just a handful of seats—and saw a real chance to become Speaker if the Republicans took control in 2022. But while historical trends favored Republicans, because the party not in control of the White House tends to pick up seats in the midterms, it would not be easy for McCarthy to herd a disparate group of GOP lawmakers to win a Speaker's vote. And his biggest concern was the growing number of loyal MAGA representatives, and not just Trump allies like Jim Jordan and Devin Nunes. He also would need to win over the ascendant new members of the Far Right, like Lauren Boebert of Colorado and Marjorie Taylor Greene of Georgia, who were proving remarkably adept at stealing the spotlight and raising money even though their views were considered extremist by many of their Republican peers.

And McCarthy kept looking at one number in particular: the 139 Republicans in the House who voted against certifying Biden's win on January 6. McCarthy was one of them. They believed the Big Lie. He needed their support. And most of all, he needed Trump's support. He needed to go kiss the ring.

The result: a deeply awkward photograph. The two men stood

together in a gilded sitting room, both in suits, only Trump in a tie. The smiles seemed somewhat forced.

The photo was a curiosity: it was the first image of Trump since he left office. McCarthy was immediately blasted by Democrats on the Hill; Representative Katherine Clark of Massachusetts denounced him for associating with a "treacherous instigator," while Representative Ilhan Omar, the progressive from Minnesota, ripped him for spending time with a "loser insurrectionist." But McCarthy shrugged off the criticism; he got what he wanted. The photograph was the point—and the statement that came with it.

Trump was off Twitter but his newly formed political action committee, Save America PAC, blasted out an email with the image and a statement, which included the line: "President Trump's popularity has never been stronger than it is today, and his endorsement means more than perhaps any endorsement at any time."

McCarthy was willing to take the humbling at Mar-a-Lago—he apologized for his heated conversation with Trump on January 6—in order to exact two things. First, he was able to get Trump to commit to helping Republicans, putting to bed the rumors that the former president might be looking to quit the GOP to form his own political party. And, in the statement, Trump promised the House minority leader that he would help Republicans win back a majority in the lower chamber of Congress.

"They worked very well together in the last election and picked up at least 15 seats when most predicted it would be the opposite," the statement continued. "They will do so again, and the work has already started."

Trump made no mention of his own loss and stopped short of backing McCarthy's bid for Speaker. But the GOP leader quickly put out his own statement—notable for using the phrase "President Trump" as if he were still in office—which declared that "Today President Trump committed to helping elect Republicans in the House and Senate in 2022. A Republican majority will listen to our fellow Americans and solve the challenges facing our nation."

Other Republicans soon began making the trip to south Florida. From the Senate: Rick Scott of Florida, Bill Hagerty of Tennessee, Mike Lee of Utah, and Rand Paul of Kentucky all paid homage to Trump at Mar-a-Lago during his first few months out of office. Some of the most extreme Republicans in the House were also eager to be received by the former president, including Representatives Greene and Boebert, as well as Madison Cawthorn of North Carolina and Matt Gaetz of Florida. For them, elected largely by diehard MAGA supporters, it was imperative to be seen with Trump and then fundraise off the visit.

And as the weeks went by, more mainstream Republicans made the trip too. Minority Whip Steve Scalise, a longtime Trump ally, visited Trump, as did some, like Governors Ron DeSantis of Florida and Kristi Noem of South Dakota, who were rumored to have their own eyes on the White House someday. To be sure, there were still some Republicans who were eager, either publicly or privately, to turn the page on the former president. McConnell denounced him. Mike Pence would barely speak to him.

But they were in the minority. The Palm Beach pilgrimages meant something.

Trump had been the dominant figure in Republican politics for nearly six years at this point and nothing was changing. As the GOP looked to combat Biden, its most popular face remained the forty-fifth president. Poll after poll of Republican voters taken in the first months after Trump left office did not reveal a pariah, an ex-president in disgrace. They showed quite the opposite: Trump remained nearly as popular as ever with rank-and-file Republicans. He didn't need Twitter, he didn't need to be in office; GOP voters still liked him. GOP lawmakers had to continue to cozy up.

And it wasn't just that Republican voters liked him. They believed him.

A *Washington Post* poll taken that April, just three months after the inauguration, revealed just how thoroughly Trump had convinced the Republican Party that the election had been stolen. Only 19 percent of Republicans surveyed then thought that Biden was legitimately elected.

Despite fueling one of the darkest days in American history, the same lie that caused January 6 was still alive and well in the Republican Party.

* * *

Joe Biden wouldn't even say his name.

The new president took office amid a confluence of crises, including a raging pandemic and soaring unemployment. He had made two central promises to voters: that he would get the COVID-19 pandemic under control and that he would restore a sense of faith in government. With an eye on China, Russia, and other rising autocracies, he told the American people that he would earn their trust, that he would demonstrate that democracies could still deliver for their people. It was urgent, he declared, to restore confidence in a system of government that had been so badly strained the past four years—and he wanted them to be able to believe in it again.

That included believing in the office of the president. And Biden felt that so strongly he would almost never say his predecessor's name.

During a February 2021 town hall in Wisconsin, Biden used the moniker "the former guy" as shorthand for Trump and, among many Democrats, that nickname stuck. Biden didn't want Trump to be a distraction. But despite the new president's refusal to name him, Trump shadowed the early days of the young administration. Within hours of taking office, Biden signed executive orders to undo the heart of

Trump's agenda, rejoining the Paris Climate Agreement and the World Health Organization while repealing the travel ban, revoking the permit for the Keystone Pipeline, and halting construction of the border wall. And he did so, pointedly, while wearing a mask as he sat behind the Resolute Desk, something Trump never did.

He marshaled the forces of government to battle the pandemic, which had fundamentally changed the norms of everyday society and, about a month into Biden's term, the death toll reached half a million. The president held a moment of silence outside the White House and delivered sunset remarks on the terrible American milestone. A president whose own life has been marked by family tragedy, Biden spoke at the COVID memorial in deeply personal terms, referencing his own losses as he tried to comfort the huge number of Americans whose lives had been forever changed by the pandemic.

"We often hear people described as ordinary Americans. There's no such thing," he said. "There's nothing ordinary about them. The people we lost were extraordinary.

"I know all too well. I know what it's like to not be there when it happens," said Biden, who has long addressed grief more powerfully than perhaps any other American public figure. "I know what it's like when you are there, holding their hands, there's a look in your eye and they slip away."

For a nation that had spent nearly a year of the pandemic being gaslighted about its severity, Biden's words were bracing and, to some, refreshing. Every day, he'd pull out the card tucked in his right jacket pocket, a printed version of his daily schedule. But there were other items printed on it too. Very sad ones.

The card listed the number of Americans killed in Afghanistan and Iraq, which always made him think of his son Beau, whose cancer developed not long after his return from serving in the Middle East. Also on it: the daily numbers of vaccine doses administered, the previous day's virus deaths, the daily hospitalizations, and the cumulative death toll. The weight of those numbers was seen on his face when, at public events, he would dig it out, squint, and ever-so-slowly read aloud the latest tally of COVID-19 dead.

But there was hope on the horizon. Vaccine distribution was ramping up dramatically, with shots going in arms across the nation. There were pockets of vaccine hesitancy that worried Biden officials, most of them in states that Trump won in 2020 and where citizens had listened to his skepticism about masks and the lethality of the virus. But the White House thought that would eventually fade as the vaccine became familiar and people saw that it was the ticket to returning to their normal lives. On one day in April, more than four million shots were delivered.

Biden leaned hard on his narrow majorities in Congress to pass a COVID relief bill and tangled with Senator Joe Manchin, a Democrat who had managed to be elected three times from one of the reddest states in the union, West Virginia. Manchin had long made clear, first to Harry Reid and now to the new majority leader, Chuck Schumer, that he prided himself on being an independent voice: he'd vote for something "only if I can sell it back home," he'd repeat over and over. And Manchin, though a reliable Democrat in some areas, was leery of the sweeping relief bill the White House pushed, even after a federal minimum wage hike to fifteen dollars an hour was dropped.

Foreshadowing future fights on other legislative issues, including voting rights, Manchin balked at other provisions as well, believing they were too big. After decades in the Senate, Biden was deferential to his former colleagues, mindful of their convictions and willing to give them the space to make their own decisions. Some of his aides, including new chief of staff Ron Klain, as well as some key Democratic figures like Pelosi, thought at times that Biden gave the upper chamber lawmakers too much space, that he needed to convey more urgency in getting a deal done. Eventually, Biden pushed: a series of urgent calls to Manchin and some last-minute changes got the $1.9 trillion deal done. Not a single Republican lawmaker voted for the measure.

The package was an undeniable triumph for Biden and the first step in what he wanted to be a transformative presidency, one modeled after Democratic predecessors who dramatically expanded the reach of government to confront generational crises. Born soon after Franklin D. Roosevelt's New Deal and first running for office in the shadow of Lyndon B. Johnson's Great Society, Biden had long believed in government as an instrument for good. Between the pandemic and the economic carnage it wrought, that philosophy was put to a fundamental test, and Biden's place in history was in the balance.

Biden chose to ignore the wreckage left by Trump and to have faith that the Republicans—at least some Republicans—would want to work across the aisle to do right by the country. He believed bipartisanship could still exist; he often invoked the Washington of his time in the Senate when Democrats and Republicans would bridge their divides. But that was a Washington before the Tea Party, before birtherism, before Trump, before Helsinki, before January 6. Some of even Biden's closest aides wondered if that Washington still existed.

White House aides made the following calculation about January 6 and the Big Lie that fueled it: they wouldn't ignore it but they also wouldn't tackle it head-on, at least not right away. The caravan of Republican leaders to Mar-a-Lago was noticed but Trump was still largely off the radar, and Biden wanted to ignore him. Moreover, the administration's top priority was to get as many Americans as possible to take the COVID-19 vaccines, and they were already seeing real hesitancy among Trump voters and didn't want to alienate them further. That would be the focus, Biden's aides decided, and the president also wanted to push for a long-overdue grand infrastructure package.

In the administration's first weeks, some liberal activists began to urge the administration to prioritize a defense of voting rights. A few

Democrats, including Jim Clyburn, joined them. But everything was placed on the back burner as the White House grappled with the pandemic.

* * *

A potential Republican civil war loomed.

Though Trump remained banned from social media, his voice became louder again as the spring of 2021 dawned. He started doing a few TV interviews again, with some of the usual cast of friendly cable hosts happy to ask him softball questions. His emailed statements, which were also posted on his fledgling website, also came more regularly. They did not, by any measure, carry the influence of his tweets; many news organizations simply ignored them. But they did get traction on the Right, and many Republican lawmakers used them as a gauge to deal with their own base.

And Trump was very clear about something he did not want to see happen.

"Republicans in the House and Senate should not approve the Democrat trap of the January 6 Commission," he wrote on May 19.

In the wake of the insurrection, a movement grew on Capitol Hill to form a bipartisan January 6 commission, to be modeled after a similar independent panel formed in the aftermath of 9/11 and charged with producing an objective account of what had fueled the day's violence. A number of congressional committees had already been created to examine some of the security failings that day, but this would have been the first and only one to focus on what incited the violence. This was the proper investigation that the American people deserved, one that would look into what happened at the Capitol and attempt to prevent it from ever happening again.

The commission legislation was a product of cross-party negotiations among leaders of the House Committee on Homeland Security, and it did pick up the support of some Republicans in the lower chamber. Thirty-five GOP House members joined all voting House Democrats to back the creation of a commission, and there were expectations that it would receive enough GOP support in the Senate to bring it to life.

But Trump was adamant that the commission not be created, for it was the one congressional group that would look into the origins of the riot—and it could place the blame at his feet. Some of his loyalists in the Senate, including Ted Cruz and Josh Hawley, began to balk at its formation. But the kill shot was delivered by someone who had admonished Trump just three months before but was, yet again, deciding that the political upside was worth it.

Mitch McConnell dismissed the commission as needlessly duplicative of congressional probes—and as a Trojan horse that would help Democrats in next year's midterm elections. The day before the May 28 vote, he said he would "urge my colleagues to oppose this extraneous layer when the time comes for the Senate to vote.

"I do not believe the additional, extraneous 'commission' that Democratic leaders want would uncover crucial new facts or promote healing," McConnell said.

Republican lawmakers worried they would have to spend much of the 2022 campaign season responding to its revelations about Trump's behavior while trying to avoid his wrath, when their hope was to make the year about Biden and the Democrats. And there was real concern that the Democrats would wield the commission's subpoena power to embarrass Trump and key Republicans. The fifty-four-to-thirty-five final tally in the Senate was six votes shy of the sixty needed to avoid a procedural filibuster. The GOP opposition to the measure was not moved by emotional appeals from Republican senator Susan Collins of Maine or from the family of Brian Sicknick, the Capitol police officer who had suffered two strokes and died a day after he confronted rioters at the insurrection.

"Why would they not want to get to the bottom of such horrific violence?" said Sandra Garza, the late officer's partner. "It just boggles my mind."

The defeat of the commission underscored just how much had changed since the early morning hours of January 7, when even some of Trump's closest allies had stood in the Capitol and repudiated him for causing the violence that had touched them all. Slowly but steadily in the weeks after the insurrection, it was proven that Trump retained his power over the GOP and still planned to wield it over his party to protect his own interests.

In the end, a few Republican senators did vote for the commission: Bill Cassidy (Louisiana), Lisa Murkowski (Alaska), Rob Portman (Ohio), Mitt Romney (Utah), Ben Sasse (Nebraska), and Susan Collins. They were the usual small group of GOP senators who were willing to defy the ex-president, and they were all used to being on the receiving end of Trump's ire. McConnell was willing to let the vote go, and he told aides he didn't see any advantage in punishing the apostates.

The same did not hold true in the House.

* * *

Nancy Pelosi wasn't going to wait any longer.

For months, she had signaled that her preference was a bipartisan, bicameral investigation into the Capitol riots, with Democrats and Republicans from both chambers of Congress working together as they did after the September 11 terror attacks. But after that commission died in the Senate, she vowed to move forward alone.

"January 6 was a day of darkness for our country," Pelosi said in late June. "Our temple of democracy was attacked by insurrectionists."

She launched a select bipartisan House committee, which was charged with investigating the root causes of the attack, including white supremacist and extremist groups, as well as Capitol security failures. Pelosi said that she hoped McCarthy would name "responsible" Republicans to be part of this effort, though Democrats quietly fretted that the GOP leader might name right-wing bomb throwers to submarine the commission from within.

McCarthy did just that. Of his five picks to the panel, three had objected to the certification of the 2020 election. One of them, Jim Jordan, was perhaps Trump's fiercest ally in the House. Another, Jim Banks of Indiana, was McCarthy's choice to lead the GOP representation on the panel. Pelosi rejected them out of hand, a rare move to deny the minority party's choices for a committee.

"The unprecedented nature of January 6 demands this unprecedented decision," she said.

Consulting with Trump, who had pushed for Jordan to be included, McCarthy declared that Pelosi had abused her power and "broken this institution." And then he pulled all his picks, seemingly leaving the committee without any Republican representation and denying the legitimacy of its claim to be bipartisan and impartial. McCarthy believed he had sabotaged it.

Except there would be a Republican on the committee after all. Because Pelosi named one.

* * *

The last name "Cheney" was synonymous with the Republican Party.

Dick Cheney was born in Nebraska before growing up in Wyoming. He made his way to Washington first as a congressional intern, then staffer, then White House aide, rising in the ranks to eventually become chief of staff to President Gerald Ford. He was then elected to Congress, serving for a decade before being named secretary of defense for President George H. W. Bush. A decade later, Bush's son asked Cheney to oversee the selection process for his vice presidential pick—and Cheney ended up recommending himself.

He was at the White House the morning of September 11, 2001.

With the president in Florida and then scrambled in the Midwest skies on Air Force One, Cheney manned the Situation Room. He gave the order to shoot down any rogue planes, including Flight 93 before it was taken down by passengers rebelling against the terrorist hijackers. Dubbed "Darth Vader" by Democrats, he was perceived as a driving force behind George W. Bush's ill-fated decision to invade Iraq, and he was deeply unpopular when he left office.

The daughter of such a GOP legend, Liz Cheney held several positions in the Bush administration before winning her father's old congressional seat in 2016. She quickly rose through the ranks and became the third-highest-ranking Republican in the House. A rock-solid conservative, and a definite neocon on foreign policy, she spent the first three years of the Trump administration criticizing his approach to the rest of the globe while still voting for the majority of his agenda.

But she broke with him after the insurrection. She was the first—and only—member of the House leadership to signal that she would vote to impeach him at his second trial. And she didn't do so simply by casting her ballot or by putting out a short press release. She released a scorching statement that rocked Washington and shook the foundation of the party with which her last name was synonymous.

"The President of the United States summoned this mob, assembled the mob, and lit the flame of this attack," she wrote in part. "Everything that followed was his doing. None of this would have happened without the President. The President could have immediately and forcefully intervened to stop the violence. He did not.

"There has never been a greater betrayal by a President of the United States of his office and his oath to the Constitution."

In the end, 10 of the 211 Republicans in the House voted to impeach the president. Though it was by no means a huge number, it was still the most ballots ever cast to impeach a president of the same party. There were a few surprises, including Tom Rice, of a deep-red South Carolina district. Other votes to impeach were expected, including one from Adam Kinzinger, the air force veteran who had been sharply critical of Trump. But it was Cheney, due to her lineage and leadership role, who made the biggest shock wave.

And many in her party would not forgive her for it.

That February, there was an effort to push her out of her leadership role. But despite pressure from Trump, McCarthy did not support the putsch, for fear that it would further splinter his caucus. It was easily defeated, 145 to 61. Cheney was relentless and not shy about her anti-Trump stance, speaking her conscience but also almost daring her fellow Republicans to come after her.

"The 2020 presidential election was not stolen. Anyone who claims it is spreading THE BIG LIE . . . ," she tweeted in May. This didn't sit well with many Republicans, who either didn't want to see a challenge to Trump or felt that Cheney was an unnecessary distraction during a moment when they wanted to keep the focus on Biden and the Democrats. McCarthy declared that he was "fed up" with Cheney and this time supported a move to oust her.

Liz Cheney was removed from her leadership position by a voice vote on May 12, 2021. She was undeterred, saying afterward, "I will do everything I can to ensure that the former president never again gets anywhere near the Oval Office."

She honored her word and did not shy away from Pelosi's request in July that she serve on the January 6 committee, so it would, in fact, be bipartisan. Kinzinger joined a few days later.

"It's very clear to me, as I've said, my oath and my duty is above partisanship," Cheney said.

The decisions ignited GOP outrage. McCarthy deemed them "Pelosi Republicans" and questioned their loyalty to the GOP. Representative Matt Gaetz of Florida even traveled to Wyoming in a search for Republican candidates to primary her. Soon, there would be several. Trump went on the attack, bashing both Cheney and Kinzinger via emailed statements. Traditional GOP donors closed their wallets.

Many GOP lawmakers refused to even speak to Cheney if their paths crossed on Capitol Hill.

Trumpism had won. Even a member of Republican royalty was not safe.

* * *

The Big Lie had become a litmus test.

For Trump, it wasn't enough to hold Republicans in his sway. He needed them to express fealty to his false claim that the election had been stolen. And for some in the GOP, that meant a refusal to even say the words that Joe Biden won.

Senator Roger Marshall of Kansas appeared on *Meet the Press* and would concede only that "Joe Biden was sworn into office." Arizona Republican representative Andy Biggs answered a question from a colleague about who won by saying flatly, "We don't know," and adding, "There are a lot of issues with this election that took place." Nearly a year after the election, the number-two Republican in the House, Steve Scalise, was still parroting Trump's claims of voting irregularities in swing states.

Cheney's replacement as the number-three Republican in the House, Representative Elise Stefanik of New York, embodied the transformation of the party. A once-moderate Republican who worked in President George W. Bush's White House and was a protégé of former Speaker Paul Ryan, she had morphed into a star of the MAGA universe and a die-hard Trump loyalist. In the spring of 2022, she refused to say Biden was elected lawfully.

Many of those running for office in the wake of 2020 also refused to go there. Glenn Youngkin, who was the surprise winner of the Virginia governor's race the next year, for months refused to say that Biden was legitimately elected. Five Republicans running for governor of Minnesota all danced around the question during an early 2022 televised debate, with the strongest answer being an acknowledgment that Biden "was certified by Congress as having won the Electoral College." And in a particularly grim battle for an open Senate seat in Ohio, with the hopefuls desperate for Trump's endorsement, candidate Bernie Moreno aired an ad in early 2022, more than a year after the insurrection, in which he said, "President Trump says the election was stolen, and he's right." One of his opponents, Josh Mandel, went further, saying, "I think Trump won," and calling for yet another investigation into the results from battleground states.

Fox News also stayed with Trump. Its ratings briefly fell after the insurrection but soon rebounded to lead cable again. Refusing to cede ground to OAN or Newsmax, it skewed further right. It fired the political editor who helped project a Trump loss on Election Night and tossed aside the 7:00 p.m. newscast for another opinion show. And Carlson, the unquestioned top voice at the network, leaned heavier into conspiracy theories on the vaccine and spearheaded a documentary known as *Patriot Purge*, which falsely suggested the January 6 Capitol riot was a "false flag" operation intended to demonize conservatives.

For Chris Wallace, that was enough. Considered one of the last neutral voices at the network, Wallace battled with Trump in general election debates in both 2016 and 2020. But he found the situation "unsustainable" and, in a March 2022 interview, declared, "I just no longer felt comfortable with the programming at Fox." He left for CNN's new streaming network. A Quinnipiac poll released in mid-2021 revealed that 85 percent of Republicans wanted candidates for the midterms to mostly agree with Trump—and that two-thirds of the GOP wanted him to run for president again in 2024. No other Republican, in any poll, came close to matching Trump's support.

It was still his party.

To some Republicans, that was a worry. McConnell and McCarthy had made their compromises. They both realized that they could not fully rebuke Trump if they wanted to accomplish their goals of winning their majorities and becoming majority leader and Speaker, respectively. They took different approaches: McCarthy embraced doing Trump's bidding, while McConnell kept him at arm's length and even took moments to criticize the former president and voice support for the work of the House Select Committee investigating January 6.

Naturally, they also generated different responses from Mar-a-Lago.

Trump was unsparing about McConnell, blasting him in dozens of statements, dubbing him "Old Crow," and calling for his ouster as GOP leader, a move that went nowhere. McConnell had to manage the Trumpists in his caucus, but there were no serious challenges to his power. Moreover, he and his aides began to revel in his reputation for ruthlessness, and the minority leader pointed out that Old Crow was Henry Clay's favorite brand of Kentucky bourbon. He had a drink at Trump's expense.

For McCarthy, it was a harder slog. Though he expressed far more deference to Trump, his hold on a leadership position after the midterms was far less ensured; his aides anticipated that he'd have to fend off challenges from within the caucus, including from right-wingers who felt he was insufficiently loyal to Trump. It was deeply frustrating to the California congressman; he had been obedient to Trump for years, but the one call he made on January 6—asking the president to call off the rioters—was perceived as an unforgivable sin. Trump didn't let McCarthy off the hook either, deliberately refusing to endorse him for Speaker if the GOP took control of the House in November 2022. He wanted him to twist in the wind and privately mused about supporting other candidates for the spot or even making a bid himself (an arcane House rule notes that you don't have to be a member to be a Speaker, but there was no evidence that Trump really considered it).

And both men had to deal with rising Trumpism in their ranks.

The House and Senate were filled with Trump loyalists, and the former president wanted their numbers to grow. His nascent political operation began endorsing MAGA-style primary candidates for both empty seats and, more worrisomely for GOP leaders, to take on Republican incumbents deemed insufficiently loyal to Trump.

At the top of the list: any Republican who had cast a vote to impeach Trump. Some in the GOP seemed able to shake off the challenge: for instance, Senator Lisa Murkowski had shown resilience before when winning reelection as a write-in in 2010. But not all could. Cheney was faced with a brutal primary war, a battle that became all the more pitched when McCarthy, doing Trump's bidding, took the extraordinary step in February 2022 of endorsing a primary opponent to a former member of House leadership. Cheney was still able to raise money—including from Democrats and noted Trump critic George W. Bush—but she faced a steep deficit in the polls. She vowed to fight on.

Others did not. Kinzinger announced he would not run again, voicing his unhappiness with the ugliness of politics while adding, "My disappointment in the leaders that don't lead is huge." Facing difficult primaries, three of the ten House Republicans who had voted for impeachment also announced they would not run again. And then a fourth, veteran representative Fred Upton of Michigan, announced his retirement in April. As each bowed out, Trump celebrated, keeping a running tally. He targeted governors who he believed had betrayed him as well, those who didn't honor the Big Lie and had gone ahead with certifying Biden's win in their states: Brian Kemp of Georgia and Doug Ducey of Arizona became his primary targets.

"Vote them out of office," Trump declared in yet another emailed statement. "These are two RINO (Republican in Name Only) Republicans who fought against me and the Republican Party harder than any Democrat."

Moderate Republicans in both chambers—as well as more than two dozen House Democrats, a thirty-year high—announced their retirements, not wanting to risk losing their seats to a fringe candidate or having to spend another two years in Congress pretending not to have seen the latest inflammatory thing Trump uttered.

As Trump's endorsement became coveted, middle-of-the-road Republicans became an endangered species. The calculations in the two chambers of Congress differed: McConnell needed candidates who could win statewide, an electorate inherently more diverse than one in a particularly homogenous, deep-red congressional district. But some of his moderate options, like Governors Larry Hogan of Maryland and Chris Sununu of New Hampshire, opted against leaving statehouses for runs at the Senate. In Pennsylvania and Ohio, some of the top GOP candidates held radical, pro-Trump views. And in Georgia, McConnell hoped to entice David Perdue to run again for his old Senate seat—until Perdue decided instead to embrace Trump's claims of a stolen election and mount a primary challenge to Governor Brian Kemp. That left McConnell with little choice but to back Trump's pick for Senate, hometown football star Herschel Walker, whose deeply problematic candidacy included questions about domestic abuse, his financial dealings, and whether or not he even lived in Georgia. In a vivid illustration of the power the former president wielded over the GOP as it faced future elections, Ted Cruz, his onetime critic, tweeted out a photo of his meeting with Walker—at Mar-a-Lago under a portrait of Trump wearing a tennis outfit.

In the House, it was a different dynamic. Thanks to increased political polarization and gerrymandering, there were far fewer competitive seats than in usual cycles. In many districts, one party's primary was, in essence, the general election. And in deep-red districts, that usually meant the winner was whoever was Trumpier. Yet at the same time, the strategy to nominate more conservative candidates in the swing districts that would likely control the House threatened to backfire, potentially resulting in GOP candidates who would be deemed unpalatable by the broader electorate in November.

Trump's demands for loyalty within the GOP threatened to hurt Republicans at the ballot box. He was ensuring that the Big Lie was at the center of the next campaign. His insistence on relitigating 2020 could prove a costly distraction as the party tried to focus on 2022. His claims that elections were rife with fraud could keep Republican voters at home again during the midterms.

He didn't care. He had nearly managed to rig and upend the system to get reelected. Plans were already underway to finish the job the next time.

Trump was eyeing 2024.

10

THE STATES

The chartered flights pulled back from the gates at Austin-Bergstrom International Airport.

It was a little after 3:00 p.m. on Monday, July 12, 2021. The runways radiated heat, the Texas summer sweltering around ninety degrees. Onboard: more than fifty of the sixty-seven Texas Democratic state representatives. And once the flights went wheels up, all of them risked arrest.

The lawmakers were fleeing the state capital in order to deny the Republican majority the quorum needed to pass new voting restrictions with, at that point, just under a month left in a special legislative session called largely for that purpose. The Texas House was set to reconvene the following morning but could not proceed without the Democrats present.

At stake was the fate of new state election legislation that would rein in local voting initiatives like drive-through and twenty-four-hour voting, and further tighten the rules for voting by mail. The measures, if passed, would also bolster access for partisan poll watchers and ban local election officials from preemptively sending out applications to request mail-in ballots.

Democrats cried foul. They argued that the measures were being

202 | JONATHAN LEMIRE

put into place on a false pretense. Republicans were using Trump's erroneous claim of voter fraud, and the resulting doubt he had created in the nation's elections, in order to ram through proposals that would dramatically cut back turnout, particularly among Democrats. Those efforts, the Democrats claimed, were in response to a surge in voting during the pandemic and were meant to slow down Texas's evolution into a swing state.

The flight—which drew some scrutiny for its lack of masks and plethora of beer—landed in Washington a few hours later. The Democrats fanned out in hotel rooms and TV studios across the District of Columbia and took to the airwaves.

"Bottom line, there is nothing special about this special session. It's based on the big lie—Trump's claim that he won the 2020 election," said State Representative Gina Hinojosa, a Democrat from Austin.

They were hailed as heroes on the Left and did dozens of interviews, many on CNN and MSNBC. They wanted to lobby Congress to pass federal legislation that would protect voting rights across the country and overrule what would be passed in Texas. Democrats had initially stalled the bill when they had walked out of a standard legislative session in May, but then Republicans had called for the special session weeks later. The Democrats then considered flying to the home states of waffling US senators but feared that Republican governors would send them back to Texas. To block the pending legislation, the Democratic lawmakers needed to stay away through the end of the special session, which could last as long as thirty days under the state constitution.

They left families and loved ones behind as they fled Austin. It was worth it, they said, as was the risk: absent lawmakers could be legally compelled to return to the state capitol. Republican governor Greg Abbott, who made tightening election rules a priority, slammed the move as a dereliction of duty.

"Texas Democrats' decision to break a quorum of the Texas Legislature and abandon the Texas State Capitol inflicts harm on the very Texans who elected them to serve," he said.

In the end, Abbott didn't need to send the Texas Department of Public Safety to forcibly retrieve the state lawmakers and bring them back to the Lone Star State. The Democrats stayed away in solidarity for weeks, but then cracks began to emerge over strategy, personal lives, and concern that they needed to act on COVID-19 legislation. And they couldn't stay away forever: the Republicans would eventually get the votes needed to pass the measure. Time was on the Republicans' side. It was inevitable.

By late August, enough Democrats had returned to Austin to allow the special session to commence. The sweeping election laws passed, over the howls of voting rights activists and communities of color, particularly in the state's Democratic strongholds, the big cities of Houston, Austin, Dallas, and San Antonio. And the new laws' impact was swiftly felt.

On March 1, Texas held the nation's first primary of 2022. And, due to the enforcement of strict new ID and registration requirements, early in voting, a massive number of mail-in ballots were rejected in Harris County, which includes Houston, when the laws first went into effect.

Because of the 2020 election, it had become harder to vote. And it wasn't just in Texas. The Big Lie had metastasized and was now more than a talking point or a call to action.

It was translating into policy.

*　*　*

Trump's false claims of election fraud spread far beyond the White House, far beyond the 2020 election. His refusal to accept defeat created a constitutional crisis, with the president using the powers of government in a desperate attempt to hold on to power. His lies led

Americans to doubt their own democracy; they had led nearly half the nation to refuse to accept their new president as legitimate; and they had inspired thousands to storm the US Capitol and commit violence in their leader's name.

But the impact of the lie didn't end when Joe Biden placed his hand on a thick, 130-year-old family Bible to take the oath of office to become the forty-sixth president of the United States. Nor was the lie relegated to petulant emailed statements sent from Palm Beach and regurgitated in Trump-friendly corners of the conservative media.

It spread to nearly every statehouse in the country. It was picked up by state legislatures and local newspapers. It became a defining issue in congressional elections, as well as down-ballot contests for mayor and city council.

It became an excuse. It became a reason to act.

Republicans across the country used Trump's relentless claims of fraud to justify revisiting local election laws. The Big Lie was not just a former president ranting and raving on Twitter. It no longer was just the hot rhetoric that inspired an insurrection. It was now also the cold, methodical process of legislation. It infected the boring backroom process of drafting a bill and trying to quietly steer it through a legislature. Trump's false claims were the lifeblood of new policy, providing cover for something that had long been a GOP goal: to add more ballot restrictions, to tighten the election process.

And the burden of these changes would fall squarely on the shoulders of Americans—the young, the very old, voters of color—who tend to vote Democrat.

In short, the Republicans were making it more difficult to vote. And that's not all they were doing.

Elections for secretaries of state are usually little-noticed affairs, with candidates typically benefiting from voters who cast straight-ticket ballots: if a voter is casting a ballot for a Democratic candidate for governor, for instance, they tend to pick Democrats in the other races too. But in 2021 and 2022, money began pouring into the campaigns for secretaries of state and other legislative elections. And support and endorsements began flowing from Mar-a-Lago.

Why?

Because in the United States, national elections are conducted on the local level. Outside of the final certification stages that take place under the Capitol dome, elections are held in the states. Regulations are set in state legislatures, and how the votes are counted—and which votes are counted—are determined at the state level, through election boards, legislatures, and secretaries of state. A GOP stranglehold over those seemingly minor offices would allow the party to both tighten voting laws and, potentially, certify the election results only if its favored candidate were to win.

By the fall of 2021, Trump's emailed statements became so frequent that they were easily ignored, becoming almost the white noise of the political discourse. Often, they were endorsements for one Republican lawmaker or another, a blessing highly coveted in GOP circles but often unnoticed by the mainstream political press. But one endorsement that September raised eyebrows: it was for State Representative Mark Finchem, who was running for Arizona secretary of state.

That is a race usually too local for a former president to offer an endorsement. But Trump was drawn to Finchem, who had promoted QAnon conspiracy theories, attended the January 6 "Stop the Steal" rally, and was photographed later that day at the US Capitol. Trump's statement saluted him for his "incredibly powerful stance on the massive Voter Fraud that took place in the 2020 Presidential Election Scam." And it wasn't even the first time Trump had backed a candidate for a state secretary of state: he did the same in Michigan and Georgia. All three of his chosen candidates supported his lies about the election and were vying for jobs in battleground states where the position's current occupant had opposed Trump's efforts to overturn the election. Trump was trying to stack the deck. There was no "2020 Presidential Election

Scam." But this time, elections could actually be rigged. And Trump and his allies were trying to rig them. Trump's claims were not dead: they were alive and well and shaping the battle for the ballot. The Big Lie would not just define the 2020 election. It was intent on dominating 2022 and 2024 as well.

In spring of 2021, advisers to Donald Trump agreed to an interview for this book to take place later that year. But as more about its subject was released, the former president backed out of the interview.

* * *

The right to vote is perhaps America's most sacred right. It also has a torturous, violent history. And it has truly been available to all Americans for only a short time.

When the Constitution was ratified, the right to vote was given only to white male property owners. Over the next few decades, the property requirements were dropped, but the franchise remained an exclusive privilege. Women have had the right for a century, after the decades-long women's suffrage movement finally resulted in the ratification of the Nineteenth Amendment in 1920. The Fifteenth Amendment sought to protect the voting rights of Black men after the Civil War but, after a brief flurry of progress during Reconstruction, a series of discriminatory practices and legal barriers—namely the Jim Crow laws in the South—deeply restricted their right to cast a ballot and be recognized as equal citizens. Poll taxes, literacy tests, new laws, intimidation, and outright violence were used to keep Black people from voting. It took the Voting Rights Act of 1965 for those barriers to be outlawed at the state and local levels.

And an extraordinary set of circumstances was needed for it to happen even then. President John F. Kennedy had been wary at first of fully and publicly embracing the cause of civil rights, for fear of the backlash it could provoke among Southern Democrats whose support he needed for his reelection bid. The president believed in the cause, but he and his brother Robert, the attorney general, tried to signal that it would be a second-term priority. But events overtook them, as the Freedom Riders moved across the South, sit-ins were held throughout segregated states, and violence erupted.

And when Governor George Wallace blocked the door of the University of Alabama to prevent it from being integrated, Kennedy was compelled to act, proposing a civil rights bill and, in a televised national address, declaring it both a constitutional and "moral" issue. Kennedy later hosted Dr. Martin Luther King Jr. and other leaders of the March on Washington the same day that King gave his famed "I Have a Dream" speech, on the steps of a monument to the man who had ended slavery a century before.

That was August 28, 1963. Kennedy was killed in Dallas less than three months later.

But the new president, Lyndon B. Johnson, took up that mantle and benefited from the goodwill of a nation mourning the assassination of a beloved young president. Johnson, a master of the Senate, was also particularly well positioned to take advantage of the moment: he knew how to navigate Capitol Hill and, as a southerner, could better relate to those opposed to the efforts. The Civil Rights Act of 1964 was a significant step, making discrimination in public facilities and federally funded programs illegal.

The following year, after a landslide reelection, Johnson pushed for the Voting Rights Act and, as he made his final case, drove his point home by quoting "We Shall Overcome," a gospel song that had been turned into a protest anthem for the civil rights movement.

"It is the effort of American Negroes to secure for themselves the full blessings of American life," Johnson said. "Their cause must be our cause too. Because it is not just Negroes, but really it is all of us, who must overcome the crippling legacy of bigotry and injustice. And we shall overcome."

John Lewis, the civil rights activist who later became a legendary congressman, watched the president's speech with King. Lewis said Dr. King wiped a tear from his face when Johnson quoted the song. It was an important step on a journey that, just over four decades later, would lead to the election of the nation's first Black president. Lewis cried his own tears that night.

But the battle for voting rights would still flare up every few election cycles. One front: gerrymandering, the fight every decade to draw new borders to congressional districts that would stack the deck for one party over the other. That has long resulted in bizarre sights: districts that resemble no traditional geographic shape at all but rather are drawn to keep a lawmaker in power or keep one voting bloc together. In early 2022, for instance, the GOP tried to redraw North Carolina's congressional districts in order to stuff Democratic cities into tiny blue districts and spread other Democrats across light-red areas, diluting their influence. The result: even though Trump had narrowly edged out Biden in the state, 50–49 percent, the new map would yield ten red seats and just three blue ones. A federal judge tossed it out.

Republicans have traditionally bested Democrats in the process, and voters of color have tended to pay a steep price in the gerrymandering cycle. But, as of early 2022, the conventional wisdom was that the two parties had played to a draw, and neither party looked likely to gain a large number of congressional seats as a result of the altered lines. It remains a deeply cynical, problematic process. Normally, Republicans would want to tighten election security, which in turn would tend to restrict access to the ballot. Democrats would usually go the other way, aiming to make it easier for more people to vote.

For decades, those fights, though important, would mostly be contested out of sight in the courthouses and back rooms of American democracy.

The aftermath of the 2020 election brought them to center stage.

Republicans wasted no time. Most of the new state legislatures elected that November were seated two months later, in early January 2021. Within a month, thirty-three states introduced, prefiled, or carried over 165 measures to restrict ballot access, well over four times the number of measures being considered in that same period a year before. The reasons were clear, if not plainly spoken: it was a backlash to the historic voter turnout in 2020 and grounded in a series of baseless and, at times, racist claims of voter irregularities and fraud.

And that was just the beginning, before much of the political world was paying attention. A new battlefield was quickly drawn, in which there would be a pitched partisan conflict over the future of American democracy.

Broadly, Republicans focused on two pieces of the electoral system: the administration of elections and restrictions on voting, particularly mail-in ballots that were widely used during the pandemic. Some areas sent mail-in ballots to all voters, even if not requested. Other localities expanded voting hours or placed twenty-four-hour drop boxes or drive-through areas for people to place their completed ballots. Forty-three percent of voters cast ballots by mail in 2020, making it the most popular method, according to the Census Bureau. Another 26 percent voted early in person, while 27 percent voted on Election Day itself, far less than normal, according to the Pew Research Center. Democrats in particular flocked to the two forms of early voting, far outpacing the GOP in some states—a trend that raised significant alarm among Republicans.

The GOP, nodding to Trump's lies, moved to curtail absentee-ballot drop boxes by claiming without evidence that they were susceptible to fraud. New laws restricted identification requirements for voting by mail and banned states from proactively sending out mail-in ballot applications to all citizens. Other provisions aimed to shorten the time frame during which absentee ballots could be requested. And many of these measures appeared poised to disproportionately affect voters of color, who often relied on drop boxes and polling stations with longer hours.

The efforts, to many, evoked the nation's long history of racial discrimination at the polls. One such flash point was the renewed Republican push to require voters to show valid identification—and the debate over what constitutes valid ID—in order to vote. This GOP talking point predated Trump but was given new life in early 2021 after the former president repeatedly declared, without evidence, that some of the votes for Democrats were actually being cast by noncitizens, illegal immigrants, and dead people.

Democrats have long argued that voter ID laws depress turnout, particularly among low-income voters of color for whom it would be more difficult to obtain a driver's license or other government-issued identification card. The American Civil Liberties Union has long opposed such measures, noting that the voters they would impact are disproportionately low-income, racial and ethnic minorities, the elderly, and people with disabilities.

Republicans have countered that IDs are required for many aspects of daily life, including boarding an airplane or picking up a package at the post office—and, therefore, should be required to vote too. They also argue that a requirement to show ID would prevent fraud. But statistics don't back up that claim. In a widely respected study, research by a Loyola law professor found that between 2000 and 2014, there were only thirty-one incidents of voter ID fraud out of one billion ballots cast.

But that wasn't all. Some of the legislatures took aim at how elections are overseen, stripping some local officials of their powers or pursuing partisan reviews of election results. And it didn't happen only in battleground states. In Arkansas, for instance, the GOP-run legislature passed a bill that allowed a state board of election commissioners—composed of six Republicans and just one Democrat—to investigate when issues arise at any level of the voting process, from registration to voting to ballot counting to the certification of results. And if needed, the legislation authorizes that panel to "institute corrective action." It was all but a free pass to change a result it didn't like. In Utah, an effort to stop mail-in balloting was defeated in February 2022, but supporters of the measure filled five overflow rooms in the Salt Lake City capital, the biggest crowd veteran reporters could remember gathering there. The bill's proponents vowed to try again.

The targeting of state and local election officials was a new frontier in trying to game the system. Not usually in the spotlight, the officials became vulnerable simply by doing their jobs. In a grim irony, they became political pawns because of the commitment to duty—in the face of threats—displayed by some of their brethren after the 2020 election.

State secretaries of state came under fire. Georgia's Brad Raffensperger needed security after he refused Trump's demand, in that infamous recorded phone call, "to find" the 11,780 votes it would take for the president to flip the state. Several armed protesters menacingly stood around Michigan secretary of state Jocelyn Benson's home in December 2020. A tweet sent to Colorado secretary of state Jena Griswold, a Democrat, read "Bullet. That's a six-letter word for you" and "I'm really jonzing to see your purple face after you've been hanged." A voice mail left for Arizona secretary of state Katie Hobbs in September 2021 included this message, which she shared with CNN: "I am a hunter—and I think you should be hunted. You will never be safe in Arizona again."

The threats didn't appear to be organized nationally, since many came from the officials' home states. None of the public servants were ready for this. Their offices didn't have the budgets to monitor threats, nor had any of them been assigned regular security before. No systems were in place at the state or federal level to support them, and the Department of Justice acknowledged that the federal government did not have the infrastructure needed to handle the situations. And the targets weren't just secretaries of state, who at least had gotten a taste of public scrutiny during their runs for statewide office. They were city commissioners, town clerks, volunteers. Nearly one in three local election workers said they felt unsafe because of their jobs, with about 17 percent of those who responded saying they had received threats, according to an April survey on behalf of the Brennan Center for Justice, which tracks voting bills and advocates for federal election legislation.

One of them was Al Schmidt.

* * *

A bespectacled bureaucrat and father of three, Al Schmidt didn't look like a person who would draw the wrath of violent extremists. He was one of the three Philadelphia city commissioners charged with overseeing election-related affairs for the city. He was even a Republican.

A week before Election Day, an ominous voice mail was left for him, declaring that the election board members were "the reason why we have the Second Amendment." A short time later, two men were arrested for making threats against the Pennsylvania Convention Center, where ballots were to be counted and where Schmidt and his colleagues were to be stationed. The men were armed with two loaded semiautomatic Beretta pistols, one semiautomatic AR-15-style weapon, as well as dozens of rounds of ammunition.

After Pennsylvania was called for Biden, giving him the White House, Schmidt appeared in the media to defend his role in the process. That drew Trump's attention.

"A guy named Al Schmidt, a Philadelphia Commissioner and so-called Republican (RINO), is being used big time by the Fake News Media to explain how honest things were with respect to the Election in Philadelphia," Trump tweeted. "He refuses to look at a mountain of corruption & dishonesty. We win!"

The death threats followed. Schmidt's wife and children moved out of their family home. Schmidt's and his parents' houses received around-the-clock security for months into 2021.

Perhaps even less likely perpetrators of a global conspiracy to deny Trump a second term were the mother-daughter duo of Ruby Freeman and Wandrea "Shaye" Moss. Moss was a clerical worker in the election office of Fulton County, Georgia, where Atlanta is located. Freeman, her mother, took on a temporary job to help count ballots. Their alleged plot? The two Black women were accused of cheating Trump by pulling fake ballots from suitcases hidden under tables at a ballot-counting center.

Rudy Giuliani falsely claimed that video footage showed the women engaging in "surreptitious illegal activity" and acting suspiciously, like drug dealers "passing out dope." In early January, Trump himself singled out Freeman, by name, eighteen times in his infamous call with Georgia's secretary of state. He called the sixty-two-year-old temp worker a "professional vote scammer" and a "hustler" who "stuffed the ballot boxes." And a publicist for the rapper Kanye West—the hip-hop and fashion mogul briefly considered a presidential run but largely aligned himself with Trump—even visited Freeman and pushed her to admit to the alleged offense.

The women were terrified. Freeman called 911 several times in December, saying, according to records, that she had gotten a wave of "threats and phone calls and racial slurs." She told police: "It's scary because they're saying stuff like, 'We're coming to get you. We are coming to get you.'"

Two days later, a panicked Freeman called 911 again, after hearing loud banging on her door just before 10:00 p.m.

"I don't know who keeps coming to my door," she said in a recording, which was first obtained by Reuters.

"Lord Jesus, where's the police?"

Freeman quit her job. Moss took a leave of absence. No one was charged in connection with the harassment.

These incidents across the two states underscored something many Americans never thought about: that election workers are often low-paid employees and, in lots of cases, volunteers. So many of them showed real bravery at their posts during the pandemic—as well as taking on an unprecedented wave of harassment and threats. And now, some states were passing legislation that put them under more scrutiny and undermined their authority.

The GOP rhetoric that accompanied the move to make the voting changes fueled widespread doubts about the integrity of American elections and delivered fervent partisan gamesmanship to parts of the democratic process that once relied largely on orderly routine, helpful volunteers, and good faith. New measures that would impose even relatively modest restrictions on voting could have an outsize impact: in 2020, two key battleground states, Georgia and Arizona, were decided by fewer than twelve thousand votes each.

It was a full-on assault on the voting process, at a time when the nation was reeling from the pandemic and the intense political battles of the last decade. Preoccupied by the pandemic, the Biden administration didn't truly react to the growing GOP movement until six months into its term. Meanwhile, the restrictions were cheered on by Trump in exile and, soon, the cause would be embraced by Republicans in Washington.

And at the forefront of the local movement were three states that were battlegrounds in 2020—and will be again four years later.

* * *

Arizona was a sore subject for the Republican Party. With the exception of Bill Clinton winning it during his 1996 landslide, the state had gone for the GOP in every election for seventy years, until Biden squeaked out a victory over Trump. Fox News calling it for the Democrat still ate at Trump months later. The state's demographics were tilting toward the Democrats: Phoenix was exploding in size; more Latinos were registering to vote; some liberal California voters were moving east and bringing their politics with them. Yet while Biden had won it, the state government was still dominated by Republicans—and they moved to take steps to help ensure that a Democrat wouldn't win there again soon.

The GOP in the state proposed a series of stand-alone bills that took on specific aspects of the voting process and were viewed as complements to a series of restrictive voting laws passed in 2016 and upheld by the Supreme Court four years later. Those laws allowed only voters, their family members, or their caregivers to collect and deliver a completed ballot. Further gutting a Voting Rights Act protection, the Supreme Court in July 2021 also upheld a long-standing state policy requiring election officials to throw out ballots accidentally cast in the wrong precincts, which drew an angry response from Democrats who said the state had a history of switching polling places more often in minority neighborhoods and putting them in places intended to cause mistakes.

The state party rolled out several new measures in the wake of Trump's loss. It passed a law to change the state's popular Permanent Early Voting List, which determines who receives mail ballots each election cycle. The new rules require that voters who do not cast a ballot at least once every two years will have to respond to a government notice to avoid being removed from the list and in order to continue getting a mail ballot.

Another law stripped power from Hobbs, the Democratic secretary of state, by spreading her power around. It would now also allow third parties designated by the legislature to flag ineligible voters for removal and would give voters far less time to fix any mistakes with their early ballots.

In total, the measures are expected to remove an estimated 150,000 voters who don't vote frequently from Arizona's early ballot mailing list.

Biden won the state by fewer than 10,500 votes.

Trump, meanwhile, won Florida. Twice. And the election there ran smoothly. Twice. But that didn't matter.

Florida had long been a state praised for counting its votes quickly and for its long and successful history of using early and mail-in voting. Yet Governor Ron DeSantis, elected with Trump's help and considered a White House hopeful himself, soon signaled support for widespread election reforms after the 2020 election. Despite anger on the Left, DeSantis in May 2021 signed into law a measure that, as one key provision, required voters to renew their mail voting application every two years and to submit a form of identification.

The use of drop boxes was curtailed, as was the ability of someone to drop off ballots for nonfamily members. The law also gave partisan election observers more access to the ballot-counting process. And initially, a provision was added to prevent behavior undertaken with the intent of influencing a voter—meaning it could be applied to anyone bringing food or water to someone standing in line outside a polling place. That controversial provision was later dropped from the bill.

And then there was the state that became the first flash point for the efforts to restrict voting rights: Georgia.

Georgia was, in many ways, the epicenter of the 2020 election, and it appeared poised to remain that way through the next four years. It arrived as a swing state ahead of its time, seemingly following the southern progression from Virginia to North Carolina (not so much South Carolina) as deep-red states turned purple. Atlanta had exploded, a vibrant hub for the nation's Black community, and more and more educated and affluent voters flocked to the city and its suburbs. Women in those suburbs, in particular, were turned off by Trump. And Democrats, with help from the voter registration efforts of rising political star Stacey Abrams, saw an opportunity.

Biden's narrow win there—only the second Democratic victory in the state since Georgia native Jimmy Carter captured it in 1976—was only the beginning of the role the Peach State would play in the election. It was, of course, where Trump harangued the secretary of state to find him more votes. And it was also where Trump's disinterested performance and claims of voter fraud submarined GOP voter turnout and helped hand two Senate seats—and the entire Senate—to Democrats, dramatically altering the course of Biden's presidency.

It didn't take long for Governor Brian Kemp to direct a course of action. He had come under tremendous fire from Trump and his allies for, correctly, noting that Biden had won and refusing to support efforts to overturn the votes. Moreover, Kemp had a tough 2022 reelection fight on his hands, likely against Abrams. So he and the state Republican legislature moved that March to create a new voting rights package, which combined elements from more than a dozen existing bills.

The rules were strict: they prevented proactively sending ballots to voters, cut the time for the application process, and required voters to submit identification as they applied. They also stripped power from the secretary of state, cut the number of mail-in ballot drop boxes, and prohibited any organization from bringing food or water to anyone standing in line to vote.

The reactions were swift: Biden called it "Jim Crow in the 21st century" and "an atrocity," declaring that the Justice Department was "taking a look" at the measure. While the regulations were being debated that March, Biden and Vice President Kamala Harris scheduled a trip to Atlanta to discuss them, but the visit was largely upstaged by a wave of anti-Asian violence in the area. While the spa shootings became the focus of the president's speech at Emory University, he still touched on the voting rights debate.

"The fact that you held a free and fair election in Georgia that stood up to recount after recount, court case after court case, is something you should be proud of," Biden said. "But as this state, home to Martin Luther King and John Lewis, knows better than most: the battle for the right to vote is never, ever over. And it's not over here, in this state of Georgia."

Trump also weighed in and, after taking more swipes at Kemp, declared that GOP lawmakers in Georgia "learned from the travesty of the 2020 Presidential Election." He said that a Republican loss in the state "can never be allowed to happen again" and said it's "too bad" the law wasn't implemented before the 2020 election.

Tensions soared as the debate broke into the national media cycle. Some major Atlanta-based corporations, including Delta and Coca-Cola, came out in opposition to the measure. Abrams and Georgia's two new senators, Raphael Warnock and Jon Ossoff, were inescapable on cable TV. Conservatives defended the bill, noting that some provisions expanded access to voting, including guaranteeing a minimum number of ballot drop boxes in each county and providing more resources for localities to address long lines for in-person voting. Some on the Right noted that a few deep-blue states, like New York, also had archaic and, at times, restrictive voting measures.

Amid the debate, a few of the bill's provisions were dropped, including a crackdown on Sunday voting, which was considered to have predominantly hurt Black voters whose churches organize post–church services "Souls to the Polls" trips to polling places. But the bill was passed amid explosive debate. Georgia state representative Park Cannon was arrested and removed from the state capitol after passage of the bill, her hands cuffed behind her back.

The restrictions were not as draconian as the Jim Crow laws, but they absolutely could have outsize effects in racially diverse, densely populated areas where polling places frequently moved and lines were longer. The outcry from Washington and corporate America was swift. An unlikely focal point: Major League Baseball, which was slated to have its 2021 All-Star Game in Georgia. That decision had already come under some scrutiny, since the Atlanta Braves had recently left their not-even-twenty-years-old downtown ballpark for a far whiter suburb without much access to public transit. In the wake of the voting rights law, several MLB stars—including some of its most prominent Black players, like Los Angeles Dodgers star Mookie Betts—communicated privately but in no uncertain terms that they would not play in an

All-Star Game held in Atlanta. Baseball made the change, pulling the game out of Georgia and moving it to Colorado.

The impact of the new laws was felt right away: in a late 2021 election in the state, half of the rejected absentee ballots missed the new deadline for returning mail ballots. And two high-profile races loomed for 2022: Warnock faced an immediate reelection challenge from football star Herschel Walker. And Kemp would likely get a rematch with Abrams, if he first was able to survive the Trump-backed primary challenge from former senator David Perdue.

Trump praised the efforts and urged other states to follow suit.

"Republicans in State Legislatures must be smart, get tough, and pass real Election Reform in order to fight back against these Radical Left Democrats," he wrote in a July statement. "If they don't, they'll steal it again in 2022 and 2024, and further DESTROY our Country!"

But Georgia, Florida, and Arizona were far from alone in tightening their election laws. All told, nineteen states, most of them controlled by Republicans, enacted thirty-four laws in 2021 that made voting harder, according to an analysis done by the Brennan Center for Justice. Some of the most extreme bills did not make it past state legislatures, with Republicans often choosing to dial back their farthest-reaching proposals. But numerous new laws—and much of the proposed legislation that failed the year before—sought to exert more partisan control over election administration and make it easier to cast doubt on future election results through partisan ballot reviews. Without question, the process of conducting elections themselves had become more political.

And voters, particularly Democrats in swing states, were staring at a future in which it would be harder to cast their ballots. Many wondered, angrily: How could this be allowed?

One answer: the Supreme Court let them.

* * *

The Voting Rights Act that Lyndon Johnson signed into law in 1965 set off a wave of enfranchisement of Black citizens, with more than 250,000 registering to vote before the end of that year alone, according to the American Civil Liberties Union. The bill was widely considered the most effective piece of civil rights legislation in the nation's history. And only after its passage, most historians agree, could the United States claim to have a measure of voting equality. It has been renewed five times with large bipartisan majorities, including most recently in 2006.

But the Supreme Court steadily hollowed out the landmark Voting Rights Act over the last decade, deeply cutting into the Justice Department's authority over voting and giving states new latitude to impose restrictions. The Voting Rights Act had contained several provisions protecting the right to vote as well as banning racial gerrymandering and any voting measures that would target minority groups. It also required states with a history of discrimination at the polls to obtain clearance from the Justice Department before changing their voting laws.

The Supreme Court's 2013 decision lifted the requirement for the states to receive that preclearance to enact any voting law changes. The court was divided along ideological lines, and the two sides drew markedly different lessons from the history of the civil rights movement and the nation's progress in curtailing racial discrimination in voting. At the center of the disagreement: whether racial minorities continued to face barriers to voting in states with a history of discrimination.

The law had applied to nine states, almost all in the South: Alabama, Alaska, Arizona, Georgia, Louisiana, Mississippi, South Carolina, Texas, and Virginia. It also was in use in scores of counties and municipalities in other states that had seen discrimination.

Barack Obama, whose election as the nation's first Black president was cited by the court's majority as to why there was no longer a need for all the act's restrictions, declared that he was "deeply disappointed" by the ruling. Chief Justice John Roberts wrote that Congress remained free to try to impose federal oversight on states where voting rights were at risk but needed to update its thinking and not focus "on 40-year-old facts having no logical relationship to the present day.

"Congress—if it is to divide the states—must identify those jurisdictions to be singled out on a basis that makes sense in light of current conditions," he wrote. "It cannot simply rely on the past."

The decision knocked down the federal barrier and paved the way for the states to push forward with many of the restrictions enacted in 2021. Those restrictions spread like wildfire. There were some options still available to voting rights advocates. They could still challenge voting laws in federal court on other grounds, including under the Fourteenth and Fifteenth Amendments, and they could also cite state constitutional protections in state courts.

But the legal process can sometimes take years. And the midterms were on the horizon.

* * *

His political fortunes suddenly on the upswing, Trump and his allies in mid-2021 returned to their familiar playbook of misdirection and falsehoods. So much of the former president's rhetoric, some political analysts long said, could fall under two categories: confession or projection. Trump would, in fact, sometimes say the quiet part out loud: when, for instance, early in 2022, he admitted in a statement that, yes, he absolutely had wanted Pence to take the unconstitutional step of overturning the results of the election one year prior.

And sometimes it would be projection, when he would attack someone for doing the very thing he was doing. As a fierce political debate erupted over states, particularly Georgia, restricting access to the ballot, much of the conservative movement—led by the former president—seized upon the moment to claim that the Democrats and media were overstating its impact, that they were exaggerating what it would do. And many Republicans, Trump supporters and critics alike, did so with a very specific phrase.

The Big Lie.

"All the facts disprove the big lie," said Mitch McConnell in spring 2021, bringing up polls that showed support for some of the measures, like voter ID requirements, incorporated in Georgia's package of laws.

McConnell added that "a host of powerful people and institutions apparently think they stand to benefit from parroting this big lie." And even Liz Cheney voiced support for the new wave of election restrictions, claiming that they weren't inspired by Trump.

Other conservatives slammed Biden for his Jim Crow comparison or for not recognizing that some of the more extreme measures in the law had been dropped. Newt Gingrich, Georgia native and former House Speaker, tweeted that Democrats were "engaged in big lie smear against Georgia." And Trump took to using the phrase "Big Lie" to describe both the Democrats' attacks in Georgia and the nonsensical (in his estimation) claim that Biden had been elected at all. Some of the familiar faces on Fox News—notably Tucker Carlson, who had rapidly become the most dominant voice on the network—also railed against the pushback to the new laws.

The Trumpist smoke machine had kicked up, trying to turn an undeniable fact—that some of the state measures would make it harder to vote—into something far murkier. It was whataboutism, a "both sides" effort to confuse those who only caught a snippet of the news via an ambiguous cable chyron or misleading tweet.

Of course, the claim was faulty. Though Republicans like Kemp argued that the state's bill was about streamlining the process, plenty of others in the GOP framed the new voting restrictions as a response to concerns about election legitimacy. And the bill stripped Raffensperger of power just after he became a crucial obstacle to Trump's efforts to overturn the results.

There was no denying any other conclusion: Trump's claims had both spawned and provided a cover for the tighter election laws. But that was just one part of the new political landscape that had formed with stunning speed after Trump's exit from office. He wasn't a pariah; his power remained. William Barr, his former attorney general, wrote a book—titled *One Damn Thing After Another: Memoirs of an Attorney General*—after leaving his post that sharply decried Trump's behavior after Election Day; but when asked in interviews, Barr acknowledged in March 2022 that he would vote for him again. State laws were being rewritten, Trump enemies purged from vital election posts. The Republican Party was, with few exceptions, still in his thrall.

Democrats tried to push back.

Some blue and battleground states looked to expand voting laws. By the end of 2021, at least twenty-five states enacted sixty-two laws with provisions that expanded access. For the most part, these states—almost all run by Democratic governors—made it easier to request and cast mail-in ballots and expanded early voting periods. The laws, in some states, also lengthened the deadlines for ballots to be counted as well as improved access for the disabled, elderly, and non-English speakers. Three states—New York, Connecticut, and Washington—expanded voting rights to those with past convictions, while six others enacted automatic voter registration laws. And eight extended or made permanent policies first implemented during the pandemic, including sending mail-in ballots to all voters, implementing curbside voting, and allowing no-excuse early voting.

But these were modest measures, for the most part not put into place in states that would dictate the control of Congress in 2022 or the presidency in 2024. Only federal legislation would be able to truly protect the vote, worried and angry Democrats increasingly believed. Activists marched. Voters picked up phones. The Texas lawmakers boarded their planes for Washington. The Big Lie could not go unanswered.

Congress would need to do it. Congress would need to be pushed. They looked to the White House.

11

CHALLENGES

"Have you no shame?"

The president's words, nearly yelled, echoed off the modern concrete walls onto which a giant red, white, and blue image of the United States flag had been projected. They reverberated down the hallway, past the sleek screens displaying the words "We the People." They resonated over the exhibits showcasing the nation's founding documents. And they washed over the people in the crowd, many of them Black, who felt that their arguably most sacred right—one whose torturous path to being achieved was archived all around them—was in more peril than it had been in decades.

President Joe Biden chose the National Constitution Center in Philadelphia to be the living backdrop for what would be one of the most consequential and impassioned speeches of his young term. American democracy was under assault; the right to vote was being stripped away. And it was under siege from the same forces that had led to an insurrection that jeopardized the very principles to which the building was devoted.

"We're facing the most significant test of our democracy since the Civil War. That's not hyperbole. Since the Civil War," Biden said that July day in 2021. "The Confederates back then never breached the Capitol as insurrectionists did on January the sixth."

The rebellion at the Capitol had loomed over Biden's first six months in office, but the threats that worried Democrats and preoccupied the president were those that had spread out across the nation in the months since the riot. His predecessor's lies about the 2020 election, his false claims of fraud, had fueled not just the riot, but now a sweeping series of voting restrictions being put in place in statehouses across the nation. In a speech that some allies thought was long overdue, Biden was going to place the defense of the vote at the very center of his presidency in order to push the federal government to protect one of the most fundamental rights of its citizens.

Philadelphia was an easy choice for a venue. Along with Boston, it was one of the centers of the American Revolution and where the foundation for American democracy was laid. Biden's home in Wilmington, Delaware, was only about a half hour away, with visitors to the region surprised that, spiritually, the city was both a center for corporate headquarters and a suburb of Philadelphia. The very next stop for a northbound Amtrak train boarded at the Joseph R. Biden station in Wilmington was Philadelphia, and Biden, while in Congress, had spent so much time in Philadelphia's bigger media market—an easier venue from which to raise a national profile—that he was jokingly referred to at the time as "Pennsylvania's third senator." His wife, Jill, also made no secret that she hailed from Philadelphia and, as First Lady, would vigorously root for the Phillies, Eagles, Flyers, and 76ers. Along with Pittsburgh to the west, Philadelphia was a totem for Biden, and where he headquartered his campaign. It was fitting, the president frequently said, that Pennsylvania was the state that had pushed him over the 270 Electoral College votes needed to be president.

As senator, Biden would famously take the train back and forth from Washington, but now, as president, he had a better ride. Air Force One touched down a little after 2:00 p.m., and the presidential motorcade quickly wound its way through the sweltering city streets to the Constitution Center. The center had opened on July 4, 2003, built on the northern end of Independence Mall, one of the most historically significant stretches of land in the nation. Just to its south is the Liberty Bell, which, though in truth a fairly underwhelming American landmark, still draws big crowds. And anchoring the other end of the mall stands the far-more-impressive Independence Hall, which was a gathering place for some of the most famous names in American legend: Washington. Hamilton. Franklin. Jefferson.

Those men did not give the right to vote to all Americans, but they took the first steps on that journey there. Biden wanted to make sure that no further backtracking would occur, believing that the defense of voting rights would be—along with the pandemic and healing the wounds caused by Trump—one of the generational challenges his presidency would face. Two federal bills were languishing in Congress. There had been growing rumblings on the Left that he should be using the presidential bully pulpit to do more. There was fierce debate over the future of the Senate filibuster. Biden had weighed in on the Georgia election law debate months before, to no real avail. And since then, more states were enacting restrictions. The Big Lie was not fading. It was gaining steam.

"We will be asking my Republican friends—in Congress, in states, in cities, in counties—to stand up, for God's sake, and help prevent this concerted effort to undermine our election and the sacred right to vote," Biden said. "We're going to face another test in 2022. A new wave of unprecedented voter suppression, and raw and sustained election subversion. We have to prepare now. . . . The denial of full and free and fair elections is the most un-American thing that any of us can imagine, the most undemocratic, the most unpatriotic, and yet, sadly, not unprecedented."

The president took square aim at the new laws, deeming them restrictive and antithetical to American principles. He reviewed the unprecedented efforts to safeguard the election and validate his own victory, noting that rigorous reviews and recounts found no evidence of fraud.

He never mentioned Trump by name but warned about the "bullies and merchants of fear" who trolled in the "darker and more sinister" underbelly of American politics.

"No other election has ever been held under such scrutiny, such high standards," Biden said. "The big lie is just that: a big lie."

His address was met with thunderous applause. Biden lingered for nearly an hour after the speech, which had taken place during a lull in the COVID-19 pandemic, shaking hands and posing for photos. He had delivered the speech with fire but had stopped short of committing to push for a change in the filibuster, which more and more Democrats believed would be the only way to deliver the federal legislation that could override the state restrictions.

The Reverend Al Sharpton watched Biden work the rope line.

In recent years, Sharpton had become one of the most influential voices in the civil rights movement and Democratic Party. He had been a New York City activist—at times a very controversial one—for decades, then became more of a national figure when he briefly ran for president in 2004. His group, the National Action Network, grew in prominence, and Sharpton got an MSNBC show and, sometimes, President Barack Obama's ear. He became a powerful voice on police injustice and a moving speaker at the funerals of young Black men killed by law enforcement. And both publicly and behind the scenes, Sharpton urged Biden to remember the Black voters who, more than any other group, had put him in office.

Sharpton looked around the Philadelphia museum as Biden posed for selfies. He summoned me and made sure to stress that it was "a good speech." But he made clear that they would be "just words" if the filibuster didn't change and the voting restrictions were allowed to remain in place. Sharpton then told me that he had indicated to Biden that "I told him that I was going to stay on him."

Sharpton looked up toward the podium where Biden had stood

earlier to deliver his speech. The presidential seal had been removed but the preamble to the Constitution was still projected behind it.

"The stakes couldn't be higher."

* * *

A half dozen historians sat around a long table in the White House's East Room. One by one, they spoke of the most transformative presidents, from Abraham Lincoln to Franklin Roosevelt to Lyndon Johnson. Michael Beschloss was there, as were Doris Kearns Goodwin and Jon Meacham, who had become an unofficial White House adviser. They spoke about what made previous presidents successful and what lessons could be drawn for the present. They pointed to momentous action, not incremental change.

Their audience of one listened. He asked questions. And he agreed. Joe Biden wanted to go big; he wanted to embrace the parallels to FDR and LBJ. He had been elected at a time when the nation faced its greatest array of crises in nearly a century. He pledged to restore unity to a divided country, tame a killer pandemic, and steady a shaky economy.

He made real progress. But his first year in office was almost evenly bifurcated between success and struggle.

In his first six months, he steered the $1.9 trillion COVID-19 relief bill to passage, surging funds to American families, schools, and businesses battered by the pandemic. His administration rolled out a massive vaccine distribution program that made the protective shots available to every American just months after they were approved for use. He unveiled a series of economic policies that, by the end of his first year in office, would help cut unemployment from nearly 9 percent on Inauguration Day to under 4 percent a year later.

But in the late summer, the Biden administration was dramatically derailed, thrown off course both by unanticipated events and by political missteps of the administration's own making. Only weeks after Biden used July 4, 2021, to declare America's independence from the COVID-19, the lethal and highly transmissible Delta variant raced across the nation, preying largely on the unvaccinated to send death totals and hospitalizations soaring. Much as Trump had politicized masks, a number of Republican governors fought over vaccine mandates, their views echoed by some in the conservative media, including the loudest voice of all, Tucker Carlson. The Biden administration tried everything to urge those on the Right—conservatives were disproportionately dying from COVID—to get vaccines and the new boosters, but the shots had become a political land mine.

Anger flashed on the Right that Biden was infringing on their freedoms. An unlikely chant emerged: "Let's go Brandon" became a stand-in for "Fuck Joe Biden." Um, how? It came from, of all places, a flustered NASCAR reporter. She was trying to interview a winning driver—named Brandon Brown—when the anti-Biden expletive started in the crowd and was clearly audible on television. She tried to explain that they were instead chanting "Let's go Brandon" as a cheer for the driver. It was farcical, and immediately became a rallying cry for the MAGA crowd. One Oregon man even said it to Biden over the phone when the president wished his family a Merry Christmas. There appeared to be no bottom.

Another variant, Omicron, though less deadly, sent cases surging yet again into the new year. Though the deaths were even more concentrated among the unvaccinated, cases skyrocketed everywhere and slowed down the nation's hopes of returning to normal. And more political danger emerged for the White House, as supply chain shortages and other pandemic-related staffing and labor issues sent inflation spiking. There were whispered Jimmy Carter comparisons as inflation in early 2022 surged to forty-year highs.

And the world watched in horror as the United States' military withdrawal from Afghanistan in August was filled with images of tumult and violence. Biden had been set on extricating the US forces from Afghanistan since his days as Obama's vice president. He had fulfilled a campaign promise to end America's longest war, and public opinion supported him. But while the United States eventually oversaw one of the biggest airlifts in history to evacuate Americans and some allied Afghans, the opening days of its exit were full of horrors. The worst: a suicide bomb that killed thirteen American troops and at least 170 Afghans at Kabul's airport.

The combination of setbacks punctured what had been the new White House's central image of competency; the impression that after Trump's chaos, the grown-ups were back in charge. By any measure, Biden's first year in office had extraordinary successes, particularly given the difficult hand he had been dealt. Yet he ended it undeniably weaker than he began, with his poll numbers having plummeted and his party in danger of being swept out of power on Capitol Hill.

And hovering over all of it was the shadow of January 6 and the man who inspired it. Biden candidly told aides that he knew what was at stake, that he had to prove that American democracy could still deliver for its people. And he thought the way to do that was to make a good-faith effort at bipartisanship. Biden believed in American democracy, but he also believed in American government. He knew that some of the most diehard MAGA Republicans were lost causes, but he believed in his heart that there were enough in the GOP who would work together to protect something bigger than any one political party.

He tried to reach across the aisle and mostly found obstruction. And some of his most stubborn obstacles were within his own party.

What followed was more than half a year devoted to an ultimately failed legislative push, an effort that dominated the president's time and political capital at the expense of a press for voting rights. And as a distracted White House only intermittently unleashed its power on protecting the ballot, a pattern was established: the same Democratic senators who felt comfortable defying their party leader to doom

Biden's social spending agenda would do so again to block his efforts on the vote.

* * *

Biden lived and breathed the Senate.

He had spent nearly four decades there, followed its traditions, and longed for the days when senators could talk to each other as people, not just political rivals. He had missed out on some of the Capitol Hill evening hobnobbing that, for some lawmakers, defined the job; Biden instead would take the train back to Delaware each night to care for his family still reeling from that terrible car accident. But he was glad he did. The time in Wilmington kept him grounded, he long said; it made sure he didn't become a creature of Washington, even though so much of his life was lived inside the Beltway. He thought often of Beau, the memory of whom acted as a north star for some of the president's most important decisions. Biden was the most tactile of politicians: he liked a backslap and a handshake and asking about the other person's mother. And he prized the relationships he built with some of the most arch-conservatives in Congress: Trent Lott. Chuck Grassley. Even Mitch McConnell. He saw those bonds as proof that the Senate could still blur party lines to get things done.

Biden never lost hope that some Republicans, looking at a pandemic-ravaged nation, would set aside party politics to embrace parts of his agenda. He was disappointed that no one in the GOP backed his COVID-19 relief bill when it passed in the spring of 2021. His White House was fond of the claim that the bill was, in essence, bipartisan because it polled well with Republican voters, even though not a single GOP lawmaker in Washington voted for it. But plenty of GOP governors and local leaders supported it, and soon even those who worked on Capitol Hill took to touting the benefits from the relief bill even though they didn't vote for it. That hypocrisy didn't sit well with Biden, who took to carrying around a notecard listing the Republican lawmakers who extolled the virtues of the bill without casting a vote for it.

Biden was also dismayed by the GOP pushback to what he thought were commonsense public safety measures like masks. He initially didn't want vaccine mandates either, but the Delta variant changed his thinking and he didn't understand why Republicans didn't follow suit. And he was disgusted that so many in the Republican Party blocked the formation of the January 6 commission; he took to saying privately that the GOP was so beholden to Trump that "it wasn't a real party anymore."

But infrastructure, he thought, was the one thing they could agree upon. It had been a bipartisan embarrassment for decades, as Democrats and Republicans alike could see the nation's crumbling highways and bridges. Airports were outdated; too many pipes seeped lead into the drinking water; schools and ports were falling apart. The Trump administration had tried to pivot toward infrastructure several times but its efforts at doing so—branded "Infrastructure Week"—inevitably failed, overwhelmed by controversies usually of the president's own making. "Infrastructure Week" became a Washington joke, and one Biden himself enjoyed.

Considering his blue-collar background and longtime associations with trains, as well as his relationships with some in the GOP caucus, Biden believed he was the president to get a bill over the finish line. But it wouldn't just be a $1 trillion infrastructure bill. The White House wanted to pair it with a $3.5 trillion social spending plan that would reshape the government's relationship with its citizens, dramatically expanding the social services safety net and lifting tens of thousands of Americans out of poverty. It set out to broaden well-known programs—for example, adding dental, vision, and hearing aid benefits to Medicare and continuing the Obama-era health law's temporary subsidies that helped people buy insurance during the pandemic.

The "Build Back Better" plan, as it was dubbed by the White House, would be one of the most expansive government spending programs ever and key, Democrats believed, to keeping control of Congress in 2022. They planned to pass it with a congressional trick known as budget reconciliation, which would allow them to do it on a party-line vote. But, of course, since they had only fifty Senate votes—with Vice President Kamala Harris set to break the tie—they couldn't afford to lose a single Democrat. That, in turn, gave each single Democratic senator extraordinary power over the proceedings; and a few senators soon made clear they planned to use it.

The White House charted the course: it would get a bipartisan infrastructure deal through Congress first, then move to Build Back Better. And once the massive legislation agenda was passed, Biden would turn toward voting rights. But he didn't ignore voting rights completely. In June, he traveled to Tulsa, the city Trump had alienated the year before by trying to hold his comeback rally on Juneteenth. Biden arrived to mark the hundredth anniversary of the race massacre that had destroyed a thriving Black community in that Oklahoma city. He declared that he had "to help fill the silence" about one of the nation's darkest—and long-suppressed—moments of racial violence.

"Some injustices are so heinous, so horrific, so grievous, they cannot be buried, no matter how hard people try," Biden said. "Only with truth can come healing."

In 1921, a white mob, including some people hastily deputized by authorities, looted and burned Tulsa's Greenwood district, which was referred to as Black Wall Street. As many as three hundred Black Tulsans were killed, and thousands of survivors were forced into internment camps overseen by the National Guard. Burned bricks and a small piece of a church basement were about all that survived of the historically Black district that had stretched over more than thirty blocks.

"Just because history is silent, it does not mean that it did not take place," said Biden, in a deeply emotional speech that left many in the audience blinking back tears. And he connected the moment to the ongoing struggle to protect the ballot, announcing that Harris would lead the administration's voting rights efforts.

It was a start. But then the movement was again placed on the back burner, not to take center stage again until after the congressional spending negotiations. A growing number of Democrats and civil rights activists worried that it would be too late.

* * *

For a while, things seemed to be going according to plan.

It was, by any estimation, a slog to get the bipartisan infrastructure deal done. There was some momentum for a few weeks behind a deal put forth by the junior senator from West Virginia, Shelley Moore Capito. Biden got heavily involved, talking to senators on both sides of the aisle. He had been frustrated earlier in the year, when the pandemic had made it impossible to safely host lawmakers at the White House. He had learned to hate remote meetings, both domestically and with foreign leaders. For most of his career, Biden was used to trotting the globe, first as part of the Senate Committee on Foreign Relations and then as vice president. He had always envisioned a possible presidency that way, but he was older now and the toll of the travel was real. And White House aides were leery of any circumstance that could put him at risk of exposure to the virus. Biden understood, but he hated it: "I can't do diplomacy by fucking Zoom," he'd complained to aides more than once.

But the early weeks of summer offered a respite: he was able to take his first foreign trip, to world leader summits on England's Cornwall coast and in Brussels, and then to a high-stakes meeting with Vladimir Putin in Geneva. He was greeted in Europe with a sigh of relief by Western leaders: he was not Trump. And Geneva was no Helsinki: Biden warned the Russian leader against any election interference by cyberattack. Putin, for his part, smiled quietly while his security guards forcibly pushed me and other reporters out of the summit room for trying to ask him questions.

Deals were made between allies over global vaccine distribution; NATO was recommitted to. There was still some underlying anxiety among the Europeans that perhaps Biden would be an aberration, that an isolationist "America First" foreign policy could return in four years with Trump or someone like him. But for now, they celebrated a return to normalcy even as concerns would soon grow as to what Putin might be planning.

And Biden was able to finally host senators at the White House and have them fan out around his chair in the Oval Office. Though he had spent much of his adult life trying to get there, it turned out Biden didn't really like living at the White House all that much. He found it stiff and formal, "like a museum." He didn't like staff being present at all hours to wait on him; he much preferred to just shuffle over to the kitchen himself to get some late-night ice cream. The then seventy-eight-year-old chief executive much preferred his house back in Delaware, with his family nearby, some favorite restaurants, and the familiar features of home. Much to the chagrin of the traveling White House press pool, Biden favored heading to his home in Wilmington more weekends than not.

But the White House still carried with it a lot of power, and Biden knew it was undeniably useful as a leveraging tool to get things done. So there he was, bursting through the doors of the West Wing, past the marine standing guard, to make a surprise appearance on the White House driveway with a bipartisan group of senators. He had an infrastructure deal. Or at least the start of one.

"When we can find common ground, working across party lines, that is what I will seek to do," said Biden on that sunny June 2021 day. He deemed the infrastructure agreement "a true bipartisan effort, breaking the ice that too often has kept us frozen in place."

The bill's price tag was $973 billion over five years, or $1.2 trillion over eight years, and it was a scaled-back but still central piece of Biden's agenda. And it was indeed a bipartisan effort: Senator Rob Portman, Republican of Ohio, was a driving force, and in the end the bill would collect nineteen GOP votes, including Mitt Romney, Lindsey Graham, and, at the last minute, Mitch McConnell. It was just step one: the reconciliation bill would come later. But it was a triumph for Biden and a reaffirmation of his belief that he could still reach across the aisle. That was the hard part, his aides thought. It gets easier from here.

They were wrong. Democrats would prove to be a surprise obstacle, given the competition between the liberal and moderate wings in the House, and two stubborn senators in particular. And as the Big Lie picked up steam in the states, that trouble would soon spill over in his push to battle the coming storm over voting rights.

* * *

Biden was tired of Joe Manchin.

To be clear, the two men were friends. They had a fine relationship, shared a folksy style. And Biden could live with political disagreement. That came with the job. White House aides were keenly aware of the dynamic at play: Manchin had pulled off the unlikely feat of getting elected as a Democrat in one of the reddest states in the country—three times as senator and twice before that as governor. In fact, only Wyoming had voted for Trump at a higher rate in 2020 than West Virginia. And Manchin was happy to remind his Senate colleagues and White House aides that, in essence, if they didn't like dealing with him, they could deal with the Republican who would follow him. He made clear, as he had during the COVID-19 relief bill debate months earlier, that he would only vote for what he could explain to his constituents back home. It wasn't clear how he explained the houseboat he docked along the Potomac or the Maserati he drove. But Manchin was also very much aware of the power that he, or any Democratic senator, now wielded in a fifty–fifty chamber of Congress.

And Manchin loved being the center of attention.

Even before his newfound power in 2021, Manchin was not shy about hopping on camera. He was quick to do television interviews, eager to supply a quote to the Capitol Hill reporters lingering in hallways. He would quietly work as an unnamed source for print reporter and TV anchor alike. And suddenly, he was in demand and in the conversation like never before. As was another, unlikelier, senator.

Kyrsten Sinema was once so liberal that the Democratic Party wasn't lefty enough for her. As she came of age politically, she joined the Green Party and worked for Ralph Nader's 2000 presidential bid. After a failed run for office, she switched to the Democratic Party and was elected first to the Arizona state legislature and then to Congress. She was a triathlete and bisexual. She began to moderate her politics, driving hard to the center and associating with other Blue Dog Democrats. And then, after Trump bullied Jeff Flake out of the Senate, Sinema took a run at his open seat and secured a win in 2018. She modeled herself in some ways on the legendary Arizona senator John McCain in that she prized herself for being unpredictable, a real maverick. But her ideology, at times, seemed less than consistent, making her more like an enigma. And as much as Manchin loved the media spotlight, Sinema shied away from it—she rarely gave interviews outside of her home state press.

The two of them couldn't be more different. But they soon became linked, as "Manchin and Sinema" or "Sinema and Manchin" (Manchinema?) were uttered together in one breath on cable news shows and among frustrated Democrats. And that's because they emerged as a huge roadblock to getting Biden's agenda through Congress.

Biden himself confused matters when, after the bipartisan infrastructure deal passed, he endorsed explicitly linking it to the social spending agenda. That was Nancy Pelosi's plan: she didn't want to pass one without the other. She had to try to keep her moderates and liberals in line. The moderates wanted to go ahead and pass the Senate's infrastructure deal first, then move on to the bigger spending package. Conversely, the liberals feared that doing so would cost them all their leverage; they worried that if they passed the infrastructure deal, the moderates on Capitol Hill—namely, Manchin—would walk away from the $3.5 trillion package. They wanted the two bills done at once, and when Biden voiced support for the plan, it outraged Republicans who had backed the infrastructure deal; they didn't want their votes for one package to be linked to the other, Democrats-only bill. This, of course, was all theater: the Democrats were going to try to pass both bills. But Biden backed off such an explicit endorsement.

The subsequent negotiations over the two bills showed the limits of comparing Biden to Roosevelt or Johnson. Both of those presidents had been blessed with huge Democratic majorities in both houses of Congress. Biden had a fifty–fifty Senate and only a slim margin in the House. Biden himself, though a veteran legislator, was at times too deferential, some aides thought, to the competing interests on the other end of Pennsylvania Avenue. The presidency was a bully pulpit: at some point, some of his closest advisers pressed, it was time to demand that your party back your agenda. But in his multiple trips to the Capitol, Biden listened more than cajoled, and the bills stalled.

Manchin pushed for the Build Back Better bill to shrink, which it eventually did, to around $2 trillion. His asks—some to Biden, some to Chuck Schumer—kept changing, but the answer he kept coming back with was "no." High-wire negotiations stretched late on many nights in the fall of 2021, and while a deal was struck to keep the government open, Manchin still refused to move on the spending program. It was a standoff that threatened to subsume the Biden administration.

Eventually, the progressives in the House blinked. Time and again, they proved far more willing to compromise than their conservative counterparts and, in early November, they passed the infrastructure bill in the belief that good-faith negotiations would get the larger social spending bill done too. Biden had a win, he signed the infrastructure bill into law, and federal dollars would soon begin flowing to construction projects all over the nation. And a few days later, the House passed $2.2 trillion in spending over the next decade to battle climate change, expand health care, and reweave the nation's social safety net. The bill's passage, 220 to 213, came after weeks of cajoling, arm-twisting, and legislative flexibility. It received no Republican votes and even faced a record-breaking more than eight-hour speech from Kevin McCarthy as he voiced his objections. Like most things McCarthy did, it was aimed to get the approval of one man, and Trump registered his appreciation.

Passage of these bills had taken an enormous amount of time and political capital. And it had come at the cost of other things: the more time and energy the White House poured into its legislative agenda, the less it was able to devote to combating "the most significant test of our democracy since the Civil War." The rumblings from civil rights activists about the lack of action on voting rights was growing louder. Sharpton, NAACP president Derrick Johnson, and several other civil rights leaders had gone to the White House in July to meet with Biden and Harris. They voiced their concerns, including that the filibuster loomed as an insurmountable obstacle.

"Time is of the essence. We cannot forget that justice is an ongoing struggle, and democracy an ongoing fight," Johnson said.

"This is an attack on a very fundamental value that undergirds this country. When we look at what's happening in this nation, we see an effort to impose a system, American apartheid," said Marc Morial, head of the National Urban League.

But they were told to be patient, to let the administration get through the Build Back Better agenda first, and that then voting rights would be the priority. And it finally seemed like that was about to happen. The Democrats, despite all the fits and starts and struggles, were on track.

Until they weren't.

* * *

It wasn't just what Manchin said. It was where he said it.

The West Virginia senator stared into the *Fox News Sunday* camera on December 19, 2021, and surprised the host that day, Bret Baier, with his candor. After five and a half months of tortuous negotiations among Democrats in which he was his party's chief obstacle to passage, Manchin was pulling the plug on Build Back Better and dealing a potentially fatal blow to Biden's leading domestic initiative heading into an election year when Democrats' narrow hold on Congress was already in peril.

"I cannot vote to continue with this piece of legislation. I just can't. I've tried everything humanly possible. I can't get there."

Ron Klain, Biden's chief of staff, muttered an expletive under his breath and called his staff. This was a disaster and he needed to get to the bottom of what went wrong, he said. He then called Biden. The president greeted the news with a similar expletive—he was far more foul-mouthed off camera than you'd expect—and was furious that Manchin had stabbed him and the party in the back. He knew Manchin was waffling; in fact, just a few days before, the senator had said he wanted to delay proceeding with the bill until more was known about rising inflation, which he had made his number one concern.

Biden wasn't thrilled with that delay but signaled his support for it. White House staff had then given Manchin a heads-up that the president would soon put out a statement accepting a delay in the Build Back Better Act and that it was going to mention the West Virginia senator by name. Manchin objected, asking either that his name be left out or that he not be singled out, because his family had already been the target of abuse.

But the statement went out anyway, and the only name it contained was Manchin's. The senator then snapped at White House aides and told them he was done negotiating. The West Wing interpreted that as meaning that current talks were done but could pick up again next year. But Manchin meant that he was totally walking away—which he said publicly a few days later on *Fox News Sunday*. Those at the White House were blindsided and furious, not just that Manchin had pulled the plug but that he had done so on Fox, which had spent the entire year, they felt, working to undermine their agenda. It was a slap in the face.

Biden took the high road and called Manchin that night. The two men spoke amiably, and each left the conversation thinking that the door was still open to negotiation on the package. But talks didn't resume right away, and a number of congressional aides began seeing if different pieces of the bill—perhaps lowering the cost of prescription drugs or making child care affordable—could be spun off into smaller pieces of legislation.

In February, Manchin was asked the status of talks on Build Back Better. He nearly scoffed.

"What Build Back Better bill? There is no, I mean, I don't know what you all are talking about," Manchin said. "No, no, no, no, it's dead."

The bipartisan infrastructure deal was now law and a clear victory for the president and public. But months had been spent on Build Back Better, yielding nothing. An effort to take up a smaller, limited version of the bill could be considered for later in 2022 but would only get harder to pass closer to the midterms. Biden's approval rating had plummeted to the upper thirties, a slide that began with Afghanistan and was accelerated by the pummeling that the Delta and Omicron variant waves dealt the nation. Inflation was surging and, polling revealed, Americans were sick of the gridlock and infighting on Capitol Hill.

Biden was at a low point. And then he faced an uprising.

* * *

"The judgment of history is upon us," the preacher proclaimed. "Future generations will ask, when the democracy was in a 911 state of emergency, what did you do to put the fire out?"

Raphael Warnock, who delivered sermons from the pulpit that once belonged to Dr. Martin Luther King Jr., was unleashing fire and brimstone from the floor of the United States Senate. The senior pastor of

Ebenezer Baptist Church in Atlanta, Warnock was now a senator from Georgia, elected January 5, 2021. He stared at his Senate colleagues on December 14, 2021, and declared that he had had enough, that it was time to act. He had been in office only eleven months, he was due to face voters again in another eleven months, and his state had imposed the most publicized set of voting restrictions in the nation.

And he didn't want to hear anything more about the filibuster.

Though he didn't mention them by name, Warnock aimed his verbal daggers at two of his Democratic colleagues, Senators Manchin and Sinema, who had both said that they would not vote to change the filibuster to pass federal voting rights legislation without bipartisan support. But not enough Republicans, of course, were willing to back such a move, so the two Democrats refused to play along even though their own party—and the nation's democracy writ large—stood to suffer. Warnock seethed that it was an empty commitment to bipartisanship—and that reaching across the aisle had not always led to virtuous results.

"Here's the thing we must remember: Slavery was bipartisan. Jim Crow segregation was bipartisan. The refusal of women's suffrage was bipartisan. The denial of the basic dignity of members of the LGBTQ community has long been bipartisan," Warnock thundered.

"The three-fifths compromise was the creation of a putative, national unity at the expense of Black people's basic humanity," he continued, referencing the constitutional clause that rendered a Black man less of a citizen than a white one. "So when colleagues in this chamber talk to me about bipartisanship—which I believe in—I just have to ask, 'At whose expense?'"

Despite presenting their stances as principled, Manchin and Sinema had voted just a short time before to raise the debt limit on a party-line vote that required the Senate to temporarily suspend the filibuster. Warnock, who many pundits felt faced an uphill battle to keep his Senate seat in November 2022, blasted the reversal as "a consequence of misaligned values and misplaced priorities."

An intraparty fight over voting rights had engulfed the Democratic Party not even a year after the Capitol insurrection. As Republicans put in place new voting restrictions in states across the country, civil rights activists watched with growing alarm as the White House and congressional leadership prioritized the Build Back Better agenda instead. But that had crashed against the rocks, and the window for meaningful action was already starting to narrow: with the midterms looming in November 2022, lawmakers had only a few months to legislate before they wanted to focus on campaigning. Congress's calendar, as always, was short and cynical.

But civil rights leaders drew a line in the sand. A number of leading Black activists made clear, in no uncertain terms, that they were tired of being taken for granted. Black voters had, in large part, delivered Biden the White House and Democrats the Congress. But their ability to vote was being threatened, and nothing, they felt, was being done about it.

They set a deadline: they demanded to see real action by the Martin Luther King Jr. holiday in mid-January. And if the Democrats didn't meet it, they couldn't count on Black support again.

"An inaction at this point would lead to an inaction of Black voters. People are saying, 'If they don't do this, I'm not voting,'" the Reverend Al Sharpton said to me at the time. "People are saying they feel betrayed.

"The time is now. The urgency could not be more palpable than it is now."

But familiar obstacles stood in the way.

* * *

The filibuster is not in the Constitution.

The Senate rule, at its essence, gives senators the right to derail votes with, in theory, indefinite debate. Before 1917, there was no way to end debate. But that year, a new Senate rule was put in place that allowed a two-thirds majority to end a filibuster and prompt a vote, a procedure known as "cloture." In 1975, that was lowered to three-fifths of the Senate—which is why there is a de facto sixty-vote threshold for laws to pass the Senate.

But in the middle of the twentieth century, the filibuster was the final weapon of Southern Democrats who were battling to preserve segregation and Jim Crow practices in their states. They wielded it to water down or eliminate various civil rights bills until 1964 and 1965, when a coalition of Republicans and Democrats outside the South—wrangled by President Lyndon Johnson—found enough votes to break it. But when the threshold was lowered to sixty votes a decade later, it inadvertently led to a far more frequent use of "extended debate" or the threat of the filibuster. Senators were no longer required to hold the floor for hours, so the gauzy drama of all-night sessions that might last for weeks vanished. And senators in both parties came to embrace the filibuster, or the threat to filibuster, as just another tool.

The filibuster empowered senators, particularly those in the minority. Without it, the Democrats could pass legislation—including on voting rights—with a simple up-and-down majority vote, with Harris breaking the tie. And in some cases, including on reconciliation budget bills or when the filibuster was waived, sixty votes weren't needed.

But that number would need to be hit for the two voting bills that languished before the Senate.

The first was given the name House Resolution 1 in the Congress that came to office in January 2021, a sign that it was the Democrats' top priority. Known as HR1 or the "For the People Act," the bill was a sweeping overhaul of how elections were conducted and financed. It was a broad and transformative bill that would have, among other things, created a national automatic system for registering voters and established national standards for mail-in and absentee ballots. Voter ID laws would be tossed aside, and bipartisan commissions would be created to draw the lines for legislative districts so that redistricting wouldn't favor either major party. The bill would also provide public money for campaigns and prohibit shielding the identity of dark money voters.

It was a sweeping measure intended to rewrite the way the nation votes. And it had no chance of passing.

The bill was written when Democrats were out of power, and at its heart it was what is known as "a messaging bill," an idea for candidates to tout on the campaign trail but not really crafted in a way to pass a divided Congress. Manchin—yes, him again—made clear in June 2021 that the bill went too far and his opposition quickly scuttled it.

But the West Virginia senator did indicate that he supported most of what was in House Resolution 4, which was known as HR4 or, better yet, the John Lewis Voting Rights Act, named after the legendary congressman and civil rights leader who died in July 2020. It was a comparatively narrow bill designed to fix a specific problem, in this case the 2013 Supreme Court ruling that had weakened the Voting Rights Act by making it harder for the federal government to block racially discriminatory voting laws and redistricting.

Democrats outraged by that Supreme Court decision—known as the *Shelby County (Alabama) v. Holder* case—missed something subtle. In Chief Justice John Roberts's majority opinion, he didn't close the door to the measure, nor did the ruling overturn the Voting Rights Act's ban on discriminatory voting rules. Instead, it gave Congress the opportunity to draft new, updated rules—based on present conditions and not the ones dating from the 1960s—to determine which states or local governments should be subject to preclearance. In other words, the ruling didn't end the law, it just asked Congress to fix it. And that's what the John Lewis Act was set to do. The measure also would make it easier for the Justice Department to send election observers, to safeguard that votes were tabulated and certified correctly, and for courts to block election law changes that violated the constitutional protections guaranteeing voting rights for all US citizens.

This bill was far more palatable to moderate Democrats and, potentially, had an outside chance of passing. Manchin over the summer offered his own version, which watered down some of the package but kept many of its core principles. And even in a reduced version, it would still offer far greater voter protections than what was available at the moment. But the voting conundrum remained: Either Manchin needed to find ten Republicans to support it to reach the sixty votes needed to pass or the filibuster would have to change. Otherwise, nothing would happen.

Republicans were not going to let voting rights pass with just fifty votes plus the vice president, so it would require elimination of the filibuster in what has become known as "the nuclear option." Or, at the very least, an exception to the filibuster would need to be carved out for voting rights, as had been done on occasion to raise the debt ceiling and confirm federal judges. Manchin and Sinema expressed public doubts; other Democrats did so privately. In order to change their minds, it would likely require a push from someone who served nearly four decades in the Senate and venerated all its institutions, including the filibuster.

It took him a while. But Joe Biden got there.

In his first months in office, Biden made clear that he was inclined to leave the Senate rule alone. But as the months passed and election bills ended up on the calendars of state legislatures across the country, Biden's views evolved. In October, he said in a town hall that he would consider making a one-time change to the filibuster. And then in December, as the civil rights groups laid down their ultimatum, he went further.

"If the only thing standing between getting voting rights legislation passed and not getting passed is the filibuster, I support making the exception of voting rights for the filibuster," Biden said in an interview with ABC.

And thus began, at long last, the White House's all-out push on voting rights. It was, at last, a practicable piece of policy that could push back on the Big Lie.

* * *

With the Build Back Better Act sidelined and the pressure from the Left mounting, the White House mapped out a sprint to put voting rights at the center of its agenda as the calendar prepared to turn to 2022. The clock was ticking to Martin Luther King Jr. Day, and some Black activists said they would ramp up their criticism of Democrats—and perhaps abstain from campaigning for them in the midterms—if progress was not made.

"I don't want to become too dramatic," Representative Emanuel Cleaver, a Democrat from Missouri, told *Politico*, "but voting rights may be the only thing we have to at least halt the trek away from democracy."

"I just want us to get a bill done that will help preserve this democracy because if we don't, I think we've lost this democracy," Jim Clyburn said.

Even though its public approach to voting rights was somewhat scattershot, the White House had been working diligently on the matter behind the scenes since Biden took office. Weekly staff meetings were held on the topic, and senior leadership calls were set up to discuss ways to protect election results and to assess possible pathways to federal legislation while monitoring developments in the states. Grassroots campaigns were encouraged to restore the American public's confidence in the nation's elections, to try to undo some of the damage Trump had wrought. Yet even though it animated elements of the Left, voting rights never polled very high as a major issue among most people, according to internal numbers from surveys conducted by Biden allies. Some in the president's inner circle speculated privately that a legislative defeat on voting rights might even be politically advantageous, since the fear of further GOP ballot restrictions might drive Democratic turnout in the 2022 midterms.

All along, a focus had emerged on the states; Biden aides grimly joked that the president had been in office for a year and was still facing local recounts and efforts to decertify his win. "Maybe one of these years we'll really win Arizona," one staffer joked to reporters. The West Wing knew it had to pick and choose which fights it wanted to litigate, for fear of being bogged down in court for years. Biden expressed worry about threats to election volunteers, while some of his closest aides monitored the unprecedented GOP interest in state races like secretary of state.

But while the White House knew that some of the electoral battles would need to be fought on the state level, federal legislation would be the best solution. Aides also recognized that a full-court press on voting rights—even if it was good politics—would be doomed to fail without a change to the filibuster. And while they had some skepticism that they could bring reluctant Democrats on board for such changes, they hoped a fierce push from the president on filibuster reform might help. HR1 was never an option, but there was a flicker of life to the smaller package. Aides settled on a multipronged approach: senior White House staffers would begin pushing lawmakers behind the scenes, while Biden was to start 2022 by delivering a major voting rights speech in Georgia, arguably the most important state on the electoral map as well as ground zero for efforts to restrict access to the ballot.

But first, there was one other moment to make the case.

* * *

Riot shields were now propped up around entrances to the Capitol. Metal detectors were installed, to stand guard outside entrances to the House and Senate floors. Capitol police officers patrolling the complex were still wearing black armbands memorializing their fallen colleagues.

Republicans in Congress have, so far, blocked an official display at the Capitol to commemorate the riot that took place on January 6, 2021. But exactly one year later, there were still reminders everywhere of the violence that came to that hallowed place, nearly tearing apart the nation's democracy while leaving many who were there that day still grappling with the trauma.

Precisely one year after a mob stormed the Capitol to try to prevent the certification of his election, President Joe Biden strode into National Statuary Hall, which had been invaded by throngs of Trump supporters wielding flags as weapons and threatening unspeakable violence. There had been some debate among his aides as to how to mark the day, and some advisers encouraged a small, quiet remembrance so as not to elevate the lies that had fueled that violence. But Biden chose a different path. He wanted to eviscerate those lies. And the man who told them.

"And here is the truth of it: the former president of the United States of America has created and spread a web of lies about the 2020 election," Biden said. "He's done so because he values power over principle, because he sees his own interests as more important than his country's interests and America's interests, and because his bruised ego matters more to him than our democracy or our Constitution.

"He can't accept he lost."

Biden, as was his custom, didn't use Trump's name. He didn't have to. His entire speech was aimed squarely at his predecessor in an effort to both push back against the Big Lie and to warn the nation that the threat from the former president and his followers remained undiminished. Other Democrats joined in.

"It was Donald Trump's big lie that soaked our political landscape in kerosene," Schumer said. "It was Donald Trump's rally on the Mall that struck the match. And then came the fire."

Though he had spent much of the past year trying to ignore Trump and work across the aisle, most of Biden's efforts at bipartisanship had faltered because the GOP showed no interest. He took a different path at the Capitol, swiping at the GOP by offering his most extended rebuttal of the false claim that the 2020 election was stolen, noting that multiple recounts, court battles, and inquiries had turned up no meaningful fraud. The president dismissed the rants of—and he reveled in saying this—"a defeated former president" and noted that Republicans had not challenged GOP victories for Congress and governorships based on the same balloting they claimed was illegitimate in the presidential race.

But there were no signs that many Republicans would turn away from their stance on the election. Few lawmakers even bothered to be in Washington for the insurrection commemoration, and only one elected official—Representative Liz Cheney—took part in a moment of silence put on by Democrats to remember those lost. She was joined by her father, former vice president Dick Cheney, who was greeted warmly by some of the same Democrats who once called him a war criminal. At least on this, the Democrats thought, Cheney was on the right side of history.

Other Republicans accused Biden of trying to overstate what happened a year earlier while trying to exploit the moment for political gain. Trump had initially considered holding a news conference that day but was talked out of it by aides who convinced him that his efforts at counterprogramming probably would not get the media attention he hoped. He released a statement instead.

"This political theater is all just a distraction for the fact Biden has completely and totally failed," Trump wrote. "The Democrats want to own this day of January 6 so they can stoke fears and divide America. I say, let them have it because America sees through theirs [*sic*] lies and polarizations."

Biden, in his speech, tried to reject efforts to rewrite history and cast the attackers as patriots. His frustration rising, his voice grew louder as he excoriated "those who stormed this Capitol and those who insti-gated and incited and those who called on them to do so."

He added later: "I will stand in this breach. I will defend this na-tion. And I will allow no one to place a dagger at the throat of our democracy."

Biden had tried to steer his nation out of a once-in-a-century pan-demic. He had pushed through two huge pieces of legislation to better American lives, though he'd fallen short on a third. His administration was centered on trying to restore faith in American democracy, and he seemingly couldn't reach half the country. Not because they couldn't hear him. Because they chose not to listen. They didn't think he was legitimate. And they believed others.

The threat remained. The Big Lie had become policy. Trump's power had not abated.

A year had passed since January 6. Little had changed.

12

THE CAMPAIGNS TO COME

The air raid sirens over Ukrainian cities were incessant.

Russian missiles slammed into a TV tower in Kyiv in the first weeks of war, temporarily disabling some of the nation's stations while also raining fire onto a nearby Holocaust memorial. At least five people died there, their bodies found smoldering. Rockets pummeled apartment complexes in Kharkiv, entire neighborhoods wiped out, civilians and their homes clearly targeted by Red Army weaponry. The shelling seemed to never stop at Mariupol, all but leveling whole neighborhoods in the southern port city. Russian troops opened fire indiscriminately at vehicles approaching checkpoints near the capital. One Ukrainian man was shot to death on a wooded road, his dog found whimpering beside him.

More than 4,600 miles away, Vassily Nebenzia, Russia's ambassador to the United Nations, prepared to make an implausible case.

His nation, at Vladimir Putin's direction, had invaded its neighbor in the early morning hours of February 24, 2022, realizing the war fears the West had held for months. In the fall of 2021, US intelligence noticed the beginning of what became a massive troop buildup near the Ukrainian border. Putin had made no secret of his beliefs that the collapse of the

Soviet Union was a geopolitical disaster and that Ukraine should still be part of Russia. He had invaded before, in 2014, and seized Crimea.

The Biden administration was deeply worried about the possibility of the largest land war in Europe since World War II. A military intervention was not on the table; Ukraine was not a part of NATO, and any scenario in which American and Russian soldiers started shooting at each other put the globe on an apocalyptic path. But in a concerted and highly unusual effort, the White House began loudly warning about Putin's aggressive behavior. The strategy to take intelligence public in almost real time was crafted by CIA Director William Burns and Director of National Intelligence Avril Haines and quickly endorsed by the president, who thought the effort might rattle Putin, a former KGB chief known to safeguard his secrets. The move, along with the threat of punishing sanctions, wasn't viewed as a guaranteed deterrent but a possible mechanism to slow down the Russian leader and perhaps make him reconsider.

Putin went in anyway. He waited for the Winter Olympics in Beijing to end, so as not to offend his Chinese allies, and unleashed a series of increasingly angry speeches with lies about the abuses of Russians living in a pair of separatist territories within Ukraine. Russian tanks began rolling, and the skies above Ukraine filled with rockets. But what many experts thought would be a lightning-fast Russian victory was met with fierce resistance. And as the Russian advance stalled, the world gaped in horror at the atrocities its troops left behind in places like Bucha. Ukrainian civilians slaughtered, women raped, and children executed.

In the first weeks of war, the same Ukrainian president, Volodymyr Zelenskyy, whom Donald Trump had tried to extort for damaging information about Joe Biden's family emerged as a heroic symbol of national strength. The same defense system, the Javelin missiles, that Trump had threatened to withhold were instrumental in defending Ukraine. The same alliance, NATO, that Trump had tried to undermine banded together and sent weapons to the front, while Europe and the United States unleashed wave after wave of sanctions on Russia.

And the same leader, Vladimir Putin, with whom Trump had sided over his own government, was turned into an international pariah.

But Trump also played another role in the war.

Nebenzia took the microphone to denounce a new United Nations resolution that condemned Russia's invasion and called for an immediate and complete withdrawal of all military forces from Ukraine. Moscow had forcefully rejected the resolution, calling claims that Russian troops were targeting civilians "fake" and saying other countries were hypocritical for supporting it. With the eyes of the world on him, Nebenzia singled out Washington for scorn, declaring that the United States could not be taken seriously on the matter of democracy because it was "where the legitimately elected president of the country was overthrown."

The ambassador appeared to be talking about Trump, claiming that he was the true president who had been illegally deposed due to election fraud. The headlines screamed. For years, Trump was accused of using Moscow's talking points. Now, Putin's people seemed to be using Trump's to undermine the American criticism of his invasion.

The Big Lie was being used to defend a war.

* * *

Trump's lie about the 2020 election had permeated the international and domestic discourse. Republican congressional campaigns were ramping up with defense of the claim at their centers. Trump continued to step back into the arena, loudly proclaiming that he had won while planting the seeds to successfully overturn the next election. It seemed like a federal push to protect voting rights was the only hope. Democrats were not particularly optimistic. But there was a window and they needed to take advantage of it, even if it ended up being a triumph of politics rather than policy.

As the calendar turned to 2022, Build Back Better had collapsed and was temporarily put on the shelf. Ominous signs were coming from eastern Europe, but Putin was a few weeks away from launching his assault. Democrats were looking for a win, and just as importantly in the minds of many, they wanted to show their base that they were fighting for the issues that mattered most to them. That meant voting rights. After having been on the back burner for much of 2021, the matter was suddenly Washington's main event in the days before Martin Luther King Jr. Day. Civil rights leaders hopped on cable news to keep the pressure on. Chuck Schumer pressed members of his caucus to support filibuster reform. The White House legislative affairs team, once more, set up shop on the other side of the Pennsylvania Avenue. And Biden and a team of aides, including the historian Jon Meacham, put the finishing touches on his Georgia voting rights speech.

Schumer and Democratic leaders turned their public fire on Republicans, painting them as the obstacle to voting reforms. They noted that the last renewal of the Voting Rights Bill was in 2006, when Republican George W. Bush was in office, and it had sailed through with bipartisan support. The only things that had changed, Democrats pointed out, were that a Republican wasn't in office this time around—and the GOP was in Trump's sway.

"If the right to vote is the cornerstone of our democracy, then how can we in good conscience allow for a situation in which the Republican Party can debate and pass voter suppression laws at the State level with only a simple majority vote, but not allow the United States Senate to do the same?" Schumer wrote in a January 13 letter to colleagues. "In the coming days, we will confront this sobering question—together."

Republicans were nearly uniformly against any federal voting rights legislation. The Freedom to Vote Act had no Republican support in the Senate. The John Lewis bill had one GOP backer: Lisa Murkowski of Alaska. Mitch McConnell was so opposed that he made an appearance to speak at a Senate Rules committee meeting to attack it, a rare step for a party leader. And he condemned the Democrats' efforts to change the filibuster rule and their attempt to link the first anniversary of the January 6 riot with the push for voting rights.

"No party that would trash the Senate's legislation traditions can be trusted to seize control over election laws all across America," McConnell said on the Senate floor. "Nobody who is this desperate to take over our democracy on a one-party basis can be allowed to do it.

"It is beyond distasteful for some of our colleagues to ham-fistedly invoke the January 6th anniversary to advance these aims," he said.

Even Republicans who occasionally worked across the aisle came out in opposition to the measure. Mitt Romney said the Democrats had "ventured deep into hyperbole and hysteria" in their push to alter the filibuster.

"There is a reasonable chance Republicans will win both houses in Congress and that Donald Trump himself could once again be elected president in 2024," Romney said on the Senate floor. "Have Democrats thought what it would mean for them, for the Democrat minority to have no power whatsoever?"

But Republicans were not the only problem. On the eve of Biden's speech, it was far from a sure thing that the Democrats would have enough support within their own party to change the filibuster. Neither Kyrsten Sinema nor Joe Manchin had suggested they were wavering in their opposition, though the West Virginia senator had signaled that he'd listen to the speech with an open mind. But even without a guarantee, Schumer went ahead and scheduled a procedural vote on the two voting rights bills. To make that happen, he used a quirk in the rules to allow floor debate on the bills, both of which had majority support in the fifty–fifty Senate. But advancing the measures to vote on their final passage required sixty senators to break filibusters, which Democrats had no realistic hope of achieving because of Republican opposition. Even if they were to lose, Schumer told others, senators would need "to put their names" on their votes. While that was aimed at Republicans and would create potentially good campaign ad fodder, it could also have the uncomfortable by-product of putting a spotlight on Democrats also not willing to vote to change the filibuster.

Trouble emerged: a number of Georgia civil rights groups announced they would boycott Biden's speech because they believed that it would produce only words and not actions. And then the White House was left reeling when Stacey Abrams announced that she, too, would be skipping the Atlanta speech, citing unspecified scheduling issues. That was a dubious excuse and bad optics for Biden: Voting rights was Abrams's signature issue; the president of the United States was coming to her backyard to deliver a speech on that very topic and she was skipping it? Biden gave her cover and said he had no problem with her missing the speech, but it was perceived among many in the Beltway that Abrams, facing voters at year's end, did not want to be associated with Biden and his low poll numbers. Abrams pointedly refused to reveal the alleged scheduling conflict, but people familiar with the decision said she had decided against attending the speech because she did not want to alienate the boycotting civil rights groups, knowing that she would need their full support that November.

The president took the stage on January 11, 2022, at a consortium of four historically Black colleges and universities with three target audiences for the speech: progressives, who wanted to see him fully committed to their most important issue; swing voters in Georgia, who could decide the fate of the Senate in 2022 and the White House in 2024; and, of course, Senators Manchin and Sinema, to see if they would change their minds about the filibuster.

Biden held nothing back.

He took square aim at his old home, his beloved US Senate, saying its traditions had been "abused."

"Sadly, the United States Senate, designed to be the world's greatest deliberative body, has been rendered a shell of its former self," Biden said.

He offered a full-throated endorsement of "getting rid" of the filibuster for voting rights, though he did not call for its complete elimination. His visit leaned hard on civil rights symbolism: it was held in John Lewis's old district, and Biden and Kamala Harris, the nation's first Black vice president, visited Ebenezer Baptist Church to see Raphael Warnock and pay respects to Dr. King's crypt. Invoking Trump, Biden told the audience that "the goal of the former president and his allies is to disenfranchise anyone who votes against them."

And then he went further.

"I ask every elected official in America: How do you want to be remembered?" Biden asked. "At consequential moments in history, they present a choice: Do you want to be on the side of Dr. King or George Wallace? Do you want to be on the side of John Lewis or Bull Connor? Do you want to be on the side of Abraham Lincoln or Jefferson Davis?"

Biden had equated opponents of Senate rule changes to slaveholders and drew a sharp line between men who fought for civil rights and those who fought to deny them.

Gasps could be heard in the crowd.

The reaction was predictably partisan. Republicans denounced the speech. Democrats deemed it a needed clarion call on a defining issue. Some pundits wondered if the Bull Connor reference had gone too far. Martin Luther King III, the oldest living son of the civil rights leader, and his wife, Arndrea Waters King, said they'd be "watching closely" to see if the Democrats got anything done. Manchin said Biden had delivered "a good speech" but added nothing further.

Sinema didn't say anything at all.

* * *

The Beast was already running.

The presidential limousine, nicknamed "The Beast," is a marvel of engineering. It has bulletproof armor, is sealed against a chemical attack, and weighs more than most trucks. It can, for a time, function as the seat of government. For informal trips, like to a golf course or out to dinner or church, presidents use an SUV version. But for official business, it's the limousine, which projects power and prestige.

And the limo's engine was already purring the morning of January 13, two days after the president's Atlanta speech. It was amid a motorcade of vehicles prepared for the short ride on Pennsylvania Avenue, where Biden was to attend a Senate Democratic luncheon at which he planned to ask all fifty members of the caucus to support changing Senate rules just for a carve out to allow voting rights legislation to pass. There was renewed momentum on the issue: the package of voting rights bills had just passed the House. A number of White House aides, and the traveling press pool, were already loaded in their vehicles and waiting for Biden. They planned to leave within minutes.

And then Sinema stood up to deliver a speech on the floor of the Senate.

With a few quick words, she let it be known that Biden could have saved himself the trip. She used the floor speech to once again reiterate her opposition to changing the filibuster, even in a one-time exception for voting rights. Her central argument was that the nation needed more bipartisanship and that a party-line vote to alter the filibuster would do more harm than any good that could come out of voting rights legislation.

"While I continue to support these bills, I will not support separate actions that worsen the underlying disease of division infecting our country," Sinema said. "We must address the disease itself, the disease of division, to protect our democracy, and it cannot be achieved by one party alone. It cannot be achieved solely by the federal government. The response requires something greater and, yes, more difficult than what the Senate is discussing today."

The fury from her fellow Democrats was palpable. Sinema had humiliated Biden, by not even giving him time to make his pitch before she pulled the plug on the voting rights efforts. She had given the White House a heads-up as to what she was going to say shortly before she delivered her speech, but that did nothing to calm other members of her party.

Senator Michael Bennet of Colorado declared that today's Senate was not "worthy of defense" and that it was "impossible to argue that this place functions better today than when Joe Biden was here." And Warnock, so central to the fight, likened this era's defense of the filibuster to efforts to block laws to end the Jim Crow era in the South.

"I don't think it was just because there were people who hated Black people," the Georgia senator said to reporters. "I think that often, in institutions like this, arguments about process and procedure somehow get in the way of seeing people's humanity."

But Sinema's speech delighted another senator with passionate views about the voting rights legislation.

"It was extraordinarily important and she has, with a conspicuous act of political courage, saved the Senate as an institution," Mitch McConnell said to reporters after the speech.

Despite the embarrassing setback, Biden made the trip and spoke to the caucus. He made little mention of the divisions in the Democrats' own ranks and instead focused on the Republicans' obstruction. The mood in the room was somber, several senators told others afterward. Sinema mostly stayed glued to her phone, not making much in the way of eye contact. Later, Manchin put out his own statement opposing any filibuster change, including a carve out for voting rights. White House aides were darkly grateful that he had at least waited until after the president spoke.

Biden looked visibly shell-shocked when he spoke to reporters later that day.

"I don't know whether we can get this done," he said. "But one thing is for certain—like every other major civil rights bill that came along, if we miss the first time, we can come back and try a second time.

"But I know one thing: As long as I have a breath in me, as long as I'm in the White House, as long as I'm engaged at all, I'm going to be fighting to change the way these legislatures have moved."

Biden made one more try that night, hosting both Manchin and

Sinema at the White House. Nothing came of it. It was a stinging rebuke for a president who had emphasized his long experience as a senator and his knowledge of how to get things done on Capitol Hill. Schumer delayed the vote, citing an incoming winter storm, meaning that the Democrats missed their Martin Luther King Jr. Day deadline. It was held the following week instead and the Democrats did not have the votes to break the GOP filibuster on the legislation. The voting rights bills were defeated.

The monthlong push on voting rights, culminating in the Georgia speech, had come up empty. Civil rights activists angrily blamed the White House's legislative sequencing, condemning the decision to place voting rights after other legislative priorities. The GOP-run states were free to keep passing legislation without fear of federal interference. The midterms were not even ten months away.

The Big Lie had helped secure a major victory.

* * *

As the battle over voting rights took center stage in the first weeks of 2022, the House of Representatives' Select Committee to Investigate the January 6th Attack on the United States Capitol continued to work, quietly and steadily.

A new sense of urgency had set in: the committee, from the start, had made clear that its mission was not just to probe what happened during the riot, but to prevent something like that from happening again. With Trump taking big steps back onto the political stage, the members knew their work was vital. If the former president had spurred on the riot, the investigation needed to show that, with clear facts, to make sure the American people realized that Trump was unfit to sit in the Oval Office again.

It had begun its work in the summer of 2021, with a series of intense, headline-grabbing public testimonials from Capitol police officers and other law enforcement who were injured during the riot. Then their work had moved mostly behind closed doors. Subpoenas were issued for the testimony and records from many of the most prominent members of Trump's inner circle: Steve Bannon, Mark Meadows, Roger Stone, Stephen Miller, Jeffrey Clark, Jason Miller, Kayleigh McEnany, and more. Some of the biggest names in the bunch, namely Bannon and Meadows, made a public show of refusing. The House voted to hold both Bannon and Meadows in contempt of Congress and sent along criminal referrals to the Department of Justice.

Trump railed against the proceedings constantly. He accused the committee of bias, of being a continuation of the same Democratic "witch hunt" that he claimed had dominated his time in office. He focused his wrath, publicly and privately, on the two Republicans, Liz Cheney and Adam Kinzinger, who he felt had betrayed him. The edict was clear from Mar-a-Lago: those in TrumpWorld should not cooperate with the probe.

But not everyone listened. As the committee broadened the scope of its probe, it began looking at midlevel White House aides, career government officials, and others who had been swept up in Trump's machinations. Many of them testified and handed over their records. Some senior staffers who had since turned on Trump, like communications director Alyssa Farah Griffin, did the same. And even those who refused to testify, like Meadows, found their text messages turned over to the committee and, sometimes, distributed to the public.

There were grumblings among some Democrats that the committee was moving too slowly. The political calendar was unrelenting: there would be no appetite for the work to continue into the fall of 2022, weeks before the midterm elections, so it needed to conclude and present its findings well before then. A push was made for public, potentially primetime hearings in June, to better show the American people the committee's findings. And there was growing impatience among many on the Left, including some in the White House, as to Attorney General Merrick Garland's slow pace in deciding whether to prosecute those who refused to cooperate.

But some of the documents the committee discovered were breathtaking. A PowerPoint presentation that recommended Trump declare a national security emergency to return himself to office. A document that urged Trump to claim a foreign government like China or Venezuela was trying to interfere with the election, giving him the ability to invoke emergency powers. A memo that outlined the scheme to install alternate electors. A plan later revealed by Bernard Kerik, the former New York City police commissioner and Giuliani ally, who told investigators that a scheme was concocted—but never utilized—to seize voting machines.

Mike Pence became a particular focal point. He had been at the center of the plan to overturn the election and had held his ground; some in the committee thought he might testify. But Pence opted against. Though in public remarks he continued to insist that he did the right thing on January 6, he was not going to risk his own political future by cooperating with a probe that most in the GOP felt was illegitimate. Some of Pence's aides, however, did cooperate.

But even without appearances from many of those most intimately involved in the scheme—and many of them would have invoked the Fifth Amendment and not said anything anyway—the committee used reams of documents and files and emails and text messages as it built its case. Trump moved to use executive privilege to block release of records, his lawyers claiming that they should stay shielded even though he was no longer in office. Biden rejected the claim, triggering the release of documents and White House visitor logs from January 6 to be turned over to the committee from the National Archives, where they were sent after Trump left office. An appeals court ruled against Trump. And then, in February 2022, it was discovered that Trump had wrongly absconded to Mar-a-Lago with boxes of documents that should have been sent to the National Archives. Some of them were deemed classified, prompting spasms of outrage from Democrats who remembered what a flashpoint Hillary Clinton's handling of classified information was during the 2016 campaign. Some of this material, too, was sent to the January 6 committee.

And then late one night in early March, a court filing was quietly released that suddenly brought the contours of the shadowy investigation into the light. In the filing, the House committee argued that former president Trump and members of his campaign were part of a conspiracy to overturn the 2020 election results. The language was simple: the committee "has a good-faith basis for concluding that the President and members of his Campaign engaged in a criminal conspiracy to defraud the United States."

Criminal conspiracy.

The filing mostly focused on John Eastman, the conservative lawyer, and his plan to overturn the election results, and it made the claim that Trump and his team may have tried to enact "a corrupt scheme to obstruct the counting of electoral college ballots and a conspiracy to impede the transfer of power," the committee said in a statement. It was the most direct line yet that the committee had tried to draw connecting Trump, his allies, and potential criminal activity surrounding the election. Three distinct crimes were cited: obstruction of an official proceeding, interfering in election certification, and spreading false information about the results. But determining whether Trump violated criminal law on January 6 would be a complex undertaking, and a tricky calculus emerges when considering charging a former president.

Trump's lawyers downplayed the filing, and the ex-president railed against it, using his not particularly clever nickname for the congressional body investigating the riot.

"The actual conspiracy to defraud the United States was the Democrats rigging the Election, and the Fake News Media and the Unselect

Committee covering it up," he said. And then he may have tipped his hand about his true concern.

"The Unselect Committee's sole goal is to try to prevent President Trump, who is leading by large margins in every poll, from running again for president, if I so choose."

* * *

The White House tried to regroup.

After the defeat of the voting rights measures on Capitol Hill, anger rippled through some quarters on the Left. Biden was chastened. Civil rights groups were furious: they felt abandoned, but vowed to fight on.

"Anything short of protecting the right to vote is a death sentence for democracy," said Derrick Johnson, the NAACP president. "This fight is far from over."

The weekly White House meeting on voting rights continued, as did efforts within the Democratic campaign arm. They would proceed on two tracks: while the push for overarching federal legislation was not going to be abandoned, there was recognition that it was unlikely to pass in 2022 with the current makeup of the Congress. Other avenues would have to be pursued to safeguard the vote.

Within the White House, there was a mixture of frustration and resignation. Some Biden aides thought that too much was being made of the states' efforts to change election laws; Republicans had tried this before, a few thought, and would again. Others acknowledged that when Democrats were in power at the state level, their party was also not above efforts, like gerrymandering, to stack the deck. Within the West Wing, there was also some annoyance around how the process had played out, and not just at Sinema and Manchin (although both of them, to be clear, were not exactly beloved at 1600 Pennsylvania Avenue). There was a lot of second-guessing about HR1, the messaging bill that never stood a chance, because it was so expansive; it gave

Republicans an easy target that enabled them to paint all the voting bills—even more modest ones—with the same extremist brush. There also was a sense that if a federal bill had passed, it likely would have been tied up in the courts through the midterms and potentially tossed by the conservative-leaning Supreme Court.

The focus shifted. First, Democrats needed to repair relations with some in the civil rights community to make sure they would be engaged and motivated in elections going forward. Second, they would need to focus on turnout, to push voters to the polls in such huge numbers that they would be able to withstand the obstacles and legal challenges sure to be put in their paths by the new state laws. Third, they'd need to draw lessons from how local officials and business leaders pushed back against the GOP in states like Arizona and Georgia; they'd need to cultivate other civic-minded individuals and organizations to do the same. And fourth, they'd need to restore the American people's faith in the election system; polls suggested that the onslaught of rhetoric about rigged elections had led even some Democrats to doubt their trustworthiness.

And attention shifted to a smaller piece of legislation that had a narrow aim: to eliminate the provision by which Trump and his allies tried to have Pence block Biden's victory.

The vice president's role in the certification of the results was based in the ambiguously phrased Electoral Count Act of 1887 and barely considered again until Eastman and other Trump advisers concocted the plan to have Pence throw out some states' electors. The new legislation would eliminate the loopholes and make clear that the vice president's role was only ceremonial. It picked up support on both sides of the aisle, including from Joe Manchin, Lisa Murkowski, and Susan Collins.

"The peaceful transfer of power shouldn't require heroes," Collins wrote in a February 2022 op-ed endorsing the measure.

The White House signaled support for the revision; it was small but necessary. The lack of progress on larger voting rights legislation ate at Biden, who truly feared that the nation's democracy could slip away if things didn't change soon. More than most on his staff, he still believed that some Republicans were redeemable. He remembered how Washington used to work. He wasn't naive; he realized things had changed. But he was dismayed that they had changed this much.

"I still think enough Republicans will stand up and do the right thing," Biden told a close confidant in early 2022 after the voting rights effort failed. "But I'm less confident than I was a year ago."

* * *

Arizona. Georgia. Iowa. Florida.

The Trump rallies were back. Beginning in the second half of 2021 and accelerating as the political world raced into a midterm year, Trump began hitting the road again as an in-your-face display of his continued sway over the Republican Party. Gone was Air Force One, gone was "YMCA" as the closing song. One other change: for a little while, Trump touted the COVID-19 vaccines and booster shots, only to abandon that take when it was met with indifference and even hostility by some in his crowd. He had created the MAGA monster but he couldn't always control it.

But so much was the same. Biden was weak, Democrats were socialists who loved crime, Republicans needed to be tough on immigration, and he had won the 2020 election. Yep, he was still at it. In dark and divisive speeches, he continued to rail against his defeat, claiming without evidence that the result had been rigged. And he demanded Republicans toe the same line. In a Texas rally in late January 2022, the state's lieutenant governor, Dan Patrick, called out, "Well, we all know who won in 2020, don't we? Who won?"

No one in the crowd seemed to think it was Joe Biden. At an Arizona rally weeks earlier, Trump was even blunter.

"The Big Lie is a lot of bullshit," were among the former president's first words, ones that were greeted with rapturous applause.

"I ran twice and we won twice and we did better the second time. We did much better the second time," Trump said.

The crowds ate it up. These were the diehards, people who lived their lives safely nestled in a Fox News cocoon. The Big Lie was dogma. The former president mocked Democrats' concerns about the insurrection and instead continued to repeat claims of election improprieties and that the other party had taken advantage of the pandemic to steal the election with fraudulent mail-in voting.

"Why aren't they investigating November 3, a rigged and stolen election?" he said. "The people are very angry. They got duped and they found out what happened. The people have to be free to find the answers and if not, they will never trust again and our country will be absolutely decimated."

At the Texas rally, Trump floated the idea of pardons for the January 6 rioters were he to become president again. He portrayed those who had desecrated the US Capitol as some sort of martyrs, victims of overzealous Democratic persecution. The suggestion was met with rare pushback from Republicans, many of whom seemed to feel that the Capitol riot was one of the very few safe spaces from which to criticize the former president. The story died down after a day or two.

But the attempts to read the tea leaves did not. Did Trump hint that he was going to run for president again in 2024?

Though the presidential race was years away, speculation had already begun about the possible front-runners. Biden would be eighty-one years old on Election Day 2024. During the 2020 campaign, he had privately talked about being a "transition" president, and some aides even briefly considered a pledge that he would serve only one term. But since taking office, he had publicly declared that he planned to run again. Of course, he had to do that: declaring he would not would immediately make him a lame duck and curtail his political clout. Privately, though, many of his closest allies wondered about Biden's ability to withstand the rigors of another run: the job already seemed to age him, and he wouldn't be able to campaign from his basement the next time.

And one thing a divided Washington agreed upon: if Biden opted not to run, the Democratic field would not clear for Harris. The vice president had a series of political setbacks and little to show for her role leading the administration's efforts on immigration and, of course, voting rights. It was an inherently thankless job and she had a tough portfolio. She had undeniable strengths but loads of Democrats would be expected to line up to run against her, including some familiar faces from 2020.

But it was the speculation about Trump's future that truly ran rampant. There were some Republicans who wished he would stop litigating 2020 and focus on the future, but they largely remained silent. The Big Lie wasn't going to hurt Trump's chances at the presidency among Republicans; it might only enhance them. The party remained his. He offered teases and hints about running. One day at his Florida golf course, a passerby asked if he could take a photo with the "forty-fifth president." Trump smirked and responded, "forty-fifth *and* forty-seventh." His new exit song at the end of rallies? A 1966 classic from Sam and Dave whose title was viewed by many as both a hint and a reassuring message to his supporters: "Hold On, I'm Comin'." Be patient, Trump seemed to be saying. I'll be back soon.

In private conversations, he would quiz aides and advisers as to the best moment to announce his candidacy, even though he would talk in ambiguous circles and never fully commit to another campaign. He did wonder about his health, and he didn't want to risk losing twice, although, of course, he wasn't admitting that he had lost even once. Some of his allies urged him to do so sooner than later, reasoning that declaring might ease his legal jeopardy; it would already be a huge leap to indict a former president, but even more of one to target the front-runner for the GOP nomination.

The swirling multiple investigations were never far from Trump's mind. Though the January 6 committee's investigation posed some political peril, the former president was more unnerved by the dueling probes underway in Manhattan—one civil, one criminal—into the Trump Organization, led by the New York State attorney general and the Manhattan district attorney, respectively. He didn't like the pressure on his business or his family. Neither was certain to bring a case, particularly the Manhattan DA. But he instructed his lawyers to fight.

He waited to decide on 2024. He knew that if he were to jump in, even late, he'd be the overwhelming front-runner for the GOP nomination. He also knew that if he opted not to run, the moment he made that official would be the very moment his clout within the GOP would begin to fade. So, he waited. There was no harm in waiting.

Except to the other Republicans with eyes on the White House. Trump had frozen the field.

* * *

The conundrum for the rest of the possible 2024 GOP field was obvious: if someone was to declare a candidacy without waiting for Trump, that person risked alienating the most powerful—and vengeful—voice in the Republican Party. Moreover, they knew their potential opponents were also paying close attention to the degree of loyalty they showed to the former president. Some likely 2024 contenders created campaigns-in-waiting—hiring trusted advisers, meeting with donors, and visiting all-important primary states despite knowing it could all be for nothing if the former president entered the race. But few dared acknowledge that they would plunge ahead if Trump ran.

Some White House hopefuls, like Nikki Haley, the former South Carolina governor and Trump's ambassador to the United Nations, made a trip to Mar-a-Lago and explicitly said they would not run if Trump did. Others, like Florida senator Marco Rubio and South Dakota governor Kristi Noem, were slightly more subtle, declaring that if Trump ran, he would be the party's nominee and would have their support. The list went on: Senators Josh Hawley and Tim Scott also suggested that they would bow out if Trump announced a candidacy.

A few broke ranks. Chris Christie didn't commit to running but said he would make his eventual decision without factoring in Trump. Mike Pompeo, Trump's former secretary of state, traveled to those key early primary states, Iowa and New Hampshire, and refused to rule out a bid.

And in early 2022, a series of polls showed Florida governor Ron DeSantis emerging as Trump's most potent intraparty contender. This rankled Trump; he had "made DeSantis," he told others, with an endorsement that had propelled him to the governor's mansion in Tallahassee. Plus, Trump was a Florida Man now and he didn't like the backyard insurgency. Florida was without question the new spiritual home for Trump's Republican Party; but the state wasn't big enough for the both of them, Trump thought. DeSantis also toned down some of his formerly fawning rhetoric about Trump and made the political calculation to—somehow—move to the right of Trump on a number of pandemic issues, including fighting local districts over mask mandates in schools, upbraiding a group of high school kids for sporting face coverings as they stood behind him for a photo op, and refusing to say whether he had received a COVID-19 booster shot. Even for Trump, that was too much, and he demanded that everyone should have to say whether they had gotten a booster or not (Trump had). And most galling of all to Trump: DeSantis was no longer showing him the proper deference and refused to proclaim—to say the "magic words," Trump told associates—that he would not run if the former president did.

And then there was the curious case of Mike Pence.

On Election Day 2020, it would have been hard to imagine that Pence, the epitome of a loyal vice president, would ever cross Trump, and downright unthinkable that he would challenge him for the Republican nomination. But after January 6, their dynamic was irrevocably altered, and Pence began eyeing the terrain in Iowa, New Hampshire, and South Carolina. Trump was less worried about Pence, who he thought had burned bridges with much of the conservative base for failing to go along with the plan to overturn the election. That still infuriated the former president who, in a classic case of saying the quiet part out loud, all but confessed to his electoral scheme in a statement shortly after the first anniversary of the insurrection, declaring of Pence that, "Unfortunately, he didn't exercise that power, he could have overturned the Election!"

But as Pence moved to possibly take on his former boss, he continued to defend his decision. His aides scheduled an address to a chapter of the influential conservative group the Federalist Society and previewed to reporters that Pence would take a stand. And he did just that, declaring, "President Trump is wrong.

"I had no right to overturn the election," Pence told the crowd gathered in Orlando. "The presidency belongs to the American people, and the American people alone. And frankly there is almost no idea more un-American than the notion that any one person could choose the American president."

Op-ed boards and media pundits praised Pence for doing the right thing, for affirming his commitment to the rule of law. Tellingly, his comments were met with near silence by the conservative crowd.

But there were roars from another GOP crowd, gathered in that same Florida city three weeks later.

*　*　*

"We did it twice, and we'll do it again. We're going to be doing it again a third time."

It wasn't quite a declaration of a 2024 run at the White House but it wasn't far off. Trump, just over a year after allegedly being sent off to political exile, was the star attraction at the Conservative Political Action

Conference's annual meeting in late February 2022. He wore his familiar blue suit and his trademark red tie; he sported a tan. Maybe he had lost a little weight since the last time many in the audience had seen him. But, really, little had changed. It was his show.

Over the last two decades, CPAC had become a bellwether for where the Republican Party stood. It drew a who's who of the Right, particularly the Far Right, where GOP donors and activists and superfans gathered to revel in the conservative buzz of the moment. Formerly held in Washington, it too had relocated to Florida to be in line with the current GOP zeitgeist. And the conference held a special significance for Trump: in his first appearance there, back in 2011, he had delivered a speech that electrified the crowd and, to many, was the first sign of his possible political power. The groundwork for his eventual presidency, some of his closest aides believe, was laid in that speech.

His hold over the audience had only grown eleven years later. His speech was the only time the cavernous conference room was full all weekend. Many of the attendees at CPAC believed Trump had been robbed in 2020. He easily won the straw poll asking whom the attendees wanted to be the next nominee, usually a good read on the pulse of the party.

Trump flags hung from right-wing media booths where the former president's allies and former White House officials talked about "America First" policy, raged against culture war issues, and railed on the Biden administration. Bedazzled MAGA hats and "Trump was right" buttons were spotted everywhere. Supporters ignored other events to try to work their way into a free VIP reception with Trump. The menu? A buffet of his favorite McDonald's fast-food items.

It felt like a campaign speech, two years before the 2024 primary season was to officially begin. Of course, he launched into the familiar grievance-filled tirade that the election was stolen from him. But he also looked ahead, touching on current events. He slammed the Biden administration's handling of inflation and the border. And he ignored his own fawning words for Putin to claim that Biden's withdrawal from Afghanistan emboldened Russia to invade Ukraine.

And he played to the crowd's desire for him to run again, at one point declaring, "As your president . . ." and then stopping to soak in a thunderous ovation. He spoke like a candidate. And he finished his speech just as he had done so many times before.

"We will make America powerful again," Trump said. "We will make America wealthy again. We will make America strong again. We will make America proud again. We will make America safe again.

"And we will make America great again."

It was 2016. It was 2020. It was 2024.

* * *

Biden was still tinkering with the speech on his ride to the Capitol.

The last time he had made this precise journey, he was dealt a stinging defeat by members of his own party on the push for voting rights. This time, he made the trip to deliver his first State of the Union address, in which he again would rail against Republican efforts to restrict the access to the ballot.

"The most fundamental right in America is the right to vote—and to have it counted," Biden said. "And it's under assault. In state after state, new laws have been passed, not only to suppress the vote—we've been there before—but to subvert entire elections."

But in a reflection of the moment's political reality, Biden didn't dwell on concrete measures to protect the ballot. He offered only a brief endorsement of federal legislation that had little chance to succeed due to fellow Democrats' continued opposition to filibuster reform. It was an implicit acknowledgment that the battle for democracy at home had been delivered a setback. This night, though, Biden needed to rally the nation to help defend democracy abroad.

It was not the speech the president and his team had planned to give. But after Russia invaded Ukraine, the topics that had once been front and center—COVID-19, inflation, and economic recovery—took a back seat, in another reflection of a presidency that had been forced to respond to events rather than shape them. He was able to tout his new Supreme Court pick, Ketanji Brown Jackson, whom he had nominated just days before to be the first Black woman on the nation's highest court. Biden had fulfilled the promise he had made to Jim Clyburn nearly two years before, a promise that had helped lead him to that very moment, in which he addressed the nation as president.

But his focus was the war raging an ocean away. Biden vowed that the United States would emerge from years of division and disease to protect and expand freedoms at home and abroad.

"While it shouldn't have taken something so terrible for people around the world to see what's at stake, now everyone sees it clearly," the president said. "In the battle between democracy and autocracy, democracies are rising to the moment, and the world is clearly choosing the side of peace and security."

The central premise of the Biden presidency was being played out in real time. The United States, he believed, needed to prove that its own government could work so that it could unite with democracies around the globe to push back on rising authoritarianism. Putin may have thought that the United States' withdrawal from Afghanistan meant that he had free rein to move in. But he was also clearly inspired by what he saw as the aftermath of Trump's four years: strained alliances, deep divisions at home, doubts about the integrity of democracy itself. That, too, was a legacy of the Big Lie.

But in the war's first weeks, the alliances held. Trump praised Putin for being savvy, an assertion briefly amplified by the fringes of the conservative media and movement, only to be drowned out by a number of Republicans who denounced the Russian president as a dictator. At least on matters of Russia, much of the GOP was still willing to defy the former president. But Trump hovered over the war, with Western allies uncertain if they could count on America to continue to stand with them after the next election.

Biden delivered his speech against the backdrop of a pandemic that ignored borders and had touched every corner of the globe for the past two years. It came a year after an insurrection, the aftershocks still felt. Trump was back, inflation was rising, trust in government sinking. Biden had been in Washington a long time, had achieved the pinnacle of power, had been tasked with steering the nation through an unimaginable series of crises. But he still thought of himself as a guy from Wilmington, a guy who understood average Americans, a guy who talked plainly and made sense. He knew Americans were tired and frustrated, that the nation was divided as it had been few times before. He knew harder times could lie ahead.

It was not a time for soaring rhetoric. It was a time for a simple message, one that acknowledged the hard times but offered reassurance, that still believed that the experiment that was American democracy, though battered, would not fall. He delivered that message midway through his speech.

"I know the news about what's happening can seem alarming," Biden said.

"But I want you to know that we are going to be okay." The nation hoped he was right.

* * *

The Big Lie was born in 2016. Over the next six years, the man who gave it life used it to undermine the nation's faith in its civic institutions and in the process of democracy itself. It had, via cable news, corrupted viewers and inspired dictators. It was faithfully repeated by political allies who were afraid of Trump and his followers. It was used to justify an abuse of power and the workings of government. It had challenged Democrats to battle among themselves to protect the ballot.

It inspired an insurrection at the US Capitol, posing the greatest threat to the republic itself since the Civil War.

And it lives on.

It dominated the Trump White House and shaped Biden's presidency. It was used to justify restricting access to the ballot and put the battle for voting rights center stage again. It hovered over the Democratic agenda and posed as a litmus test for Republicans. It was a defining issue for the 2022 midterms and, no matter who is on the ballot, will be for the 2024 presidential campaign. It threatened to undermine Americans' faith in every election going forward.

The Big Lie was now officially doctrine within the Republican Party.

The Republican National Committee held its annual winter meeting in Salt Lake City in February 2022 and made clear, in no uncertain terms, who was the leader of the party. The GOP censured Cheney and Kinzinger, the Republicans who had most loudly attacked Trump and his lies, condemning them specifically for being part of the January 6 committee, which, the party said, was participating in the "persecution of ordinary citizens engaged in legitimate political discourse."

Legitimate. Political. Discourse.

The Capitol riot, an explosion of violence at the most sacred space in American democracy, was now being explained away as a form of legitimate political discourse. A fatal insurrection was being rationalized and justified. There was some pushback, as a few Republicans objected to the language. And after the vote, party leaders aimed to clarify the resolution, saying it did not apply to the mob that stormed the Capitol.

But that wasn't true. The censure was carefully negotiated in private among party members and made no distinction between the rioters and anything else that happened on January 6. The language was enshrined in official party policy. It was the strongest effort yet to minimize Trump's actions in the moments before the insurrection. Republicans had forcefully—and officially—turned on two of their own for daring to condemn what Trump did.

Coming just over a year after the insurrection, the censure in many ways completed the GOP's journey. The Republican Party had allowed itself to be hijacked by Trump, tethering itself to him to fulfill its agenda while turning a blind eye to his tumult and lies. And in just twelve months' time, party leaders had gone from condemning the Capitol attack, and Trump himself, to downplaying it, and finally to coming to terms with it.

It was now part of the Republican Party's core belief: the actions and lies that led to the insurrection, and the violence itself, were acceptable.

The Big Lie was who they were.

ACKNOWLEDGMENTS

These next few pages have long stood as the most daunting of the entire book to write, for there is no question that I will fail in adequately expressing my heartfelt thanks to so many people who have supported me over the years. This is a team effort—the book is, life is, everything is. And I've been blessed with the best teammates and can only hope that I've made you proud. These brief words of thanks will not nearly convey the depth of my gratitude. My apologies, also, for those I will surely forget to thank. Any omission is the fault of fatigue and deadlines and not a lack of appreciation for all that you have done over the years.

None of this, or anything, would be possible without my wife, Carrie Melago. She is my partner, my most trusted adviser, my first editor. She has been there with me every step of the way and has supported me at every turn. She is a remarkable journalist whose judgment I value above all others. She is a wonderful mother, whom our two boys are lucky to have; candidly, we'd be lost without her. She takes on so much and sacrifices so much and always puts others' needs first. She also makes me laugh like no one else. Thank you, Carrie. I couldn't do it without you.

To my sons, Beckett and Flynn: I love you. Every day, I am reminded how lucky I am to be your dad. My favorite thing in the world is to play with you and cheer you on and watch you grow into such sweet boys. You both make me proud every day, and you are the world to me. Everything, it's all for you. I can't wait to see what's next.

I owe more than I can possibly to say to my parents, Robert and Susan Lemire. You both instilled in me a love of history, politics, and the written word. But my parents did far more for me than just teach me to love and care about the news. They supported and loved me and trusted me no matter what decisions I made, and they have been there every step of the way as wonderful confidants, sounding boards, and grandparents. My father is the most electric teacher I know, his eyes alive at bringing the past to life. My mother is the kindest person I have ever met. Thank you forever.

A lucky thing is when your brother is your best friend. Joe Lemire has been my closest pal and confidant since the moment he was born. We have the same mannerisms, can finish each other's sentences, and inevitably share the same panicked concerns about the Boston sports teams. He is an extraordinary guy, a terrific journalist, a wonderful father. He is outrageously funny and also never complains when I constantly beat him in Wiffle ball and Tecmo Super Bowl. Thank you, Joe.

I am extraordinarily fortunate to be blessed with so many friends and to have worked at a number of remarkable places. It'll be impossible to name everyone, but let me try my best to give even a semblance of the appropriate gratitude.

First, my thanks to those who made this book possible, namely my patient and brilliant and kind editor, Zachary Wagman. You believed in me and the idea and helped shepherd it through. Thank you. And to the rest of your team at Flatiron Books: Bob Miller, Megan Lynch, Maxine Charles, Marlena Bittner, Nancy Trypuc, and Alexus Blanding. Thanks also to Elisa Rivlin and my fact-checker Ben Kalin for your careful eyes.

Let me also praise the remarkable team at Creative Artists Agency, starting with David Larabell and Alan Berger. Thank you for taking a chance on me when I didn't have any TV or book experience to my name and for making me feel like part of the team at CAA. You have been valuable resources, advocates, sounding boards, and friends.

MSNBC has become a second home to me and not just because I spend more hours at the studios each morning than I do in my apartment. The *Morning Joe* and *Way Too Early* teams are more than co-workers, they are family. They have the hardest jobs in news and they do it with grace and humor and lots and lots of coffee. Don't kid yourself, folks: it's early. Joe Scarborough and Mika Brzezinski, thank you for an opportunity of a lifetime and so many smart conversations and deep laughs. I can never express my gratitude enough. Willie Geist, thank you for being a friend and sounding board and someone who never hits the wrong note. Mike Barnicle hates being thanked and will really hate when I take this moment to note that he's one of the most generous people I have ever met. Alex Korson and Dan Norwick have some of the toughest gigs in TV yet bring their A game each day long before the sun is up. Cat Rakowski: thanks for being a dear friend and for being so damn good at your job. And thanks also to the rest of the *MJ* family, including Rachel Campbell, Michael del Moro, Lauren Schweitzer, Adam Tzanis, Mike Buczkiewicz, Liza Anderson, Eliza Ranieri, Meg Gillan, Drew Katchen, and Ali Bonaviso.

Thank you, of course, to Rashida Jones for your leadership at MSNBC and support and for giving me this chance. I can't wait to see what the future holds. So many people at the network have taught me so much; thank you for letting me be a small part of the legacy of NBC News and MSNBC. I have far too many people to thank for their friendship and generosity, but I shall try my best: Nicolle Wallace, Brian Williams, Katy Tur, Andrea Mitchell, Jesse Rodriguez, Phil Griffin, Jeff Shell, Cesar Conde, Elena Nachmanoff, Jessica Kurdali, Hallie Jackson, Chuck Todd, Stephanie Ruhle, Chris Hayes, Eddie Glaude, Elise Jordan, Richard Haass, Reverend Al Sharpton, Steve Rattner, Jon Meacham, Kasie Hunt, John Heilemann, Katty Kay, Alex

Witt, Peter Alexander, Kristen Welker, Ali Vitali, Kelly O'Donnell, Chris Matthews, Mike Memoli, Liza Pluto, Querry Robinson, Marci Santiago, Eric Greenberg, Laura Roberts, Paul Driscoll, Joey Barroso, and Tammy Caputo.

I have been so fortunate to hit the ground running at *Politico*, a place that will always have my gratitude for welcoming me with open arms. The place does sharp, powerful, terrific work, and I'm glad to be aboard. Thank you, in particular, to Matt Kaminski. My thanks also to Sam Stein for being a friend who is also a smart editor with no shortage of story ideas or ability to make my copy a little punchier. My thanks to my White House team: Laura Barrón-López, Eugene Daniels, Chris Cadelago, Alex Thompson, Max Tani, and Adam Cancryn. And a few of the other sharp, hardworking journalists at *Politico*: Meridith McGraw, Burgess Everett, Elana Schor, Emily Cadei, Karey Van Hall, Ryan Lizza, Rachael Bade, Daniel Lippman, and Dafna Linzer.

The Associated Press has done arguably the most important, vital, and far-reaching journalism in the world, not just today but throughout its storied history. I say with no exaggeration that it was a true honor to spend eight years there and it will always be part of me. My thanks begin with Julie Pace, who believed in me when I was a young White House reporter and was my most tireless advocate. Thank you to Nancy Benac and Michael Tackett, who never failed to make my stories better and who are just as good people as they are editors. My thanks to David Scott and Steven Sloan for leading the way during the two most extraordinary and exhausting presidential campaigns we've ever seen. To the extraordinary White House team, thank you for sharing the story of a lifetime with me; plus, I can't think of anyone else with whom I'd want to sit in a cramped booth. My thanks to Zeke Miller, Jill Colvin, Darlene Superville, Josh Boak, Aamer Madhani, Alexandra Jaffe, Ken Thomas, Julie Bykowicz, Kevin Freking, and Vivian Salama. And a special "hey, buddy" to Evan Vucci; there is no one I'd rather have had alongside for this wild ride. Thanks, pal, I've learned more from you than I'll ever admit.

My everlasting gratitude to all of those who make the AP the essential place that is, I learned from all of you: Colleen Long, Andrew Harnik, Bob Furlow, Lisa Mascaro, Michelle Price, Steve Peoples, Lisa Lerer, Bill Barrow, Thomas Beaumont, Kathleen Hennessey, Jennifer Peltz, Jake Pearson, Jim Mustian, Gary Pruitt, Brian Carovillano, Noreen Gillespie, Wendy Benjaminson, David Ake, Lauren Easton, and Sally Buzbee. And a special nod to those who gave me my start at AP: James Martinez, Amanda Barrett, David Caruso, and Karen Testa Wong.

Though Washington has a reputation for being a cutthroat place, I can't say enough about the generosity shown to me by so many others on the White House and political beats. I'm proud to be in the same profession and proud that many of you are my friends. I have learned so much. My thanks to Sopan Deb, Eli Stokols, Michael Bender, Reid Epstein, Nick Corasaniti, Jerome Cartillier, Steve Holland, Jeff Mason, James Oliphant, Josh Wingrove, Justin Sink, Jordan Fabian, Jennifer Jacobs, Annmarie Hordern, Josh Dawsey, Ashley Parker, Seung Min Kim, Phil Rucker, Tyler Pager, Robert Costa, Bob Woodward, Maggie Haberman, Peter Baker, Michael Shear, Michael Grynbaum, Matt Flegenheimer, Doug Mills, Annie Karni, Ted Mann, Julie Mason, Mike Allen, Jake Sherman, Anna Palmer, Margaret Talev, Roberta Rampton, Yamiche Alcindor, and Jeremy Diamond.

The *New York Daily News* remains the lifeblood of the greatest city in the world and I'm proud to have gotten my start there. Beginning my career there exposed me to so much, and not just City Hall, the NYPD, and FDNY. It was a privilege to tell the stories of the people who live there, their triumphs and tragedies, as the city faced its greatest tests. I'm so grateful to have worked alongside—and against!—so many legends at the city's papers. Just to name a few: Kerry Burke, Wil Cruz, Zach

Haberman, Pete Donohue, Tom Namako, Amber Sutherland-Namako, Oren Yaniv, Perry Chiaramonte, Dean Chang, Kirsten Danis, Jere Hester, Henry Goldman, Yoav Gonen, Erica Orden, Sara Germano, Grace Rauh, Jillian Jorgensen, Mara Gay, Anna Sanders, Rocco Parascandola, Joe Kemp, Sean Gardiner, John Doyle, Azi Paybarah, Joel Siegel, Ian Bishop, Thomas DeFrank, Adam Lisberg, and Erin Durkin.

My deepest love and thanks to the rest of my extended family, who have been such a remarkable support system for my entire life: Rita Lemire, Stephen Lemire, Gary and Margaret Persichetti, Ed and Judy Lemire, Richard and Mary Beth Lemire, Dan and Brenda O'Brien, Marian O'Brien, Howard and Mary Patton, Penelope Lemire, Spike and Linda Melago, and Tim and Kathy Melago. And the cousins: Matt, Tom, Sean, Justin, Jessica, Sarah, Robert, Laura, Ashley, Grace. And I miss you: Red, Anna, Moe, and Gerry.

My thanks to my support systems at Columbia University, namely Alex Sachare and Greg Corsico, and all of those at the *Columbia Daily Spectator*. It was my first newspaper, and I learned so much. It was an honor to attend such an extraordinary school. And my thanks also to the teachers and friends (and track team) at Central Catholic High School as well as those at Ste Jeanne d'Arc school in Lowell.

It's hard to put into words my gratitude for these friends who have been with me for years and years. These guys don't fit into any neat box, they have simply been there when I have needed them the most: Colby Hamilton, Andrew Pagano, Dan Rosen, John Lauinger, Lee Baler, Josh Fay-Hurvitz, Mike Mirer, Marc Dunkelman, Leo Lopez, and Jonathan Selib.

And, lastly, thanks to the 2004 Boston Red Sox. You really did change my life.

SOURCES

This book primarily emerged from my nearly seven years of covering the White House, President Donald Trump, President Joe Biden, and the 2016 and 2020 presidential campaigns for the Associated Press, MSNBC, and *Politico*, as well as my coverage of then–private citizen Trump for several years with the *New York Daily News*. It is grounded and informed by both on-the-record and background interviews with dozens of administration and campaign officials, lawmakers, elected officials, informal advisers, and friends. I thank them for sharing memories, documents, messages, and photographs. The book also draws from Twitter, Factbase, and the Trump Twitter Archive, as well as the archives of the Associated Press and NBC News.

In addition, I relied on the following published and broadcast sources, often in more than one chapter.

PROLOGUE: "RIGGED"

"Arnold Sports Festival 2016: Everything You Need To Know." WBNS 10 CBS (Columbus), February 26, 2016.

Berenson, Tessa. "Donald Trump: 'The Election's Going to Be Rigged.'" *Time*, August 1, 2016.

"January 6 Insurrection: The *Washington Post*'s Investigation." *Washington Post*, 2021.

Lemire, Jonathan. "Trump Suggests General Election Could Be 'Rigged.'" Associated Press, August 1, 2016.

Lemire, Jonathan, Brian Slodysko, and Zeke Miller. "Biden Blasts 'Un-American' Voting Limits; Texas Dems Act." Associated Press, July 13, 2021.

Vitali, Ali. "Trump Says He's 'Afraid' Election Is 'About to Be Rigged.'" NBC News, August 1, 2016.

I: THE BEGINNING

Blake, Aaron. "A Brief History of World Leaders Laughing at Trump." *Washington Post*, December 4, 2019.

Chozick, Amy, and Michael Barbaro. "Hillary Clinton, Mocking and Taunting in Debate, Turns the Tormentor." *New York Times*, October 19, 2016.

Colvin, Jill, and Jonathan Lemire. "Trump Closes Door on One Falsehood, Opens Door to Another." Associated Press, September 17, 2016.

Diamond, Jeremy. "Trump: 'I'm Afraid the Election's Going to Be Rigged.'" CNN, August 1, 2016.

"Donald Trump Stumps in Mechanicsburg." *York Daily Record*, August 2, 2016.

"Full Transcript: Third 2016 Presidential Debate." *Politico*, October 19, 2016.

Gibney, Alex. "Meet the Leader of Eliot Spitzer's Smear Campaign." *Atlantic*, October 13, 2010.

Healy, Patrick, and Jonathan Martin. "Donald Trump Won't Say if He'll Accept Result of Election." *New York Times*, October 19, 2016.

Kessler, Glenn. "Trump's Outrageous Claim That 'Thousands' of New Jersey Muslims Celebrated the 9/11 Attacks." *Washington Post*, November 22, 2015.

Lemire, Jonathan. "Trump Suggests General Election Could Be 'Rigged.'" Associated Press, August 1, 2016.

Lemire, Jonathan, and Zeke Miller. "Trump Challenges UN, Boasting of America's Go-It-Alone Might." Associated Press, September 25, 2018.

Nash, Charlie. "Roger Stone on the *Milo Show*: How Trump Can Fight Voter Fraud." Breitbart, July 29, 2016.

Pace, Julie, and Lisa Lerer. "Debate Stunner: Trump Won't Say He'll Accept Election Result." Associated Press, October 19, 2016.

Toobin, Jeffrey. "The Dirty Trickster." *New Yorker*, May 23, 2008.

Walker, Shaun. "Vladimir Putin Calls Donald Trump a 'Very Colourful and Talented Man.'" *Guardian*, December 17, 2015.

Weigel, David. "For Trump, a New 'Rigged' System: The Election Itself." *Washington Post*, August 2, 2016.

Yee, Vivian. "Donald Trump's Math Takes His Towers to Greater Heights." *New York Times*, November 1, 2016.

Zeitz, Joshua. "Why Do They Hate Her?" *Politico Magazine*, June 3, 2017.

2: 2016

"Billion Dollar Blowup." *People*, February 1990.

Blake, John. "Of Course Presidents Lie." CNN, November 24, 2013.

Buettner, Russ, and Charles V. Bagli. "How Donald Trump Bankrupted His Atlantic City Casinos, but Still Earned Millions." *New York Times*, June 11, 2016.

Cathey, Libby. "Legacy of Lies—How Trump Weaponized Mistruths during His Presidency." ABC News, January 20, 2021.

"Chapter 11 for Taj Mahal." Reuters, July 18, 1991.

Colvin, Jill. "Trump Shrugs Off Widespread Outrage over Proposed Muslim Ban." Associated Press, December 9, 2015.

Crary, David. "New Burst of Attention for Old Doubts about Obama." Associated Press, July 23, 2009.

D'Addario, Daniel, and Joyce Lee. "How *The Apprentice* Shaped Donald Trump's 2016 Presidential Campaign." *Time*, June 21, 2016.

DelReal, Jose A., and Katie Zezima. "Trump's Personal, Racially Tinged Attacks on Federal Judge Alarm Legal Experts." *Washington Post*, June 1, 2016.

Dovere, Edward-Isaac. "How Clinton Lost Michigan—and Blew the Election." *Politico*, December 14, 2016.

Enrich, David. "The Money behind Trump's Money." *New York Times*, February 4, 2020.

Farenthold, David. "Trump Said He Raised $6 Million for Veterans. Now His Campaign Says It Was Less." *Washington Post*, May 21, 2016.

Fisher, Marc, and Will Hobson. "Donald Trump Masqueraded as Publicist to Brag about Himself." *Washington Post*, May 13, 2016.

Goldman, Adam, and Alan Rappeport. "Emails in Anthony Weiner Inquiry Jolt Hillary Clinton's Campaign." *New York Times*, October 28, 2016.

Grynbaum, Michael M. "Donald Trump and New York Tabloids Resume Their Elaborate Dance." *New York Times*, April 11, 2016.

Haberman, Maggie, and Alexander Burns. "Donald Trump's Presidential Run Began in an Effort to Gain Stature." *New York Times*, March 12, 2016.

Haberman, Maggie, and Jonathan Martin. "Trump Once Said the *Access Hollywood* Tape Was Real. Now He's Not Sure." *New York Times*, November 28, 2017.

"'Ivana Better Deal': Mrs. T Brands Donald's $25M Pre-Nuptial Pact a Fraud." *New York Daily News*, February 13, 1990.

"Ivana to Donald at Secret Sitdown: Gimme the Plaza! . . . the Jet and $150 Million, Too." *New York Post*, February 14, 1990.

Kaczynski, Andrew, and Em Steck. "How Donald Trump for Years Used the Royal Family to Gin Up Publicity for His Properties." CNN, June 5, 2019.

Katersky, Aaron, and M. L. Nestel. "Judge Finalizes $25 Million Settlement for 'Victims of Donald Trump's Fraudulent University.'" ABC News, April 9, 2018.

Kessler, Glenn, Salvador Rizzo, and Meg Kelly. "Trump's False or Misleading Claims Total 30,573 over 4 Years." *Washington Post*, January 24, 2021.

Lemire, Jonathan. "Trump, before Debate, Appears with Bill Clinton's Accusers." Associated Press, October 9, 2016.

Lemire, Jonathan. "Trump Elbows into 2016 Race." Associated Press, June 16, 2015.

Megerian, Chris. "What Donald Trump Has Said through the Years about Where President Obama Was Born." *Los Angeles Times*, September 16, 2016.

"Plaza Hotel Files for Bankruptcy Protection under Trump Plan." UPI, November 4, 1992.

Poniewozik, James. "Donald Trump Was the Real Winner of *The Apprentice*." *New York Times*, September 28, 2016.

Schnurr, Samantha. "Meeting Donald Trump, a Confrontation with Marla Maples and Life in Trump Tower: Juicy Revelations from Ivana Trump's Memoir." E! News, October 10, 2017.

Tennery, Amy. "Trump Accuses Cruz of Stealing Iowa Caucuses through 'Fraud.'" Reuters, February 3, 2016.

Trump, Donald J., and Tony Schwartz. *The Art of the Deal*. New York: Random House, 1987.

"Trump Once Impersonated His Own Spokesman to Claim Madonna, Kim Basinger Wanted to Date Him." *Week*, April 12, 2016.

"Trump's Castle and Plaza File for Bankruptcy." UPI, March 9, 1992.

Vilensky, Mike. "Trump Roasted and Skewered at White House Correspondents' Dinner." *New York Magazine*, May 1, 2011.

3: THE TRUMP PRESIDENCY

Baker, Peter. "Trump's Wiretapping Claims Puncture Veneer of Presidential Civility." *New York Times*, March 7, 2017.

Cathey, Libby. "Legacy of Lies—How Trump Weaponized Mistruths during His Presidency." ABC News, January 20, 2021.

Dale, Daniel. "The 15 Most Notable Lies of Donald Trump's Presidency." CNN, January 16, 2021.

Dale, Daniel. "Trump Makes Yet Another False Claim about California Voter Fraud." CNN, June 24, 2019.

Dale, Daniel. "Trump Walks out of News Conference after Reporter Asks Him about Veterans Choice Lie He's Told More Than 150 Times." CNN, August 9, 2020.

Davis, Julie Hirschfeld, and Matthew Rosenberg. "With False Claims, Trump Attacks Media on Turnout and Intelligence Rift." *New York Times*, January 21, 2017.

Dilanian, Ken, Alex Moe, and Ali Vitali. "Nunes Had Secret White House Meeting before Trump Monitoring Claim." NBC News, March 27, 2017.

Finnegan, Michael, and Mark Z. Barabak. "How the Phony Conspiracy Theory over Wiretapping Caught Fire." *Los Angeles Times*, March 22, 2017.

Flavelle, Christopher. "NOAA Chief Violated Ethics Code in Furor over Trump Tweet, Agency Says." *New York Times*, July 9, 2020.

Flavelle, Christopher, and Lisa Friedman. "NOAA Officials Feared Firings after Trump's Hurricane Claims, Inspector General Says." *New York Times*, August 6, 2020.

Ford, Matt. "Trump's Press Secretary Falsely Claims: 'Largest Audience Ever to Witness an Inauguration, Period.'" *Atlantic*, January 21, 2017.

Gonzales, Richard. "NOAA Contradicts Weather Service, Backs Trump on Hurricane Threat in Alabama." NPR, September 6, 2019.

Ignatius, David. "'Who Do You Believe?' a Reporter Asked Trump. His Answer Was Stunning." *Washington Post*, July 16, 2018.

Lemire, Jonathan. "An Angry Weekend Follows on Heels of Frustrations for Trump." Associated Press, March 6, 2017.

Lemire, Jonathan, Jill Colvin, and Vladimir Isachenkov. "Trump Embraces Longtime US Foe Putin, Doubting Own Intel." Associated Press, July 16, 2018.

Lucey, Catherine, Jonathan Lemire, and Zeke Miller. "Trump Tells AP He Won't Accept Blame if GOP Loses House." Associated Press, October 17, 2018.

Nelson, Ella. "Trump: Boy Scouts Thought My Speech Was 'Greatest Ever Made to Them.' Boy Scouts: No." Vox, August 2, 2017.

Olorunnipa, Toluse, and Josh Dawsey. "'What I Said Was Accurate!': Trump Stays Fixated on His Alabama Error as Hurricane Pounds the Carolinas." *Washington Post*, September 5, 2019.

Parker, Ashley. "Spin, Hyperbole and Deception: How Trump Claimed Credit for an Obama Veterans Achievement." *Washington Post*, October 23, 2020.

Parker, Ashley, Philip Rucker, Josh Dawsey, and Carol D. Leonnig. "Trump's Putin Fallout: Inside the White House's Tumultuous Week of Walk-Backs." *Washington Post*, July 21, 2018.

Payne, Adam. "Trump Walked out of a Press Conference after a Reporter Challenged His Repeated False Claim That He Signed Veterans Choice into Law." Insider, August 9, 2020.

"Read the Transcript of AP's Interview with President Trump." Associated Press, October 17, 2018.

Shear, Michael D., and Emmarie Huetteman. "Trump Repeats Lie About Popular Vote in Meeting With Lawmakers." *New York Times*, January 23, 2017.

Stark, Liz, and Grace Hauck. "Forty-Four States and DC Have Refused to Give Certain Voter Information to Trump Commission." CNN, July 5, 2017.

Stokols, Eli. "Trump Accuses Obama of 'Wire Tapping' Trump Tower Phones." *Politico*, March 4, 2017.

Tackett, Michael, and Michael Wines. "Trump Disbands Commission on Voter Fraud." *New York Times*, January 3, 2018.

Taylor, Jessica. "Trump Administration Goes to War with the Media over Inauguration Crowd Size." NPR, January 21, 2017.

Thrush, Glenn. "Trump's Voter Fraud Example? A Troubled Tale with Bernhard Langer." *New York Times*, January 25, 2017.

"A Timeline of Trump's Hurricane Dorian, Alabama Controversy." *Time*, September 8, 2019.

Villeneuve, Marina. "Report: Trump Commission Did Not Find Widespread Voter Fraud." Associated Press, August 3, 2018.

Vogel, Kenneth P., and Cory Bennett. "Nunes Asks FBI to Investigate Trump Leaks." *Politico*, February 17, 2017.

Volz, Dustin. "Justice Department Affirms No Evidence Obama Wiretapped Trump." Reuters, September 2, 2017.

Wallace, Gregory. "National Park Service Edited Inauguration Photos after Trump, Spicer Calls." CNN, September 9, 2018.

4: THE DEMOCRATS

Cadelago, Christopher. "Trump Owns the Shutdown. And He's OK with That." *Politico*, December 23, 2018.

Cohn, Nate. "Democrats Are Bad at Midterm Turnout. That Seems Ready to Change." *New York Times*, April 5, 2017.

Davis, Julie Hirschfeld, and Mark Landler. "Trump Nominates Neil Gorsuch to the Supreme Court." *New York Times*, January 31, 2017.

Dawsey, Josh. "Trump Derides Protections for Immigrants from 'Shithole' Countries." *Washington Post*, January 12, 2018.

DeBonis, Mike, and Seung Min Kim. "'All Roads Lead to Putin': Pelosi Questions Trump's Loyalty in White House Clash." *Washington Post*, October 17, 2019.

Flegenheimer, Matt. "What's a 'Covfefe'? Trump Tweet Unites a Bewildered Nation." *New York Times*, May 31, 2017.

Flynn, Meagan. "Trump Tried to Insult 'Unhinged' Pelosi with an Image. She Made It Her Twitter Cover Photo." *Washington Post*, October 17, 2019.

Heller, Nathan. "A Dark Night at the Javits Center." *New Yorker*, November 9, 2016.

Johnson, Ted. "Trump Slams Sen. Kirsten Gillibrand in Suggestive Tweet." *Variety*, December 12, 2017.

Kellman, Laurie, and Lisa Mascaro. "About That Photo: Trump, Pelosi Clash amid Impeachment." Associated Press, October 17, 2019.

Lopez, German. "Trump Last Week: I'll Own the Shutdown. Trump Now: It's the Democrats' Fault." Vox, December 21, 2018.

Nilsen, Ella. "How Nancy Pelosi and Chuck Schumer Got Trump to Own a Government Shutdown." Vox, December 12, 2018.

Shear, Michael D., and Helene Cooper. "Trump Bars Refugees and Citizens of 7 Muslim Countries." New York Times, January 27, 2017.

Stevenson, Peter W. "The Iconic Thumbs-Down Vote That Summed Up John McCain's Career." Washington Post, August 27, 2018.

"Trump's Executive Order: Who Does Travel Ban Effect?" BBC News, February 10, 2017.

5: CONSERVATIVE REINFORCEMENTS

Baker, Peter. "In Trump's Ukraine Phone Call, Alarmed Aides Saw Trouble." New York Times, September 26, 2019.

Bauder, David. "Did Fox's Tucker Carlson Play Role in Calming Iran Pressure?" Associated Press, January 9, 2020.

Bertrand, Natasha, Darren Samuelsohn, Josh Gerstein, and Kyle Cheney. "Mueller Complained to Barr about Russia Report Memo." Politico, April 30, 2019.

Colvin, Jill, Jonathan Lemire, and Zeke Miller. "Trump Unleashes Impeachment Fury in Acquittal 'Celebration.'" Associated Press, February 5, 2020.

Committee on the Judiciary, Impeachment of Donald J. Trump President of the United States, House of Representatives Report 116–346, December 15, 2019.

"Donald Trump on Mueller's Appointment: 'This Is the End of My Presidency. I'm F—d.'" CNBC, August 18, 2019.

Fandos, Nicholas. "Trump's Ukraine Call Was 'Crazy' and 'Frightening,' Official Told Whistle-Blower." New York Times, July 29, 2019.

Fandos, Nicholas, Michael S. Schmidt, and Mark Mazzetti. "Some on Mueller's Team Say Report Was More Damaging Than Barr Revealed." New York Times, April 3, 2019.

Flegenheimer, Matt. "The Best Words: Trump, Zelensky and a Very Explosive Phone Call." New York Times, September 25, 2019.

Grynbaum, Michael M. "Fox News Once Gave Trump a Perch. Now It's His Bullhorn." New York Times, July 1, 2018.

Grynbaum, Michael M. "Fox News Stars Trumpeted a Malaria Drug, Until They Didn't." New York Times, April 22, 2020.

Grynbaum, Michael M., and Maggie Haberman. "Fox News Is Trump's Chief TV Booster. So Why Is He Griping About It?" New York Times, August 13, 2019.

Harrington, Rebecca. "All the Terrible Things Trump and Ted Cruz Said about

Each Other before the President Decided He Was 'Beautiful Ted.'" Insider, October 23, 2018.

Kennedy, Dan. "How the Media Blew the 2016 Campaign." *U.S. News & World Report*, November 6, 2016.

Lemire, Jonathan. "Business Promotion and Politics Par for Trump's Golf Tour." Associated Press, June 25, 2016.

Lemire, Jonathan. "Giuliani Tells AP: Trump Won't Answer Obstruction Questions." Associated Press, September 8, 2018.

Lemire, Jonathan. "Giuliani Trying to Influence Perception of Mueller Probe." Associated Press, June 8, 2018.

Lemire, Jonathan. "Trump, in Scotland, Links Brexit Vote to His Campaign." Associated Press, June 24, 2016.

Lemire, Jonathan, Michael Balsamo, and Lisa Mascaro. "Trump, in Call, Urged Ukraine to Investigate Biden's Son." Associated Press, September 20, 2019.

Lemire, Jonathan, and Eric Tucker. "Trump's Legal Team Breathes a Sigh, Takes a Victory Lap." Associated Press, April 20, 2019.

Levine, Mike. "The Russia Probe: A Timeline from Moscow to Mueller." ABC News, July 23, 2019.

Mannion, Connor. "AP Reporter: Trump 'Feels Like Fox Should Be on His Side' Because He Gets Advice from Hannity and Tucker." Mediaite, August 30, 2019.

Mascaro, Lisa, Mary Claire Jalonick, and Jonathan Lemire. "Trump Ordered Aid Frozen; More Democrats Want Impeachment." Associated Press, September 24, 2019.

McCammond, Alexi, and Jonathan Swan. "Scoop: Insider Leaks Trump's 'Executive Time'–Filled Private Schedules." Axios, February 3, 2019.

Mueller, Robert S., III. *Report on the Investigation into Russian Interference in the 2016 Presidential Election*. Washington, DC: Department of Justice, March 2019.

"Mueller Report Findings: Mueller Rejects Argument That Trump Is Shielded from Obstruction Laws." *Washington Post*, April 18, 2019.

Olorunnipa, Toluse, and Mike DeBonis. "Trump Lashes Out at Democrats in Cheering His Acquittal as Pelosi Declares Him 'Impeached Forever.'" *Washington Post*, February 6, 2020.

Parker, Ashley, and Robert Costa. "'Everyone Tunes In': Inside Trump's Obsession with Cable TV." *Washington Post*, April 23, 2017.

Peters, Jeremy W. "Where Fox News and Donald Trump Took Us." *New York Times*, February 5, 2022.

Rucker, Philip, Robert Costa, Laurie McGinley, and Josh Dawsey. "'What Do You Have to Lose?': Inside Trump's Embrace of a Risky Drug against Coronavirus." *Washington Post*, August 6, 2020.

Rutenberg, Jim. "Roger Ailes: The Man Who Mined a Divided America." *New York Times*, May 18, 2017.

Sillito, David. "Donald Trump: How the Media Created the President." BBC News, November 14, 2016.

Stewart, Emily. "Donald Trump Rode $5 Billion in Free Media to the White House." Street, November 17, 2016.

Stracqualursi, Veronica. "'I'm Not Trying to Pretend to Be a Fair Juror Here': Graham Predicts Trump Impeachment Will 'Die Quickly' in Senate." CNN, December 14, 2019.

Stracqualursi, Veronica. "Trump in Scotland: Brexit, Bagpipes and British Comedian's Swastika Golf Balls." ABC News, June 24, 2016.

Tur, Katy. *Unbelievable: My Front-Row Seat to the Craziest Campaign in American History*. New York: William Morrow, 2017.

Yan, Holly. "Donald Trump's 'Blood' Comment about Megyn Kelly Draws Outrage." CNN, August 8, 2015.

Zapotosky, Matt, and Devlin Barrett. "Mueller Did Not Find the Trump Campaign Conspired with Russia, Attorney General Says." *Washington Post*, March 24, 2019.

6: 2020

Abutaleb, Yasmeen, Josh Dawsey, Ellen Nakashima, and Greg Miller. "The U.S. Was Beset by Denial and Dysfunction as the Coronavirus Raged." *Washington Post*, April 4, 2020.

Allen, Jonathan, and Amie Parnes. *Lucky: How Joe Biden Barely Won the Presidency*. New York: Penguin Random House, 2021.

Baker, Peter, Maggie Haberman, Katie Rogers, Zolan Kanno-Youngs, and Katie Benner. Videos by Haley Willis, Christiaan Triebert, and David Botti. "How Trump's Idea for a Photo Op Led to Havoc in a Park." *New York Times*, June 3, 2020.

Belvedere, Matthew J. "Trump Says He Trusts China's Xi on Coronavirus and the US Has It 'Totally Under Control.'" CNBC, January 22, 2020.

Buchanan, Larry, Lazaro Gamio, Lauren Leatherby, Robin Stein, and Christiaan Triebert. "Inside the White House Event Now under Covid-19 Scrutiny." *New York Times*, October 3, 2020.

Cathey, Libby. "Trump, Downplaying Virus, Has Mocked Wearing Masks for Months." ABC News, October 2, 2020.

Colvin, Jill, and Jonathan Lemire. "Trump's India Visit Prioritizes Pageantry over Policy." Associated Press, February 24, 2020.

Cramer, Richard Ben. *What It Takes: The Way to the White House*. New York: Vintage, 1992.

Dovere, Edward-Isaac. *Battle for the Soul: Inside the Democrats' Campaigns to Defeat Trump*. New York: Penguin Random House, 2021.

Forgey, Quint, and Matthew Choi. "'This Is Deadly Stuff': Tapes Show Trump Acknowledging Virus Threat in February." *Politico*, September 9, 2020.

Freking, Kevin, and Jonathan Lemire. "Trump's Intended Show of Political Force Falls Short of Mark." Associated Press, June 20, 2020.

Glueck, Katie, Jonathan Martin, and Thomas Kaplan. "What Went Wrong for Joe Biden in Iowa." *New York Times*, February 7, 2020.

Haberman, Maggie, and Annie Karni. "The President's Shock at the Rows of Empty Seats in Tulsa." *New York Times*, June 21, 2020.

Knickmeyer, Ellen, and Jonathan Lemire. "Trump Rally on Juneteenth in Tulsa Called 'Slap in the Face.'" Associated Press, June 12, 2020.

Korecki, Natasha, Marc Caputo, and Maya King. "'Blood in the Water': Biden Campaign Reels after New Hampshire Trouncing." *Politico*, February 12, 2020.

Lemire, Jonathan. "Cavalier White House Approach to COVID Catches Up to Trump." Associated Press, October 3, 2020.

Lemire, Jonathan. "Lafayette Square Could Decide Trump's Legacy—and Election." Associated Press. June 17, 2020.

Lemire, Jonathan. "Trump Wears Mask in Public for First Time during Pandemic." Associated Press, July 11, 2020.

Lemire, Jonathan, Jill Colvin, and Zeke Miller. "Trump Said to Be Improving but Next 48 Hours 'Critical.'" Associated Press, October 3, 2020.

Lemire, Jonathan, Michelle L. Price, and Kevin Freking. "Trump Lashes Biden, Defies Pandemic on White House Stage." Associated Press, August 28, 2020.

Lemire, Jonathan, and Calvin Woodward. "Trump's Leadership Is Tested in Time of Fear, Pandemic." Associated Press, July 6, 2020.

Lipton, Eric, David E. Sanger, Maggie Haberman, Michael D. Shear, Mark Mazzetti, and Julian E. Barnes. "He Could Have Seen What Was Coming: Behind Trump's Failure on the Virus." *New York Times*, April 11, 2020.

Lorenz, Taylor, Kellen Browning, and Sheera Frenkel. "TikTok Teens and K-Pop Stans Say They Sank Trump Rally." *New York Times*, June 21, 2020.

Miller, Zeke, Jill Colvin, and Jonathan Lemire. "Trump, Stricken by COVID-19, Flown to Military Hospital." Associated Press, October 3, 2020.

Ortiz, Erik. "National Protests over George Floyd's Death Was 'Conflagration Waiting to Happen.'" NBC News, May 29, 2020.

Osnos, Evan. *Joe Biden: American Dreamer*. New York: Simon & Schuster, 2020.

Phelps, Jordyn, and Ben Gittleson. "Trump Looks to Act on Call to Slow Down Testing He Falsely Blames for Surge in Cases." ABC News, July 20, 2020.

Shear, Michael D., Sheri Fink, and Noah Weiland. "Inside Trump Administration, Debate Raged over What to Tell Public." *New York Times*, March 7, 2020.

Superville, Darlene, Aamer Madhani, and Jonathan Lemire. "Wary of Irking China, Trump Offers Rosy Take on Virus Threat." Associated Press, January 30, 2020.

Totenberg, Nina. "Justice Ruth Bader Ginsburg, Champion of Gender Equality, Dies at 87." NPR, September 18, 2020.

Woodward, Bob. *Rage*. New York: Simon & Schuster, 2020.

Woodward, Bob, and Robert Costa. *Peril*. New York: Simon & Schuster, 2021.

7: THE ELECTION

Alemany, Jacqueline, Emma Brown, Tom Hamburger, and Jon Swaine. "Ahead of Jan. 6, Willard Hotel in Downtown D.C. Was a Trump Team 'Command Center' for Effort to Deny Biden the Presidency." *Washington Post*, October 23, 2021.

Baker, Peter, Maggie Haberman, and Annie Karni. "Pence Reached His Limit with Trump. It Wasn't Pretty." *New York Times*, January 12, 2021.

Balsamo, Michael. "Disputing Trump, Barr Says No Widespread Election Fraud." Associated Press, December 1, 2020.

Barry, Dan, and Sheera Frankel. "'Be There. Will Be Wild!': Trump All but Circled the Date." *New York Times*, January 6, 2021.

Bella, Timothy. "Trump Requests a Mail-In Ballot after Months of Falsely Crying 'Fraud' on Mail-In Ballots." *Washington Post*, March 10, 2021.

Bender, Michael C. *"Frankly We Did Win This Election": The Inside Story of How Trump Lost*. New York: Twelve Books, 2021.

Blake, Aaron. "'What's the Downside for Humoring Him?': A GOP Official's Unintentionally Revealing Quote about the Trump Era." *Washington Post*, November 10, 2020.

"Completed Wisconsin Recount Confirms Biden's Win over Trump." Associated Press, November 30, 2020.

"Counting Electoral Votes: An Overview of Procedures at the Joint Session, Including Objections by Members of Congress." Congressional Research Service, December 8, 2020.

Crowley, Michael. "Trump Won't Commit to 'Peaceful' Post-Election Transfer of Power." *New York Times*, September 23, 2020.

Cummings, William, Joey Garrison, and Jim Sergent. "By the Numbers: President Donald Trump's Failed Efforts to Overturn the Election." *USA Today*, January 6, 2021.

Dawsey, Josh, and Ashley Parker. "Inside the Remarkable Rift between Donald Trump and Mike Pence." *Washington Post*, January 11, 2021.

Feuer, Alan, Maggie Haberman, and Luke Broadwater. "Memos Show Roots of Trump's Focus on Jan. 6 and Alternate Electors." *New York Times*, February 2, 2022.

Fischer, Sara. "How the Big Lie Spread." Axios, November 21, 2021.

Fritze, John. "Return to Sender: Trump's Strategy on Mail Ballots Divides Party before GOP Convention." *USA Today*, August 23, 2020.

Gangel, Jamie, and Jeremy Herb. "Memo Shows Trump Lawyer's Six-Step Plan for Pence to Overturn the Election." CNN, September 21, 2021.

Gardner, Amy. "'I Just Want to Find 11,780 Votes': In Extraordinary Hour-Long Call, Trump Pressures Georgia Secretary of State to Recalculate the Vote in His Favor." *Washington Post*, January 3, 2021.

"Hair Dye Don't Lie: Giuliani Sweats Election Results." Reuters, November 19, 2020.

Kessler, Glenn, and Salvador Rizzo. "President Trump's False Claims of Vote Fraud: A Chronology." *Washington Post*, November 5, 2020.

Kilgore, Ed. "Trump's Long Campaign to Steal the Presidency: A Timeline." *New York Magazine*, February 3, 2022.

Korecki, Natasha, Marc Caputo, and Christopher Cadelago. "Grief, Relief, and Jubilation: How Biden's Team Survived a Wild Five Days." *Politico*, November 7, 2020.

Lemire, Jonathan, Zeke Miller, and Jill Colvin. "Trump's Task: Resetting Campaign That GOP Fears Is Slipping." Associated Press, October 13, 2020.

Lemire, Jonathan, Zeke Miller, Jill Colvin, and Alexandra Jaffe. "Biden Wins Michigan, Wisconsin, Now on Brink of White House." Associated Press, November 4, 2020.

Lemire, Jonathan, Zeke Miller, Jill Colvin, and Will Weissert. "Biden Defeats Trump for White House, Says 'Time to Heal.'" Associated Press, November 7, 2020.

Lemire, Jonathan, Zeke Miller, and Alexandra Jaffe. "Biden Flips Arizona, Focus Turns to Michigan, Wisconsin, Pennsylvania." Associated Press, November 3, 2020.

Lemire, Jonathan, Zeke Miller, Will Weissert, and Alexandra Jaffe. "In 2020 Finale, Trump Combative, Biden on Offense." Associated Press, November 3, 2020.

Lemire, Jonathan, and Ken Ritter. "In Defiance of Nevada Governor, Trump Holds Indoor Rally." Associated Press, September 13, 2020.

Leonnig, Carol, and Philip Rucker. *I Alone Can Fix It: Donald J. Trump's Catastrophic Final Year.* New York: Penguin Press, 2021.

Linskey, Annie. "Waiting, Watching and Wilting in Wilmington for Word of an Election Result." *Washington Post*, November 6, 2020.

Liptak, Kevin, and Pamela Brown. "Heated Oval Office Meeting Included Talk of

Special Counsel, Martial Law as Trump Advisers Clash." CNN, December 20, 2020.

Murray, Sara. "Cyber Ninjas, Company That Oversaw the Partisan Arizona Election Review, Is Shuttering." CNN, January 7, 2022.

Nuzzi, Olivia. "Four Seasons Total Landscaping: The Full(est Possible) Story." *New York Magazine*, December 21, 2020.

Rupar, Aaron. "How Trump's Mail Voting Sabotage Could Result in an Election Night Nightmare." Vox, August 10, 2020.

Rupar, Aaron. "Trump's Desperate 'STOP THE COUNT!' Tweet, Briefly Explained." Vox, November 5, 2020.

Rutenberg, Jim, Jo Becker, Eric Lipton, Maggie Haberman, Jonathan Martin, Matthew Rosenberg, and Michael S. Schmidt. "77 Days: Trump's Campaign to Subvert the Election." *New York Times*, January 31, 2021.

Schmidt, Michael S., and Maggie Haberman. "The Lawyer behind the Memo on How Trump Could Stay in Office." *New York Times*, November 8, 2021.

Sneed, Tierney. "ABC News: Trump Loyalist at DOJ Circulated Draft Georgia Letter with False Election Fraud Claims." CNN, August 4, 2021.

Swasey, Benjamin, and Connie Hanzhang Jin. "Narrow Wins in These Key States Powered Biden to the Presidency." NPR, December 2, 2020.

Wolfe, Jan, and Helen Coster. "Dominion Sees No Chance of Settling Suits against Pro-Trump Lawyers Giuliani, Powell." Reuters, January 25, 2022.

8: JANUARY 6

Alemany, Jacqueline, Tom Hamburger, Josh Dawsey, and Tyler Remmel. "Texting through an Insurrection." *Washington Post*, February 16, 2022.

Barry, Ellen, Nicholas Bogel-Burroughs, and Dave Philipps. "Woman Killed in Capitol Embraced Trump and QAnon." *New York Times*, January 7, 2021.

Clancy, Sam. "Sen. Josh Hawley Renews Objection, Call for Voter Fraud Investigation after Riot at Capitol." KSDK, St. Louis NBC, January 6, 2021.

Colvin, Jill. "Trump Bids Farewell to Washington, Hints of Comeback." Associated Press, January 20, 2021.

Ferris, Sarah, Olivia Beavers, Melanie Zanona, Burgess Everett, and Marianne Levine. "Hill Chaos Turns Deadly after Rioters Storm Capitol." *Politico*, January 6, 2021.

Glantz, Aaron. "Read Pence's Full Letter Saying He Can't Claim 'Unilateral Authority' to Reject Electoral Votes." PBS, January 6, 2021.

Gregorian, Dareh, and Julie Tsirkin. "'I'm Very Fortunate': Capitol Officer Saved Sen. Mitt Romney from the Mob." NBC News, February 10, 2021.

Gross, Jenny, and Luke Broadwater. "Here Are the Republicans Who Objected to Certifying the Election Results." *New York Times*, January 7, 2021.

Haberman, Maggie, and Zach Montague. "In a New Video, Trump Addresses Violence at the Capitol and Says 'a New Administration' Will Be Sworn In." *New York Times*, January 7, 2021.

"How Pro-Trump Insurrectionists Broke into the U.S. Capitol." *Washington Post*, January 6, 2021.

Jalonick, Mary Claire. "'We Were Trapped': Trauma of Jan. 6 Lingers for Lawmakers." Associated Press, January 5, 2022.

Leatherby, Lauren, Arielle Ray, Anjali Singhvi, Christiaan Triebert, Derek Watkins, and Haley Willis. "How a Presidential Rally Turned into a Capitol Rampage." *New York Times*, January 12, 2021.

Lemire, Jonathan. "After Trump, Biden Aims to Reshape the Presidency Itself." Associated Press, January 16, 2021.

Lemire, Jonathan. "Analysis: Trump's Rage Ignites Mob Assault on Democracy." Associated Press, January 6, 2021.

Lemire, Jonathan, Zeke Miller, and Alexandra Jaffe. "Biden Takes the Helm, Appeals for Unity to Take on Crises." Associated Press, January 20, 2021.

Lonas, Lexi. "Sasse Says Trump Was 'Delighted' and 'Excited' by Reports of Capitol Riot." *Hill*, January 8, 2021.

Lonsdorf, Kat, Courtney Dorning, Amy Isackson, Mary Louise Kelly, and Ailsa Chang. "A Timeline of How the Jan. 6 Attack Unfolded—Including Who Said What and When." NPR, January 6, 2021.

Lucas, Ryan. "Where the Jan. 6 Insurrection Investigation Stands, One Year Later." NPR, January 6, 2022.

Naylor, Brian. "Read Trump's Jan. 6 Speech, a Key Part of Impeachment Trial." NPR, February 10, 2021.

Samuels, Alex, and Patrick Svitek. "After Riot at the U.S. Capitol, Ted Cruz Gets Fierce Blowback for His Role in Sowing Doubts about Joe Biden's Victory." *Texas Tribune*, January 7, 2021.

Schwartzman, Paul, and Josh Dawsey. "How Ashli Babbitt Went from Capitol Rioter to Trump-Embraced 'Martyr.'" *Washington Post*, July 30, 2021.

Serfaty, Sunlen, Devan Cole, and Alex Rogers. "As Riot Raged at Capitol, Trump Tried to Call Senators to Overturn Election." CNN, January 8, 2021.

Shafer, Ronald G. "The Electoral Count Act's History Is Clear: Vice Presidents Can't Overturn Elections." *Washington Post*, February 8, 2022.

Shear, Michael D. "Biden Calls on Trump to Go on National Television and 'Demand an End to This Siege.'" *New York Times*, January 6, 2021.

Steakin, Will, John Santucci, and Katherine Faulders. "Trump Allies Helped Plan, Promote Rally That Led to Capitol Attack." ABC News, January 8, 2021.

Subramanian, Courtney. "A Minute-by-Minute Timeline of Trump's Day as the Capitol Siege Unfolded on Jan. 6." *USA Today*, February 11, 2021.

Talbot, Haley. "Inside the House Chamber as the Capitol Was Overrun by an Angry Mob." NBC News, January 11, 2021.

Tillman, Rachel, and Austin Landis. "16 Harrowing Hours: How the Events of Jan. 6, 2021, Unfolded in Real Time." Spectrum NY1, January 6, 2022.

"The Trump Administration Officials Who Resigned over Capitol Violence." *New York Times*, January 17, 2021.

"Twitter 'Permanently Suspends' Trump's Account." BBC News, January 9, 2021.

"U.S. Senate Republican Leader McConnell Says Trump 'Provoked' Jan. 6 Riot." Reuters, January 19, 2021.

Wade, Peter. "'Look at All Those People Fighting for Me': Trump 'Gleefully' Watched Jan. 6 Riot, Says Former Press Secretary." *Rolling Stone*, January 6, 2022.

Wolfe, Jan. "Trump Wanted Troops to Protect His Supporters at Jan. 6 Rally." Reuters, May 12, 2021.

9: THE GRIP TIGHTENS

Balz, Dan. "The Senate Vote on the Bipartisan Jan. 6 Commission Showed Trump's Power and a Government under Duress." *Washington Post*, May 28, 2021.

Bash, Dana, and Michael Warren. "As Trump's Latest Intra-Party Feud Rages, Sen. Graham Heads to Mar-a-Lago on a Peace Mission." CNN, February 13, 2021.

Benen, Steve. "Mar-a-Lago Becomes the Center of the Republican Party's World." MSNBC, February 19, 2021.

Blake, Aaron. "Trump's 'Big Lie' Was Bigger Than Just a Stolen Election." *Washington Post*, February 12, 2021.

Boak, Josh, and Lisa Mascaro. "$1.9T Biden Relief Package a Bet Government Can Help Cure US." Associated Press, March 9, 2021.

Cillizza, Chris. "The Big Lie Is (Unfortunately) Winning." CNN, September 15, 2021.

Colvin, Jill, and Steve Peoples. "Whose 'Big Lie'? Trump's Proclamation a New GOP Litmus Test." Associated Press, May 4, 2021.

Edmondson, Catie, and Luke Broadwater. "After the Capitol Riot, Democrats Are Torn over Working with the G.O.P." *New York Times*, April 7, 2021.

Ferris, Sarah, and Nicholas Wu. "Cheney Joins Dems on Jan. 6 probe, Defying McCarthy Threat." *Politico*, July 2, 2021.

Field, Jeff. "Mitch McConnell 'Absolutely' Would Support Trump if GOP Nominee in 2024." Fox News, February 25, 2021.

Fram, Alan, and Lisa Mascaro. "Senate Minority Leader Mitch McConnell Calls

Trump 'Morally Responsible' for Jan. 6 Attack." Associated Press, February 13, 2021.

Friedman, Thomas L. "Trump's Big Lie Devoured the G.O.P. and Now Eyes Our Democracy." *New York Times*, May 4, 2021.

Green, Joshua. "Election Denial and $16 Spritzers: Welcome to Florida's Trump Coast." Bloomberg, June 10, 2021.

Grynbaum, Michael. "Chris Wallace Says Life at Fox News Became 'Unsustainable.'" *New York Times*, March 27, 2022.

Hagan, Joe. "'All Roads Lead to Mar-a-Lago': Inside the Fury and Fantasy of Donald Trump's Florida." *Vanity Fair*, August 10, 2021.

Holpuch, Amanda. "Mitch McConnell Savages Trump—Minutes after Voting to Acquit." *Guardian*, February 13, 2021.

Hulse, Carl. "Election Considerations Drive G.O.P. Opposition to Jan. 6 Panel." *New York Times*, May 20, 2021.

Jones, Dustin. "Pelosi Has Chosen a 2nd Republican, Rep. Adam Kinzinger, to Serve on Jan. 6 Panel." NPR, July 25, 2021.

Karni, Annie. "Elise Stefanik, Reinvented in Trump's Image, Embodies a Changed G.O.P." *New York Times*, March 27, 2022.

Kennedy, Brigid. "Is the 'Big Lie' Becoming Republicans' Midterm Blueprint?" Week, September 20, 2021.

Leary, Alex, Kristina Peterson, and Georgia Wells. "McCarthy Tries to Mend Fences with Trump." *Wall Street Journal*, January 28, 2021.

Leibovich, Mark. "Liz Cheney's Unlikely Journey from G.O.P. Royalty to Republican Outcast." *New York Times*, October 21, 2021.

Lemire, Jonathan. "After Trump, Biden Aims to Reshape the Presidency Itself." Associated Press, January 16, 2021.

Lemire, Jonathan. "Aiming Big, Biden Is Looking to Restore Faith in Government." Associated Press, April 3, 2021.

Lemire, Jonathan. "Biden Immediately Begins Selling Virus Aid Plan to Public." Associated Press, March 10, 2021.

Lemire, Jonathan, and Josh Boak. "Biden Mourns 500,000 Dead, Balancing Nation's Grief and Hope." Associated Press, February 22, 2021.

Lemire, Jonathan, Lisa Lerer, and Neal Katyal. "Biden Now Faces a GOP Totally Defined by Trump's 'Big Lie.'" Interview by Brian Williams, *The 11th Hour*, MSNBC, May 4, 2021.

Lemire, Jonathan, and Calvin Woodard. "More Action, Less Talk, Distinguish Biden's 100-Day Sprint." Associated Press, April 26, 2021.

LeVine, Marianne, and Burgess Everett. "McConnell Turns Senate Republicans against Jan. 6 Commission." *Politico*, May 19, 2021.

Parker, Ashley, and Marianna Sotomayor. "For Republicans, Fealty to Trump's Election Falsehood Becomes Defining Loyalty Test." *Washington Post*, May 2, 2021.

Peters, Jeremy W. *Insurgency: How Republicans Lost Their Party and Got Everything They Ever Wanted.* New York: Crown, 2022.

Rubin, Jennifer. "This Is How Bad McConnell Really Is." *Washington Post*, February 14, 2021.

Salvanto, Anthony, Fred Backus, and Jennifer de Pinto. "Republicans Weigh in on Liz Cheney and Direction of GOP: CBS News Poll." CBS News, May 16, 2021.

Seddiq, Oma. "Biden Says He's 'Tired of Talking' about 'the Former Guy' Trump in First Town Hall as President." Insider, February 16, 2021.

Siders, David, and Zach Montellaro. "'It's Spreading': Phony Election Fraud Conspiracies Infect Midterms." *Politico*, September 20, 2021.

Sonmez, Felicia, and Karoun Demirjian. "Pelosi Announces a Select Committee Will Investigate Jan. 6 Attack on the Capitol by a Pro-Trump Mob." *Washington Post*, June 24, 2021.

Steinhauser, Paul. "Trump's Mar-a-Lago Stays Busy as Republican Candidates Make Fundraising Pilgrimages." Fox News, March 18, 2021.

Weisman, Jonathan, and Luke Broadwater. "A Long, Hard Year for Republicans Who Voted to Impeach after Jan. 6." *New York Times*, January 5, 2022.

Werner, Erica, Jeff Stein, and Seung Min Kim. "Moderate Senate Democrats Target State Aid Fund in Biden Covid Relief Bill." *Washington Post*, February 23, 2021.

Zanona, Melanie, and Olivia Beavers. "Cheney Booted from Republican Leadership Spot." *Politico*, May 15, 2021.

10: THE STATES

Barragán, James. "After a Nearly Six-Week Exodus over GOP Voting Bill, Enough Democrats Return to Texas House to Resume Work." *Texas Tribune*, August 19, 2021.

Beaumont, Thomas. "Republicans Resist Saying Three Simple Words: 'Joe Biden Won.'" Associated Press, December 18, 2021.

Behrmann, Savannah. "Democrats Put Renewed Focus on Voting Rights: What Happened in 2021, and Where Do Proposals Stand Now?" *USA Today*, January 18, 2022.

Blake, Aaron. "Conservatives Try to Commandeer 'the Big Lie.'" *Washington Post*, May 5, 2021.

Cillizza, Chris. "Why Texas Democrats Are Doomed to Fail." CNN, July 13, 2021.

Corasaniti, Nick. "Voting Battles of 2022 Take Shape as G.O.P. Crafts New Election Bills." *New York Times*, December 5, 2021.

Corasaniti, Nick. "Voting Rights and the Battle over Elections: What to Know." *New York Times*, December 29, 2021.

Dale, Daniel. "'Incredibly Dangerous': Trump Is Trying to Get Big Lie Promoters Chosen to Run the 2024 Election." CNN, September 16, 2021.

Dale, Daniel, and Diane Gallagher. "Fact Check: What the New Georgia Elections Law Actually Does." CNN, March 31, 2021.

Devore, Isaac, and Jeremy Herb. "'It's Absolutely Getting Worse': Secretaries of State Targeted by Trump Election Lies Live in Fear for Their Safety and Are Desperate for Protection." CNN, October 26, 2021.

Elfrink, Tim. "Liz Cheney Refuses to Link Trump's False Election Claims, GOP's Push for New Voting Restrictions." *Washington Post*, May 24, 2021.

Hamburger, Tom, Rosalind S. Helderman, and Amy Gardner. "'We Are in Harm's Way': Election Officials Fear for Their Personal Safety amid Torrent of False Claims about Voting." *Washington Post*, August 11, 2021.

Izaguirre, Anthony. "As America Embraces Early Voting, GOP Hurries to Restrict It." Associated Press, April 16, 2021.

Johnson, Carrie. "How the Voting Rights Act Came to Be and How It's Changed." NPR, August 26, 2021.

Levitt, Justin. "A Comprehensive Investigation of Voter Impersonation Finds 31 Credible Incidents Out of One Billion Ballots Cast." *Washington Post*, August 6, 2014.

Liptak, Adam. "Supreme Court Invalidates Key Part of Voting Rights Act." *New York Times*, June 25, 2013.

Ponnuru, Ramesh. "Republicans Are Winning the Debate on Voter ID." *Washington Post*, October 18, 2021.

Szep, Jason, and Linda So. "Kanye West Publicist Pressed Georgia Election Worker to Confess to Bogus Fraud Charges." Reuters, December 23, 2021.

Timm, Jane C. "19 States Enacted Voting Restrictions in 2021. What's Next?" NBC News, December 21, 2021.

Timm, Jane C. "Texas Democrats Flee State in Effort to Block GOP-Backed Voting Restrictions." NBC News, July 12, 2021.

Totenberg, Nina. "The Supreme Court Deals a New Blow to Voting Rights, Upholding Arizona Restrictions." NPR, July 1, 2021.

Ura, Alexa, and Cassandra Pollock. "Texas House Democrats Flee the State in Move That Could Block Voting Restrictions Bill, Bring Legislature to a Halt." *Texas Tribune*, July 12, 2021.

Viebeck, Elise. "Here's Where GOP Lawmakers Have Passed New Voting Restrictions around the Country." *Washington Post*, July 14, 2021.

"Voting Laws Roundup: February 2021." Brennan Center for Justice.

"Voting Laws Roundup: October 2021." Brennan Center for Justice.

"Voting Laws Roundup: December 2021." Brennan Center for Justice.

"Voting Laws Roundup: February 2022." Brennan Center for Justice.

White, Ed. "Woman Charged in Threats against Michigan Election Official." Associated Press, December 23, 2020.

II: CHALLENGES

Allen, Mike. "Inside Biden's Private Chat with Historians." Axios, March 25, 2021.

Baker, Peter. "Biden Condemns Trump as Washington Splits over Legacy of Jan. 6 Attack." *New York Times*, January 6, 2022.

Bump, Philip. "Biden Warns That American Democracy Is under Threat—a Message Targeting Many in His Own Party." *Washington Post*, July 13, 2021.

Elving, Ron. "Senate Democrats Plan a Vote to Change the Filibuster. So What Is It?" NPR, January 17, 2022.

Everett, Burgess, Alex Thompson, and Jonathan Lemire. "'Going Very Poorly': Biden Can't Nail Manchin Down on Dems' Bill." *Politico*, December 18, 2021.

Everett, Burgess, Nicolas Wu, and Jonathan Lemire. "White House Lights Up Manchin after He Crushes Biden's Megabill." *Politico*, December 19, 2021.

Ferris, Sarah, Kyle Cheney, and Nicholas Wu. "Biden Decries Trump's 'Singular Responsibility' for the Capitol Riot." *Politico*, January 6, 2022.

Finn, Teaganne. "'Betrayed': House Progressives Erupt over Manchin Build Back Better Opposition." NBC News, December 18, 2021.

Fram, Alan. "Manchin, Key Dem, Says Build Back Better Bill Is 'Dead.'" Associated Press, February 1, 2022.

Hickey, Christopher, and Zachary B. Wolf. "Why Democrats Want to Change the Senate's Filibuster Rules." CNN, January 7, 2022.

Kilgore, Ed. "The John Lewis Voting Rights Act: What Would It Actually Do?" *New York Magazine*, August 21, 2021.

Kim, Seung Min, Felicia Sonmez, and Amy B Wang. "Biden Signs $1.2 Trillion Infrastructure Bill, Fulfilling Campaign Promise and Notching Achievement That Eluded Trump." *Washington Post*, November 15, 2021.

Lemire, Jonathan. "Analysis: Defiant Biden Is Face of Chaotic Afghan Evacuation." Associated Press, August 16, 2021.

Lemire, Jonathan. "Biden and Manchin Speak." *Politico*, December 20, 2021.

Lemire, Jonathan. "Biden's First Year: A Tale of 2 Presidencies." *Politico*, January 19, 2022.

Lemire, Jonathan, and Laura Barrón-López. "Biden Plans Forceful Push for Voting Rights. Aides Are Bearish on Success." *Politico*, December 16, 2021.

Lemire, Jonathan, Josh Boak, and Lisa Mascaro. "Biden Extols Bipartisan Infrastructure Deal as a Good Start." Associated Press, June 24, 2021.

Lemire, Jonathan, and Zeke Miller. "Biden's View of Job Comes into Focus after Afghan Collapse." Associated Press, August 20, 2021.

Lemire, Jonathan, Brian Slodysko, and Zeke Miller. "Biden Blasts 'Un-American' Voting Limits; Texas Dems Act." Associated Press, July 13, 2021.

Lemire, Jonathan, and Darlene Superville. "Biden Decries 'Horrific' Tulsa Massacre in Emotional Speech." Associated Press, June 1, 2021.

Mascaro, Lisa. "Big Win for $1T Infrastructure Bill: Dems, GOP Come To-gether." Associated Press, August 10, 2021.

Milligan, Susan. "The Filibuster: The Senate's Glorified Tradition of Obstruction." *U.S. News & World Report*, January 12, 2022.

Naylor, Brian. "The Senate Is Set to Debate Voting Rights. Here's What the Bills Would Do." NPR, January 18, 2022.

Parker, Ashley, and Carissa Wolf. "Biden's Critics Hurl Increasingly Vulgar Taunts." *Washington Post*, October 23, 2021.

"President Joe Biden's Speech on Voting Rights: Transcript." ABC News, July 13, 2021.

Riccardi, Nicholas. "Explainer: The Differences between Democrats' 2 Voting Bills." Associated Press, June 8, 2021.

Rogers, Katie. "'Have You No Shame?' Biden Frames Voting Rights as a Moral Reckoning." *New York Times*, July 13, 2021.

"Senator Warnock Calls for Senate Rules Change to Pass Voting Rights Legislation." C-SPAN, December 14, 2021.

Stevenson, Peter W. "How Is the John Lewis Voting Rights Act Different from H.R. 1?" *Washington Post*, June 8, 2021.

Sullivan, Sean, Seung Min Kim, and Marianna Sotomayor. "Democrats Begin to Narrow Their Differences on Biden's Social Spending Bill." *Washington Post*, October 5, 2021.

"Text of President Joe Biden's Speech Marking 1/6 Anniversary." Associated Press, January 6, 2022.

Viser, Matt, Seung Min Kim, and Marianna Sotomayor. "Biden Calls Passing Voting Legislation 'a National Imperative' and Castigates Voting Restrictions Based on 'a Big Lie.'" *Washington Post*, July 13, 2021.

Wagner, John, Amy B. Wang, Mariana Alfaro, Eugene Scott, and Felicia Sonmez. "On Jan. 6 Anniversary, Biden Calls Out Trump for 'Web of Lies' about 2020 Election." *Washington Post*, January 6, 2022.

Widdicombe, Lizzie. "What Does Kyrsten Sinema Really Want?" *New Yorker*, October 20, 2021.

12: THE CAMPAIGNS TO COME

Cohen, Rebecca, and Brent D. Griffiths. "Russia's UN Ambassador Accuses US of Helping 'Coup' in Kyiv in 2014." Insider, March 2, 2022.

DeBonis, Mike. "Schumer Sets Up Final Senate Confrontation on Voting Rights and the Filibuster." *Washington Post*, January 12, 2022.

DeBonis, Mike, and Seung Min Kim. "Sinema and Manchin Confirm Opposition to Eliminating Filibuster, Probably Dooming Democrats' Voting Rights Push." *Washington Post*, January 11, 2022.

Epstein, Reid J. "When Will Trump Answer the Big 2024 Question?" *New York Times*, September 7, 2021.

Epstein, Reid J., and Astead W. Herndon. "At CPAC, Ukraine and Policy Take a Back Seat to Cultural Grievances." *New York Times*, February 27, 2022.

Everett, Burgess, Marianne Levine, and Laura Barrón-López. "How Biden Swung for Filibuster Reform—and Missed with Manchin and Sinema." *Politico*, January 11, 2022.

Fink, Jenni. "Russia Slaps U.S. Hypocrisy in Failing to Condemn a Ukraine Coup." *Newsweek*, March 2, 2022.

Hulse, Carl. "Sinema Rejects Changing Filibuster, Dealing Biden a Setback." *New York Times*, January 13, 2022.

Isenstadt, Alex. "4 More Years: Trump Freezes 2024 Presidential Field." *Politico*, November 16, 2020.

Jaffe, Alexandra, Colleen Long, and Jeff Amy. "Biden Challenges Senate on Voting: 'Tired of Being Quiet!'" Associated Press, January 11, 2022.

Kamisar, Ben. "Florida Passes Voting Law That Includes Restrictions on Vote-by-Mail and Drop Boxes." NBC News, April 29, 2021.

Lemire, Jonathan. "Biden to America: 'We're Going to Be OK.'" *Politico*, March 1, 2022.

Lemire, Jonathan. "How the Russia-Ukraine Conflict Has Fundamentally Changed Biden's Presidency." *Politico*, March 1, 2022.

Lemire, Jonathan. "Trump's Shadow Lurks over Biden's Support for Ukraine." *Politico*, March 14, 2022.

Lemongello, Steven. "'President Trump Is Wrong': In Orlando, Pence Rebukes Claim He Could Have Overturned Election." *Orlando Sentinel*, February 4, 2022.

Linton, Caroline. "House January 6 Committee Says It Has Evidence Trump and Allies Engaged in a 'Criminal Conspiracy.'" CBS News, March 3, 2022.

McGraw, Meridith. "At CPAC, Trump Delivers a Reminder of His Muscle." *Politico*, February 27, 2022.

McGraw, Meridith. "MAGA Hats and QAnon: Inside Trump's First Rally of 2022." *Politico*, January 16, 2022.

Medina, Jennifer. "The Traveling Trump Show." *New York Times*, February 11, 2022.

Merica, Dan. "Stacey Abrams and Biden Blame Scheduling Issue for Voting Rights Speech Absence." CNN, January 11, 2022.

Nicholas, Peter. "Jan. 6 Committee Makes the Case That Trump Was Involved in 'Criminal' Activity.'" NBC News, March 3, 2022.

Orr, Gabby. "Won't-Run-If-Trump-Runs Question Leads to Waiting Game for Likely 2024 Candidates." CNN, December 9, 2021.

Oxford, Andrew. "Cyber Ninjas, Hired by Arizona Senate to Recount Maricopa

County's Ballots, Asks Court to Keep Its Procedures Secret." *Arizona Republic*, April 25, 2021.

Rogers, Katie. "Biden Calls for 'Getting Rid of the Filibuster' to Pass Voting Rights Laws." *New York Times*, January 11, 2022.

Snell, Kelsey. "Biden Says He Doesn't Know If Voting Rights Legislation Can Pass." NPR, January 13, 2022.

Strauss, Daniel, and Grace Segers. "January 6 Committee Recap: What Did Trump Do, and When Did He Do It?" *New Republic*, February 18, 2022.

Walter, Amy. "Existential Threat—Or Politics as Usual?" *Cook Political Report*, April 7, 2021.

Weisman, Jonathan, and Reid J. Epstein. "G.O.P. Declares Jan. 6 Attack 'Legitimate Political Discourse.'" *New York Times*, February 4, 2022.

ABOUT THE AUTHOR

Jonathan Lemire is the White House bureau chief at *Politico*, as well as the host of MSNBC's *Way Too Early*. A regular contributor to *Morning Joe* and NBC News, he also covered the Trump and Biden administrations for the Associated Press. *The Big Lie* is his first book.